Connecting with wildlife is such an important way to build empathy for the natural world. This is a delightful collection of stories about inspiring encounters with ocean life—everything from bioluminescent plankton to great whales. I hope it encourages everyone to get outdoors and explore for themselves.

—Julie Packard

Executive Director

Monterey Bay Aquarium

Monterey Bay and Surrounding National Marine Sanctuaries

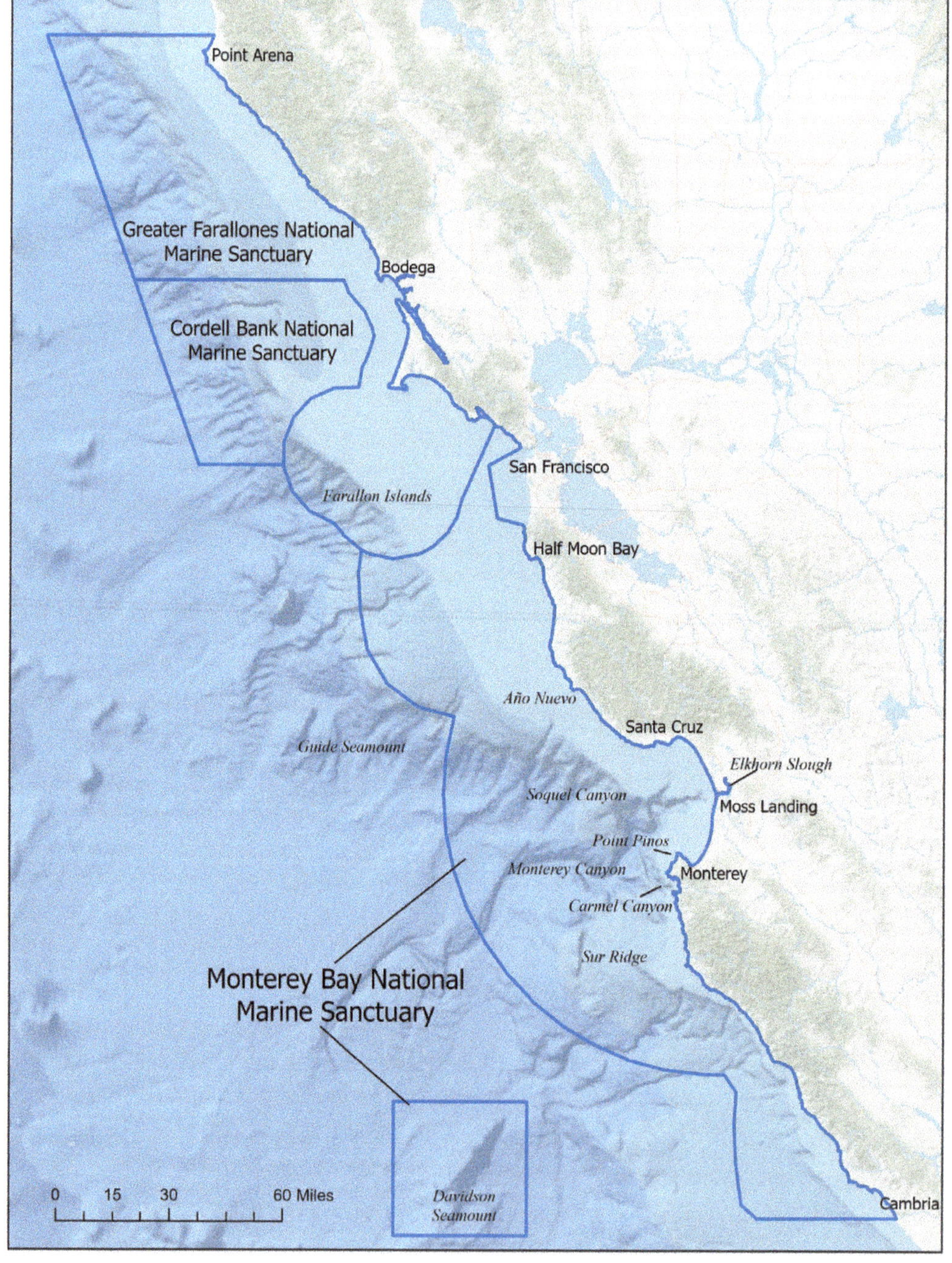

Courtesy NOAA/MBNMS

Wild Monterey Bay

Wild Monterey Bay

Up Close and Personal:

Stories of Memorable Wildlife Encounters

Edited By

Jodi Frediani and Katlyn Taylor

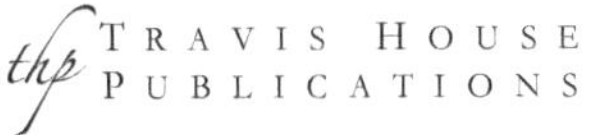

TRAVIS HOUSE PUBLICATIONS

Travis House Publications
PO Box 99
Bodega Bay, CA 94923

For all inquiries or for permission requests, contact
travishousepublications@gmail.com.

Typefaces: Apple Chancery, Garamond, Palatino, Times New Roman

Printed in the United States of America

30 29 28 27 26 25 24   1 2 3 4 5 6

Originally published as:
  https://www.wildmontereybay.com

With deep appreciation to the Safina Center of Stonybrook University
  for its support of this project.

Library of Congress Control Number: 2024911309
ISBN 978-0-9650896-1-6

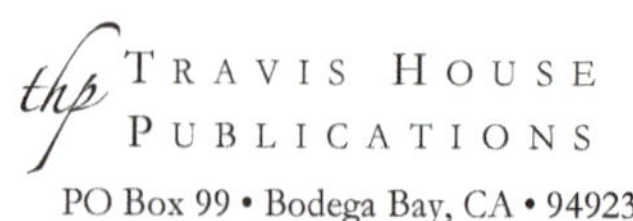

About This Book

Wild Monterey Bay started as a project asking a simple question: What's your most memorable wildlife encounter in Monterey Bay?

Storytelling is human nature. We started this project in 2016 with the hope that we could capture, through personal stories, the essence of what it's like for both people and wildlife in Monterey Bay. Scientists have been studying this place for decades and people have written books about life on its shores. Unless you combine the two—the humans and the wildlife—it's hard to get the full perspective of how amazing this place really is.

We interviewed forty people for this project, from many different walks of life. Some were just short-term visitors and others have lived on the shores of Monterey Bay for generations. Their stories involve at least twenty-five different species, from microscopic plankton to the largest animal to have ever lived on earth, the blue whale.

We originally captured storytellers' biographical information by asking them interview questions, so their responses best reflect what was relevant to them at that time. But forty people is a significant number to keep up with over the course of eight years. We have tried to make sure their background information is up to date, but as soon as this book is printed, for some it will likely be out of date again. A number of the stories also reference a specific timeline relevant to when the storytellers were interviewed. To help provide context, the dates of all interviews are listed on the top left of the story photo that begins each story.

Wild Monterey Bay is a celebration of wildlife *and* people. We began with a website, and posted each interview on YouTube. Now we have finally turned these illustrated stories into a book for people to enjoy for years to come, and we hope you will enjoy it.

A Note on Responsible Wildlife Viewing

We are pleased that you are about to enter the remarkable world of wildlife in, on and around the Monterey Bay National Marine Sanctuary. We hope you will enjoy the tales within these covers and learn a lot about many of the incredible species that live here. While we feature a large number of close encounters in this book, we want to emphasize that all our storytellers who are researchers, scientists, historians, fishermen, and boat captains followed National Oceanic and Atmospheric Administration (NOAA) marine life viewing guidelines:

(https://www.fisheries.noaa.gov/topic/marine-life-viewing-guidelines)

They conducted their work under these guidelines and regulations. Getting close to these creatures in the wild should never be undertaken without a required permit. Be respectful and refrain from approaching, touching or harassing any of our wonderful marine species. When they are disturbed, you are taking away precious energy they need for doing their other daily functions of finding food, grooming, resting and avoiding predators. For their sake and ours, engage only in responsible marine wildlife viewing. Mutual respect is the key to a healthy ocean and sustained populations of wildlife in any ecosystem.

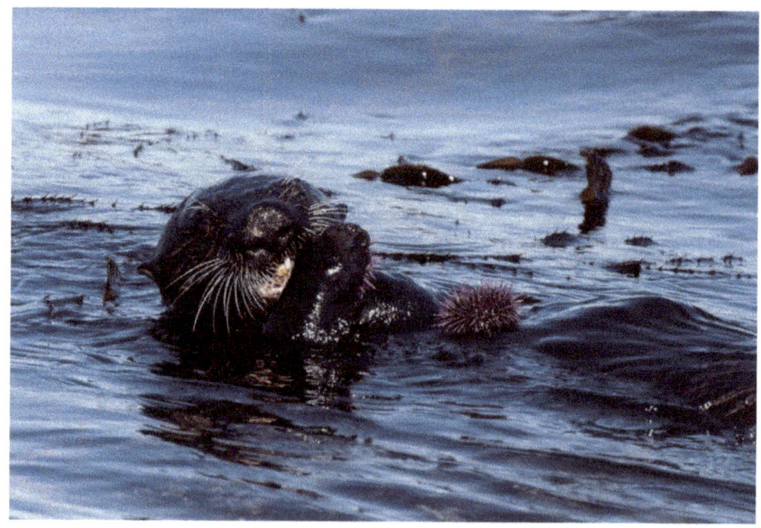

Table of Contents

What's it like taking kids who've never seen the ocean before out on a catamaran to do plankton tows and learn about navigation and conservation? Laura Barnes Walker, Education Director for O'Neill Sea Odyssey, has heard it all from "It looks fake!" to "Is this the ocean?" With her job cut out for her, she leads her charges on an exciting path of discovery as they hunt for seals, otters and, hopefully, whales.

Dakota Peebler, thirteen-year-old member of Heirs To Our Ocean (H2OO), has the good fortune to go kayaking with her family and sees a log that turns out to be a baby sea otter. Learning all about these charismatic weasels becomes one of her H2OO projects, so she can help with their conservation.

What do you do with an orphaned sea otter pup who's screaming at the top of his lungs? Why, give him to a mom in the wild whose pup has just died, of course. Easier said than done, but Michelle Staedler, Sea Otter Program Manager at the Monterey Bay Aquarium, has us on the edge of our seats as she attempts to do something that's never been done before.

Michelle Staedler's second story takes us to an abandoned cement structure in the surf off Cannery Row, where a mother sea otter is frantically swimming about. In wetsuits with salmon nets in tow, Michelle, Sea Otter Program Manager at the Monterey Bay Aquarium, and her colleague head out to see what the trouble is and find themselves in the surf in the unlikely position of pup rescuers.

Associate Professor and Researcher at the University of California at Santa Cruz, Ari Friedlaender would rather be on a boat than behind a desk. Putting suction tags on whales using a long pole while standing in the bow of a skiff is Ari's specialty. Here he takes us on one of his adventures in Monterey Bay, where the whales wear cameras, giving us a glimpse into their underwater world.

Founder and research biologist at Cascadia Research, John Calambokidis has his own whale-tagging story. While deploying those tags is a dangerous job, the rewards can be pure gold. John gives us a glimpse into the dynamic world of whales feeding on anchovies alongside sea lions, birds and other whales. And he gets us thinking about the value of those myriad little fish to the whole marine ecosystem.

Dave Cade just earned his doctorate working on cetacean foraging ecology—that is, looking in-depth at how whales feed and the world they feed in. Instead of humpback whales, Dave takes us out tagging blue whales, the largest animals to have ever lived on this planet. Getting to know your subjects is key for scientific success.

Founder of Oceanswell, Asha de Vos is Sri Lanka's foremost blue whale researcher. But seeing a blue whale in Monterey Bay was anything but routine for Asha. Her enthusiasm for her study subjects is simply contagious and Asha astounds her fellow whale watchers.

Twelve-year-old Charley Peebler graduated from Dora the Explorer to becoming a bona fide member of Heirs To Our Ocean. They give us a glimpse into one of their study topics, entangled whales, and how privileged they are to have the opportunity to see whales in the wild and learn from experts about the perils whales face.

One of the key members of the Northern California whale disentanglement team, Pieter Folkens, takes us step by step on a disentanglement mission. Pieter's storytelling carries us along on the vessel with him, wondering if we'll find the whale again, questioning whether the team will succeed, and hanging on when the whale, attached to his boat with lines, lashes out and gets everyone in the boat wet. It's quite a ride for the whale, the rescuers and readers alike.

Casper is just a youngster, but already a legend in Monterey Bay. This all-white Risso's dolphin has a fan following, and Katlyn Taylor, coeditor of *Wild Monterey Bay*, hopes we'll become a fan of this little dolphin, too.

Andrew DeVogelaere, the Research Director for the Monterey Bay National Marine Sanctuary, takes us on a journey under the sea, to a location called Sur Ridge, a mountain beneath the waves. He gives us a glimpse into the minds of scientists confronted with stunning corals, and shares how we can help care for them and help their communities thrive.

This story includes an underwater mountain 8000 feet tall, a remotely operated vehicle and some star-struck scientists who've suddenly and most unexpectedly come upon thousands of brooding octopuses, only the second such aggregation ever found. Chad King, a Research Specialist for the Monterey Bay National Marine Sanctuary, is still over the moon about this discovery. So much to learn, and he shares so much with us right here.

Sometimes it's hard to imagine how many animals there are that have never before been seen by human eyes. Lonny Lundsten is a New Age explorer who specializes in identifying critters new to science. Here Lonny, a Senior Research Technician at MBARI (Monterey Bay Aquarium Research Institute), visits a third sea mount, the Guide Sea Mount, and discovers a new type of sea slug with the ominous name of Black Tiger nudibranch.

The mysteries of the deep sea have captivated the imagination of people since the first sailors set out from shore. Geoff Shester, California Campaign Director for Oceana, takes us in a remote operating vehicle on a deep sea adventure where bright pink and purple corals and sponges grow in the company of teeny fish, tubeworms, anemones and other critters usually hidden from our view. This secret, magic world comes to life as we follow Geoff's account.

Tinker Neece is a boat captain for fishing trips and whale watch adventures with Chris' Fishing and Whale Watching. His tale combines both! Whatever was that whale doing that woke passengers from sleep before dawn? Tinker's simple style has us right there in awe of another whale encounter.

Usually, surfers are focused on the swell and the next set of waves. But Jane McKenzie, financial advisor and President and Team Captain of the Santa Cruz Longboard Union, was taken by surprise when a whale leaped out of the water right there in the surf lineup. Her life-altering experience was both awe-inspiring and terrifying.

Little can top friendly whales. Kate Cummings, co-owner and captain of Blue Ocean Whale Watch, shares two amazing encounters. The first one is about a well-known, friendly killer whale who approached their boat and showed off an elephant seal carcass he was carrying. Was he offering to share?

Because little can top friendly whales, Kate Cummings, co-owner and captain of Blue Ocean Whale Watch, couldn't decide between two amazing encounters. This second one involves a humpback whale that dove beneath their boat and lifted it up with its back. Not an everyday occurrence, mind you! You can see why it was hard to choose between the two stories.

Up close and personal clearly describes Kate Spencer's multipart story. And Kate's no ocean novice. A long-time naturalist, now owner and captain of her own whale watch vessel, the *Fast Raft*, Kate has nearly seen it all. Killer whales, humpback whales and gray whales all populate her exciting tale.

Ted Cheeseman has created Happywhale, a citizen science network for identifying humpback whales by the color patterns and scars on their tails. He can even tell us where a whale has been (to Baja California or perhaps San Francisco Bay), but when over 100 gathered in Monterey Bay to feed at the same time, Ted was totally awestruck.

Deb Gillespie had never really been out in the ocean before, though she walked daily along the shore. But the whales called her, and before she knew it, she was in over her head. Dolphins, sea lions and finally the whales made it all worthwhile—another life-transforming experience, courtesy of majestic marine mammals.

Documentary filmmaker Tom Mustill and his friend Charlotte had a once-in-a-lifetime experience with a whale that no one would wish upon their enemies. When the forty-foot-long humpback launched itself from beneath the waves like a surfacing submarine right next to their kayak and momentarily towered above them, Tom thought for sure it was all over. But his telling of this compelling tale will have readers alternating through fear, astonishment, relief, laughter and amazement.

Joy Reidenberg is a comparative anatomist at the Icahn School of Medicine at Mount Sinai, but this is her version of her good friend Tom's breaching whale story. Joy, as so many others had, first heard about the episode through the media. When she realized it was her dear friend who nearly died, she reviewed the video of the event and shares why she thinks Tom and his friend are alive today.

When a dead whale washes up on shore near a campground, the city decides it has got to go. But removing a forty-ton carcass isn't all that easy. Monte Ash, owner of TowBoatU.S. Santa Cruz, learns the ropes and shows us just how it's done. When the plan changes midday, Monte and crew find themselves dodging container ships and traveling with whale in tow through the dark, far offshore. This is another story that will have you on the edge of your seat.

Alisa Schulman-Janiger, naturalist and marine biologist, knows every killer whale in the transient population by name and its relationship to other family members. But it's the curious behavior of humpback whales who come upon killer whales hunting a gray whale calf that catches her attention. Was it altruism or something else that caused them to intervene?

Nancy Black, with the California Killer Whale Project, thought she'd seen it all, having spent thirteen years on the bay at that point. Transient killer whales and offshore orcas were the regulars who passed through. But on this day, she did not recognize any of the individuals. Another mystery was finally unraveled when she discovered these were residents from the Salish Sea who'd never before been seen south of southern Oregon. They came down on the hunt for salmon.

Orcas, or killer whales as they are most often called in Monterey Bay, are known as the top predators of the sea (except for humans), having been observed feeding on dolphins, whales and sharks. So Nancy Black, marine biologist and owner of Monterey Bay Whale Watch, was stunned to see Risso's dolphins in hot pursuit of the killer whales, a first for her. Who knows what that was all about!

Photographer and coeditor of *Wild Monterey Bay,* Jodi Frediani has heard a lot of cool stories and witnessed many more firsthand. Her own memorable encounter involves a well-known female killer whale doing what moms do best, teaching her offspring how to survive in the wild. A far cry from her distant relatives in captivity, this whale teaches us about the circle of life, while ensuring that her young have the survival skills they need to succeed.

Director of the Moss Landing Marine Laboratories Jim Harvey has done it all, or so it seems. But his latest work has turned him into a marine cowboy. Catching harbor seals in the name of science is only for the hardy. Timing, steadfastness and knowing what to do (and not to do) when a seal has latched onto your hand are only some of the qualifications needed for the job. Jim takes us out in his little boat and from there into the mud, wrestling with seals.

John Pearse, Professor Emeritus of ecology and evolutionary biology at UC Santa Cruz, was studying the impact of sea otters on the local ecosystem, so he and a student went looking for abalones off Año Nuevo, a favorite haul-out for northern elephant seals. What they found on a dive there, which gave them pause, was a headless seal. Only a shark could be responsible. Were they at risk? What should they do?

What do you do when you find your lab samples contaminated with a brown scuz? If you're a biologist, like John Pearse, you hunt for an explanation. Sherlock Holmes would have been proud. John's sleuthing took him to a Venezuelan student; a Brazilian researcher in France; a discovery in Vladivostok, Siberia; and the tide pools off Carmel, California. What he found was a species new to science right here at home, the most exciting find for any researcher.

Joy Reidenberg's seal stories are less rambunctious, but no less memorable. Confronting her first enormous elephant seals hauled out on shore only feet from her was just the beginning, an adventure in its own right for this self-proclaimed East Coast native. But as a comparative anatomist at the Icahn School of Medicine, Joy next finds herself conducting a necropsy on the monstrous head of a deceased female elephant seal, and enjoying every moment of it. This one was not the work of sharks.

Brandy Gale, a synesthetic artist, had been terrified of the water from early childhood when a bad in-water experience left its mark. But many, many years later, Monterey Bay changed all that. Brandy shares the lengths she went to to overcome her fears, how she learned to scuba dive and then how she received a welcome-back gift from a playful harbor seal.

Anemones aren't generally on the menu, at least for humans, but synesthetic artist Brandy Gale experiences critters through all her senses. This story is short, but just imagine what it is like to discover the personalities of anemones and their individual flavors.

John Mayer, co-owner of Discovery Whale Watch and J & M Sport Fishing, has been hanging out on boats since he was a teen. Clearly he's had many adventures out on the bay, but the mystical, magical lights that caught him by surprise one night long ago still rise to the top in his realm of memorable encounters.

Meg Kikkeri, a student of biology, geo-science and climate science, knows how to show friends a good time. But when Meg said, "Let's go kayaking at midnight," and didn't tell them why, they all thought it was nuts. Meg's effervescent personality overcame their reservations, and the bioluminescent adventure that followed was magic.

Randy Randazzo's an old-timer on Monterey Bay. Past owner of Randy's Fishing Trips, he's seen a lot. But it was his experience coming upon a basking shark that has stuck with him all these years. What do you do with such a beast? Well, in the old days it was worth no small change. You'll have to read Randy's story to find out what they did with that plankton-eating shark.

We confess. This story kind of snuck in here. Taking place off the Farallon Islands, it actually occurred in the Greater Farallones National Marine Sanctuary, next door to the Monterey Bay National Marine Sanctuary. But, well, since sharks travel far and wide, including Monterey Bay, and it's such a cool story, we decided to let it stay. Sal Jorgensen, shark specialist at the Monterey Bay Aquarium, shares his story about running into an old friend—a shark friend that is. How cool is that?

White sharks used to be rare in Monterey Bay, but when the warm water Blob arrived, things changed. Sal Jorgensen takes us to the white sharks' nursery with explanations of why they have taken up residence now in our bay.

Who knew that leatherback turtles had different personalities? Well, Scott Benson, National Oceanic and Atmospheric Administration (NOAA) Marine Turtle Specialist, made that discovery. Here he shares his experience capturing a 1300-pound specimen with his second-string crew. She surprised them all, and made some friends that day.

Debi Shearwater, head of Shearwater Journeys, has been leading birding trips for as long as she can remember, though it's a calling she sort of fell into by chance and circumstance. But then, chance and circumstance mixed with a good dose of instinct and adventure have led Debi and her guests around the world serendipitously finding uncommon and common birds alike. Here Debi shares with us some of those special avian moments on Monterey Bay.

Skylar Campbell, a commercial fisherman, like many who spend a lot of time on the water, finds picking just one memorable encounter to be extremely difficult. He takes us on a journey filled with orcas, octopuses, white sharks, wolf eels and more creatures than you can toss a net over.

A whole other world exists for those willing to don a wetsuit and scuba gear and venture beneath the surface of the sea. Brian Phan, a professional scuba diver and dive technician, who grew up afraid of the water, did just that and came face to face with one of the strangest fish in the sea, the *Mola mola*. At five feet in length, this particular ocean sunfish, with its enormous eyes, snub tail, and prehistoric head, made an everlasting impression on Brian and his friends who ventured into its watery world.

Only Tierney Thys could get as excited about the eyeball of an ocean sunfish as most folks get upon seeing their first whale. She is a science media producer and communicator, but her specialty is the odd-shaped fish known as the *Mola mola*. When a sea lion shows up next to her boat with a big, beautiful, but dead *mola* in its jaws, Tierney knows what she needs to do. Of course, her spontaneity gets her in trouble, but sometimes the rewards are worth the price paid.

Author and Monterey area fisheries historian Tim Thomas tells a tale, like so many of those he shares in his books and with all those who will listen. This one happened to a friend of his, rather than being one of his own adventures. It's a story about how an abalone saved his good friend's life.

Don Kelly, Warden and Patrol Captain for the California Department of Fish and Wildlife, takes his job seriously. He's out there day after day ensuring that people comply with the regulations protecting our wildlife resources. So he's seen it all! But once again, it's those whales—in this case, orcas—that make his day. Don shares his whale tales, while also giving us a glimpse into a warden's rounds enforcing the law and working with the public.

As Watershed Compliance Manager for the City of Santa Cruz, Chris Berry juggles providing quality water for the city, while protecting the natural environment. It's clear that Chris loves his work, and he takes us on a real adventure exploring a water supply watershed that empties into the Monterey Bay National Marine Sanctuary. His tale ties together an odd assortment of critters including whales, rare and endangered fish, frogs and beetles.

Foreword

By Carl Safina

Safina Center of Stonybrook University

I first visited Monterey, California a long time ago. I didn't know anyone there. I knew Monterey by name only, and didn't know what to expect of the bay itself.

On the first night in town, I thought, "What a pretty place." Touristy, yeah, but definitely pretty. A little magic in the air somehow.

I decided to walk from the Monterey Bay Aquarium down beyond Cannery Row, and to just keep walking, to see if I could go on foot all the way to Fisherman's Wharf.

But—wait a minute—is that a *sea otter?* It *is!* But aren't they endangered? Weren't they almost extinct? (Yes.) And—is that a baby? Am I actually looking at a mother and baby sea otter? (I am!)

Well… long story short (because this book is full of *great* stories), over the next few years Monterey Bay, and the Aquarium, became something like my home away from home. Several times a year I had reasons to go there for meetings and strategy sessions about the ocean conservation work I and colleagues were doing. It was, and always is, one place I always look forward to visiting. And some of my colleagues at the Aquarium, the research and academic institutions, the conservation groups… we've become friends and I value them tremendously and have traveled with some of them from Monterey Bay to far, far out in the Pacific. The bay seems to magnetically attract some of the most interesting and fantastically smart people in the world. Because: it attracts some of the world's most spectacular wild beings.

So here's the main thing: Monterey Bay itself is a unique place where the canyons of the deep ocean come right to the shore. Along most of the West Coast the continental shelf is miles wide, and then it drops away to the deep ocean. In Monterey Bay the deep ocean runs right into the shoreline.

That deep water getting shoved up along the shallow shoreline brings nutrients up into the light. And *that* ignites the whole food chain, from the drifting cells of green plankton that use light to make life, to the forests of giant kelp, to enormous schools of sardines and vast multitudes of anchovies and hordes of squid.

And all of that brings—the big stuff!

The biggest animals known to have *ever* lived *on the planet* live here. I'm talking: blue whales! And the spectacular humpbacks who launch into the air and crash into the sea like a school bus that just fell out of a cloud. And the swift minke whales. And sometimes even Moby Dick, the sperm whale, puts in an appearance. Not to mention—but I will—various kinds of porpoises and dolphins *including* the world's largest dolphins: killer whales (a.k.a. orcas). Monterey Bay is the easiest place in the continental United States to see albatrosses of two species, who are among the world's largest seabirds. That's not to mention the thousands of shearwaters who travel through the bay in one of the world's largest seabird migrations. And the incredible elephant seals. Sea lions galore. Gigantic ocean sunfish, also called *Mola mola.* And the world's largest shark with teeth, the famous and infamous great white.

So—Wild Monterey Bay is truly, and literally, deeply wild. I mean, the place is positively lit up with life. It's crazy. It's wonderful. It's magic. And it has brought us together right here right now. So, turn the page—and let's go!

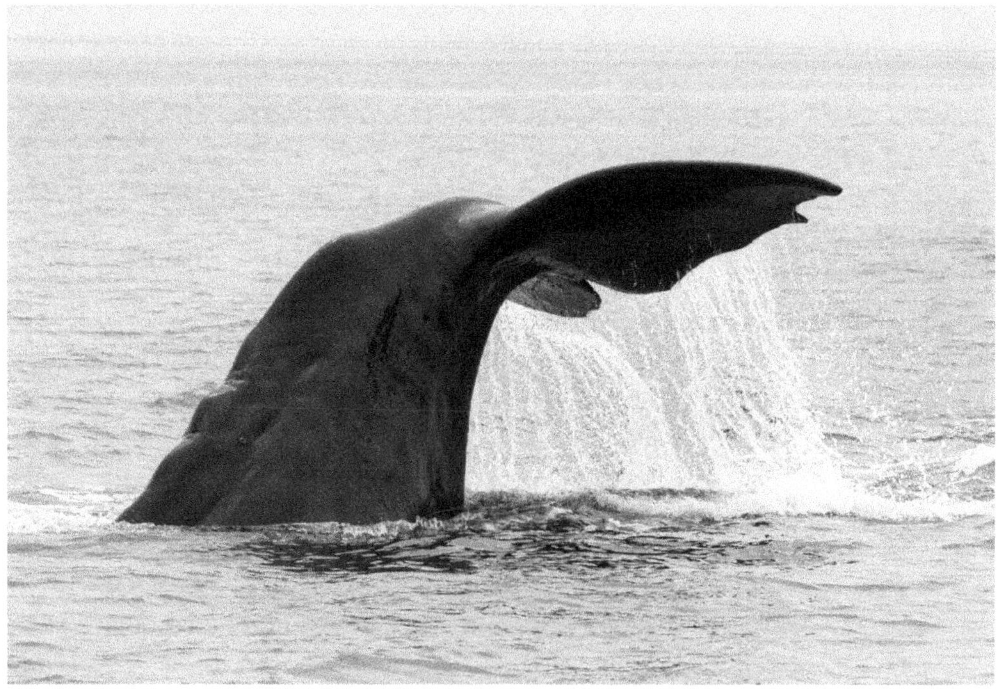

Sperm whale

How Did Wild Monterey Bay Come into Being?

This anthology was born out of a desire to share an environmental success story celebrating the extraordinary ecosystem that is Monterey Bay. We wanted to recognize the breadth of animal species that make Monterey Bay a hot spot of biodiversity and its own unique magic kingdom. We also wanted to honor and recognize the people who work and play here, including those who study, protect and appreciate the wildlife of this special coastal habitat.

We hope these stories will inspire others to care about, not only this marine ecosystem, but all of our oceans and the diverse species that inhabit them. They all need our ongoing protection to continue to flourish. While Monterey Bay gained protected status as a National Marine Sanctuary in 1992, this designation came about only because many people cared and took action.

When we set out on this adventure, we decided that storytelling would be our vehicle of choice. We were certain that anyone spending time on the bay would sooner or later experience a remarkable encounter of one sort or another. We had definitely had our own, so we concluded others must have too. And stories about those encounters could have a special sparkle and life of their own. We simply needed to find the storytellers and sit them down in front of a camera.

What is it about stories that makes them so special? Why not just some photos, or a list of species ticked off? Dr. Jane Goodall was recently quoted as saying that stories are the way to reach into the hearts of leaders and prompt change. Appealing to the brain is not good enough; one needs to appeal to the heart, and stories are the pathway. Well, we hope these illustrated stories will hold the key to opening some hearts as well.

What is it about storytelling that enchants and moves us? Stories have been with us for a very long time. While no one knows when the very first story was told, some researchers say fables were shared as far back as 6000 years ago. Perhaps the earliest stories were those painted on cave walls, dating back some 30,000 years! Many cave paintings also include animals (just as our stories do) in those now hard-to-decipher tales.

Some fables and myths have persisted in human culture over centuries, often transforming along the way, but continuing to be meaningful to those on the listening end hundreds of years after the first telling. Stories come in many forms from myths, to legends of all kinds, fables, fairy tales, trickster stories, ghost tales, hero stories and epic adventures. They once took form through song, chant and epic poetry. Today they may be found in novels, movies, on stage or in social media.

Many of the early stories were passed on through word of mouth, so we decided to ask our storytellers to do the same.

We began each interview with a brief set of questions to learn a bit about the storyteller's life, which you will find as a bio after their story. Then each tale was recounted, first person, on camera, as we tried hard not to laugh out loud at the funny bits. We wanted to have a clean auditory track on our videos.

As for the stories themselves, no questions were asked other than "What was your most memorable wildlife encounter on the bay?" Then we sat back and listened as the story unfolded and the cameras rolled. Each story was transcribed, and posted on our website and Facebook page along with the recorded video of each tale. For this book, we did some additional editing while attempting to maintain the distinct 'voice' of each storyteller.

A first-person rendition of an event usually includes facts, perhaps a bit of embellishment, sometimes strong emotion, and if the storyteller has talent, we may even be kept on the edge of our seats in anticipation of something unknown, untoward, perhaps shocking or magical. Often there is something we can fully relate to. That said, we did not choose people for their storytelling skills. Rather, we wanted a cross-section of our community who shared a love for the bay and were willing to talk about one of their special encounters.

Stories can entertain us, educate us, and give us a way to empathize with the characters. They may make us laugh, hold our breath in anticipation, inspire us or provide a bit of much-needed optimism. Stories may be brief glimpses into the past, or more in the vein of those fabled epics that take us on an unexpected, roundabout journey. But in the end, all good stories have the ability to touch our hearts. We hope that at least one of these stories will touch yours.

The Magic That Is Monterey Bay

Monterey Bay is a place of wonder, of discovery and of beauty. Thousands of marine species from phytoplankton to enormous blue whales use Monterey Bay as their home or critical habitat. Animals migrate tens of thousands of miles to this special place. Its rich ecosystem stretches miles deep and has far-reaching effects. Seawater, thousands of years old, graces the surface waters of the bay during upwelling events (a fact that Andrew DeVogelaere floored us with the first time we heard him speak). Some of the most powerful acts of nature take place right here.

But the bay is also where a confluence of people, history, literature, science, exploration and amazing wildlife come together. The bay in all its diversity and splendor has been written about in books, magazines, newspapers and blogs. It's been highlighted in film, nature specials and even an HBO TV show. People travel from every corner of the Earth to visit and experience this incredible place. World-class researchers work tirelessly to protect this indentation along the eastern Pacific Ocean and to unlock its secrets. Think tanks and celebrities find inspiration while visiting its majestic shoreline. What an amazing reputation follows Monterey Bay around the Earth!

What Else Is Monterey Bay and Where Can You Find It?

Geographically speaking, Monterey Bay, a bay of the Pacific Ocean, lies along the west coast of Central California between Santa Cruz County to the north and Monterey County to the south. The mouth of the bay is 25 miles across and to traverse the coastline from inside the bay would cover approximately 75 miles.

The predominant geological underwater feature of Monterey Bay is the vast network of deep-sea canyons. The three main interlinked canyons in this near-shore system are Monterey Canyon, Soquel Canyon and Carmel Canyon. One of the leading theories about how the canyons originally formed was that an older path of the Colorado River used to flow out to sea along this part of the coast. The canyon walls were very steep in some parts of the bay, but were continually carved deeper over time as a result of significant turbidity currents. The deepest part of the Monterey Canyon, the Monterey Fan, lies two miles (~3.2 km) deep and is an area of study that may someday shed light on this theory.

Monterey Bay is extremely rich in biodiversity and has been designated as a National Marine Sanctuary. The sanctuary extends north, south and west of the bay itself. Monterey Bay National Marine Sanctuary Superintendent Lisa Wooninck writes:

"Designated in 1992, Monterey Bay National Marine Sanctuary (MBNMS) is a federally protected marine area offshore of California's central coast. Stretching from Marin to Cambria, the sanctuary encompasses a shoreline length of 276 miles and 6,094 square statute miles (4,601 nmi^2) of ocean, extending an average distance of 30 miles from shore. At its deepest point, MBNMS reaches 12,743 feet (more than two miles). It is one of our nation's largest national marine sanctuaries, and is larger than Yellowstone National Park.

"The sanctuary contains extensive kelp forests and one of North America's largest underwater canyons and closest-to-shore deep ocean environments. Its diverse marine ecosystem also includes rugged rocky shores, wave-swept sandy beaches and tranquil estuaries. These habitats harbor an incredible variety of marine life, including 36 species of marine mammals, more than 180 species of seabirds and shorebirds, at least 525 species of fishes, and an abundance of invertebrates and algae. Known as the 'Serengeti of the Sea,' this remarkably productive marine environment is fringed by spectacular coastal scenery, including sand dunes, rocky cliffs, rolling hills and steep mountains."[1]

The sanctuary was established to protect it from harmful activities such as oil drilling, seabed mining, overfishing and other damaging activities that are prohibited today. Research, education and other compatible public uses are encouraged. The latter include regulated recreational and commercial fishing, as well as surfing, boating, diving and whale watching.

In addition to the National Marine Sanctuary designation, the bay contains many marine conservation areas, marine reserves and marine protected areas. Each one of those designations has different purposes, policies and rules—all with the aim of providing layers of protection above and beyond the general state and federal laws that protect all shorelines and coastal waters in the United States.

Who Was Here First?

We would be remiss if we did not acknowledge the first people who inhabited this amazing place. The land surrounding Monterey Bay encompasses the unceded territories of the Ohlone/Costanoan people. The tribes of the Monterey Bay area were Aptos, Cajastaca, Ichxenta, Kalindaruk, Rumsien, Uypi and Wacharon. They spoke Awaswas on the north coast, Rumsen on the south coast, and Mutsun in the lands inland from the bay. There is some

---

[1] https://montereybay.noaa.gov/intro/welcome.html

evidence to show that people inhabited this region for about 5700–6000 years before European contact.

An excerpt from the book *The Ohlone Way* describes the region's original inhabitants as

"the densest Indian population anywhere north of Mexico. Over 10,000 people lived in the coastal areas between Point Sur and the San Francisco Bay. These people belonged to about forty different groups, each with its own territory and its own chief. Among them they spoke eight to twelve different languages that were closely related but still so distinct that oftentimes people living twenty miles apart could hardly understand each other. The average size of a group (or tribelet, as it is often called) was only 250 people. Each language had an average of no more than 1,000 speakers. That so many independent groups of people speaking so many different languages could be packed into a relatively small area boggled the European mind."[2]

Much has been lost to the Monterey Bay region over time, and that includes peoples and cultures, in addition to flora and fauna.

Today we can only dream about what this area looked like in prior centuries. Another excerpt from *The Ohlone Way* gives accounts of what the bay was like in the past.

"Life in the ocean and in the unspoiled bays of San Francisco and Monterey was likewise plentiful beyond modern conception. There were mussels, clams, oysters, abalones, seabirds and sea otters in profusion. Sea lions blackened the rocks at the entrance to San Francisco Bay and in Monterey Bay they were so abundant that to one missionary they seemed to cover the entire surface of the water 'like a pavement' . . . [Another] early visitor to Monterey Bay wrote: 'It is impossible to conceive of the number of whales with which we were surrounded, or their familiarity; they every half minute spouted within half a pistol shot of the ships and made a prodigious stench in the air.' Along the bays and ocean beaches whales were often seen washed up on the shore with grizzly bears in 'countless troops'—or in many cases Indians—streaming down the beach to feast on their remains."

---

[2] Malcolm Margolin, The Ohlone Way: Indian Life in the San Francisco–Monterey Bay Area, Heyday Press, 1978.

If what we are seeing today is only a fraction of what this place used to be, we're truly in awe of the magnificence that was Monterey Bay in years past. The current richness and biodiversity is quite incredible, despite the 250+ years of commercial exploitation and changes.

A Little about Science Communication

Our goal with this book is to meld stories with science, and sprinkle in a dose of conservation awareness. One lesson Katlyn has learned from being in sales is that facts tell, but stories sell. Of course we want our book to sell, but with the intention of spreading our message about the wonder of Monterey Bay. We hope the love we have for this place shines through this compilation of first-person tales. We could tell myriad stories of our own, but the people of Monterey Bay are as important to us (and to the health and diversity of the bay) as her wildlife, so we chose to pass the microphone and let the varied cast of characters bring the vibrancy of this bay to life.

Long before humans recorded things in writing, we shared our history through the spoken word. We teach the next generation about life lessons from a young age through storytelling. Some studies have shown that narrative cognition, or learning information in a narrative format, is the default mode of human thought.

For a long time, science tried to distance itself from storytelling and narratives, but there has been a slow return to the importance of narratives. In true scientific fashion, you can find many academic articles and essays about science communication breaking down storytelling into jargon and data. What is becoming apparent in these analyses and studies is that storytelling is important to communicating science, and if it's done well, can change how people engage with science.

So, in this book you will find stories. Some of them are about how science is done, some are about how people make a living in the bay, and some of them are simply about amazing wildlife. Take from them what you will.

How Deep Is the Ocean?

L a u r a   B a r n e s   W a l k e r

(Date of Interview: 12/8/16)

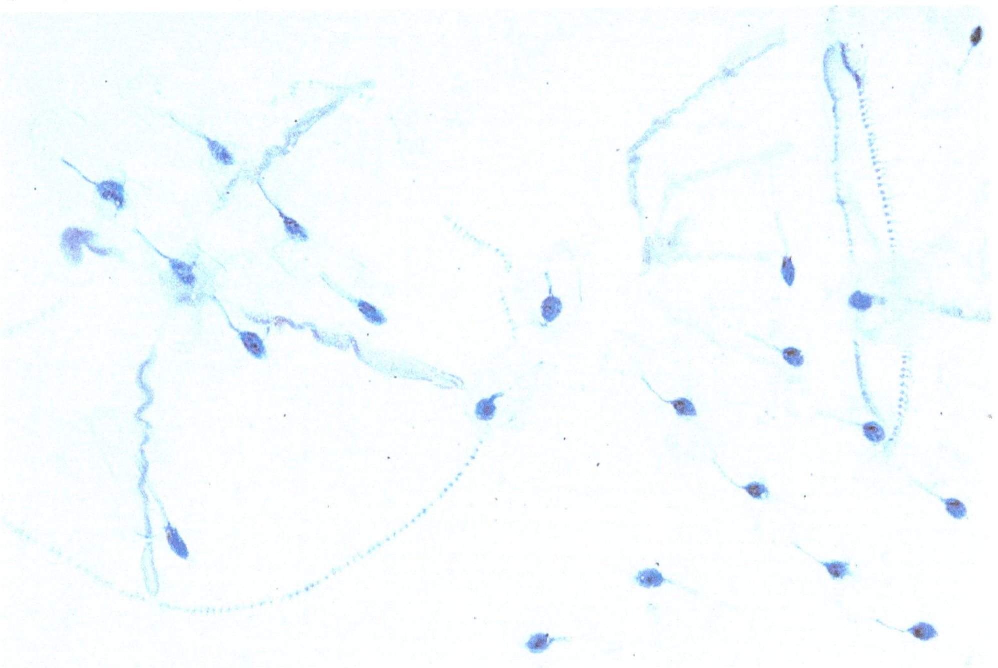

Plankton: cross jellies and salps

So, if you ask me about one particular, impactful experience that I've had on the ocean, I think I would have to say dealing with a population of kids that live twenty minutes from the ocean, but have never seen it, introducing them to the ocean and marine science. I have a lot of kids that have never been on a boat, or their only experience on the beach is maybe they took a trip to the Boardwalk in Santa Cruz on their summer break. They don't really have any idea of what's living out there, so teaching them about the ocean becomes a very memorable experience.

We get questions all the way up the dock, as we're walking with the kids. They're just shooting questions at us the whole time. "How deep is the water here?" "How deep is the ocean?" That is a really common one: "How deep is the ocean?" I go, "it depends on where you are! If you look at the depth finder right now, we're at sixty feet, but if you go out fifty miles that way, it's like two and a half miles." That's a real concept for them—about how different it is, not just one big puddle. And also, how vast it is.

They learned in school, oh you know, the ocean is more than 70% of the earth's surface. They know that, but then when they get out there and they see it, they look at me and say, "Is this the ocean?" "Is this the Pacific Ocean?" "What ocean is this?" "Where are we?" "Like, is this the ocean?" "Are we on the ocean?" "Are we going on the ocean?" There's a lot of that! Even when we're out there!

Almost every day I get kids looking at the water, and they'll say, "It looks fake." I think it's because so many kids experience things through video. When they see something that's real on video, because video looks so real, they're confused when they see reality. It's much more unusual for them to be in a real environment than in a video environment. I see that every day. I can't count how many times the kids look down at the water and say, "It looks fake." "It looks fake. Is that real? It looks fake."

So, a big hurdle we have to deal with when we're trying to introduce kids to the ocean is getting them to understand that the ocean is a living thing—it's a living habitat full of all kinds of animals that have their own reasons for doing things, their own motivations, their own destinies to fulfill.

A lot of kids will come out and some of the questions they ask heading down the dock are, "Are we gonna see whales?" "Are we gonna see dolphins?" "Are we gonna see sharks?" "Are there sharks living here?" "Can they jump up and grab us off the boat?" You know, stuff like that.

And I say to the whale and dolphin questions, "Maybe. I don't know. We might have to look for them." And they don't really get that, you know. I say, "Well, we're definitely gonna see sea lions, because they kind of hang out in one place. We're definitely gonna see sea otters, because they kind of hang out in one place. We're definitely, well, we're *probably* gonna see harbor seals, but only maybe, you know, because they don't always hang out in one place. Whales and dolphins—they have business to take care of. They're doing their thing. I don't know what that business is. Maybe they're off getting something to eat. Or migrating north, or whatever they're doing. We don't know if we're going to see them or not."

And that is a new concept, because sometimes the kids arrive and they think it's like Sea World. We can just whistle or snap our fingers—oh, there's the dolphins! You know, they're not kept anywhere. And that's another thing with language that we see from the kids a lot. We say, "Do you guys know what a sanctuary is?" And they say, "It's a place where you keep the animals."

We go, "well, we don't really *keep* them. That's not really how it works. This is where they live. It's like your house isn't where we keep you. Well, maybe it is, you know, but it's where you live, right? Your city isn't where we keep you. These animals just live here. They might show up and they might not, depending on the conditions. And the conditions are gonna change, right?"

So, it's funny, because kids who don't come here often, they get to see a lot of pictures of the beach—of the beach on TV. Even if it's cold where they live, they'll come in shorts and bathing suits, even if they live just a half hour away. So, it's really getting them to understand this is a real, natural environment. It's gonna change. You're gonna have to adapt to it. Like, it's not always gonna adapt to you the way our human environment that we can control so much does.

They have a hard time believing us, especially since they're really obsessed with sharks. The kids come out and they say, "Are there sharks here?" We have to teach science. We have to teach the absolute truth. I don't ever lie to them. I say, "yeah, there's sharks here, a lot of kinds." "What kinds?" "All kinds, you know. There are leopard sharks and great white sharks, you know, salmon sharks and all kinds of sharks." And they're like, "What are we doing out here?" because they think of sharks as this great monster enemy. But they don't jump out of the water like in the movies, and I've been working on this boat for eighteen years and I've never seen one. I wish I could. You know, they don't come up for our convenience. It's a challenge getting the kids to understand that wild animals have a mind of their own, and that they're just doing their job and fulfilling their destiny out there.

Another thing that is really fun, and one of the most impactful things we do, is show them the plankton. We get plankton samples every day and identify the different types of plankton. So, we'll get a group of kids out on the boat, and they will actually take the plankton samples themselves. I'll go, "here's your net, throw it in, pull it out, hold the jar, pour the plankton in the jar." So, they do every step, totally hands on! They pour it in the jar. They can look in and see tiny little dustlike specs in the jar. And then we come back here, and I put the plankton under the microscope, and it shows up on our TV.

And, you know, the questions we have before the sample goes up on the TV are like, "What does plankton look like?" "How can you tell phytoplankton from zooplankton?" We go, "Well, they all look different. And, you know, how do you tell a daisy from a redwood tree? How do you tell a dog from a rosebush?" It's very important that they know that there are thousands of types of plankton, and not just one.

So, we get here in the lab, and the plankton have such endearing characteristics, even for the kids. When they see a baby barnacle, they just go, "oh, look at that guy, it's so cute." I talk about the plankton, their life cycle, what they eat and what they do and how their life is and some of the challenges they go through just to survive, especially meroplankton[3]. You know, so much meroplankton exists just to be eaten, so that a single one can survive. And getting the kids to understand that? Well, it doesn't really happen. They don't really get it until the very last ten seconds of the program.

The kids will look at the plankton on TV and we'll identify the species, and they'll *ooh* and *ahh*. Then at the very end, we take the slide out from under the microscope, and we pass it around right under the kids' noses so they can see that those little specs of dust right there are what they just saw on TV. And that is the only moment when they really get it, because, you know, we pass that slide around and they go, "No way!" And then the inevitable questions, "When you're swimming, are they all over you?" "What happens if I swallow them?" "Are they going to swim around inside my stomach and live?"

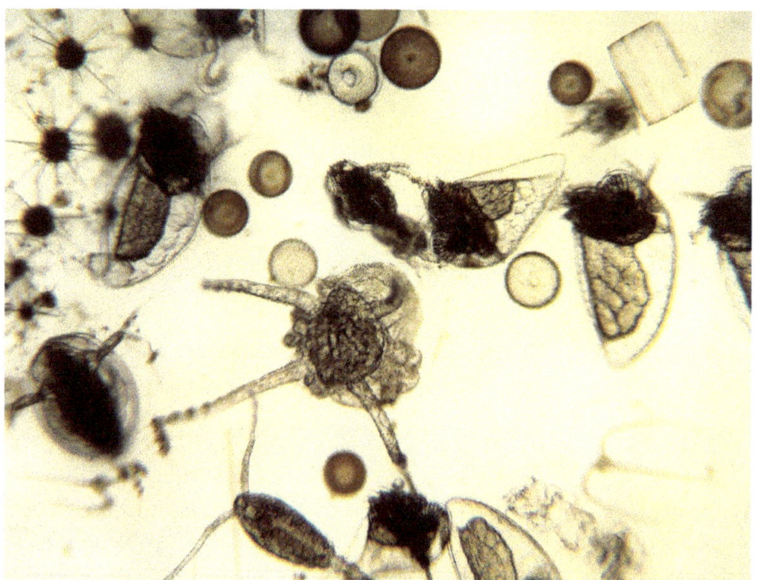

Radiolaria and other zooplankton
© O'Neill Sea Odyssey

So, we have to put a lot of those fears to rest. But the kids really start to care about these tiny little microscopic creatures. By the end, they're thinking about, "Well what are you going to do with them now?" "Are you going to put them back?" Like, they're really interested!

We see a lot of pregnant Cladocera[4], and the kids are like, "Well, she's gonna have babies! You've got to put her back in the ocean!" "What about that fish egg we saw?" "You have to put these back." So we'll take the samples and put them in

---

[3] Meroplankton are only planktonic for part of their life cycle. They include larval forms of such marine animals as sea urchins, starfish, crabs, octopus and most reef fish.

[4] They are also known as water fleas, tiny crustaceans that are holoplankton—planktonic for their entire lives. They have live offspring, which is very different from most other holoplankton crustaceans, which lay eggs.

a cup and ask the kids to take them and pour them off the dock back into the harbor. Pretty much every day.

And that makes them feel connected. You know that makes them feel like this cup of water, which before they would have just poured onto their sand castle, *this is alive!* These are living creatures, they're just not the same size as us. So that, I think, is one of the things that I enjoy most about my job—having the kids make that connection—and I think it takes the whole three hours to get there.

Honestly, you think it's gonna happen right when they get on the boat, but they are questioning their reality so much throughout the whole process, that I really think it does take the whole program for them to get it, a lot of times. Especially if they're kids that haven't been exposed to the ocean environment before.

LAURA BARNES WALKER

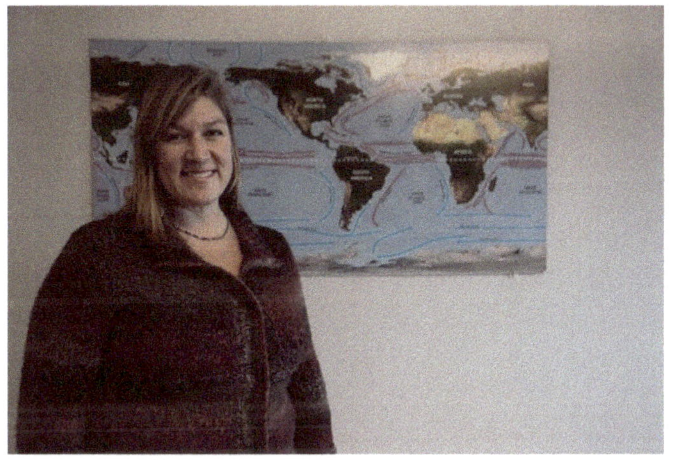

Laura Barnes Walker currently works for the Ocean Conservancy's Global Ghost Gear Initiative, a team that works internationally to prevent, mitigate, and remediate environmental harm from lost and abandoned fishing gear.

At the time of this interview, Laura held the position of Program Manager for O'Neill Sea Odyssey (OSO), which provides hands-on educational experiences for young students, encouraging them to protect and preserve our marine environment. The program takes fourth- through sixth-grade kids out on Monterey Bay in a catamaran. The students do a three-station program that includes marine biology, marine ecology and navigation, which serve as an introduction to marine science. Most of these kids have never been on a boat before.

Her duties at OSO included onboard deckhand work, and the teaching of all three learning stations aboard the catamaran. She also researched and wrote all of the OSO curricula, managed grants, scheduled teachers, paid for buses out of OSO's scholarship fund, mopped up, scrubbed life jackets, and designed visual aids. Laura was an OSO employee from 1999 to 2021.

She was born in Santa Barbara, California and grew up there. Her dad worked on the water, so Laura grew up on boats. Her first job was scrubbing the bottom of her dad's boat, for which she earned an allowance.

Laura studied humanities at San Francisco State University because she wanted a well-rounded education. However, the ocean life continued to call. Immediately after graduating, she worked for the Maritime Museum Association in San Francisco. Then North Sails offered her a job making sails for the America's Cup, a job she held until the races ended a year later.

After the job at North Sails ended, Laura really wanted to travel but didn't have the necessary funding, so she got a job as a tour guide in Alaska. There she spent a couple of years working in the eco-tourism industry, leading camping tours, and subsequently worked on Prince William Sound as a naturalist on a glacier and on a wildlife day-tour charter boat.

Upon Laura's return to California, a friend suggested Santa Cruz as an antidote to big city life, which would have been hard after experiencing the wilderness of Alaska. Once settled, Laura went to the harbor to look for a job. She approached Save Our Shores (SOS), as she wanted to do something good for the environment. During her time in Alaska, Laura was shocked by the lack of environmental awareness she often observed in the tourism industry.

It turned out that SOS didn't have any job openings at the time, but they did have a Sanctuary Stewardship Program, which included 100 hours of training about the ecology of Monterey Bay. Laura completed the ten-week course, plus 100 hours of community service public outreach.

Near the end of that program, SOS told her that O'Neill was looking for someone with boat experience who had worked as a naturalist. Laura was hired and started as an instructor in the Sea Odyssey program in 1999. A few years later she was asked if she'd like the Education Coordinator position to write their curriculum as a book, which led in time to the Program Manager position. Laura said yes and worked at O'Neill Sea Odyssey for the next twenty years!

A Log or a Baby Sea Otter?

Dakota Peebler

(Date of Interview: 11/12/16)

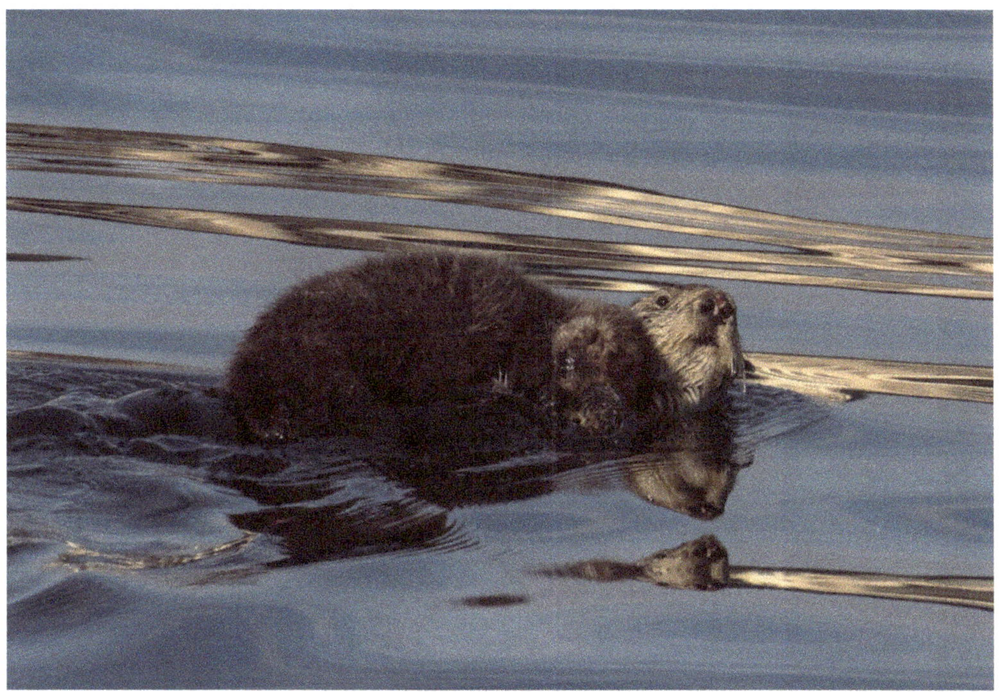

Southern sea otter mother and pup

My family and I went kayaking in Monterey Bay, and we were hoping to see some wildlife. We were kayaking along and we saw this little log, and we thought it was a baby sea otter, but it wasn't. And then we thought it was a baby sea otter again! And then we thought it was a log. Then we thought it was a baby sea otter! It actually *was* a baby sea otter!

It was crying for its mom, and we were just like going, "Oh no, what are we going to do; it doesn't have its mom?" And then its mom just popped up and grabbed the baby sea otter. It was a really fantastic experience, just seeing the baby sea otter reunited with its mom.

So, after that, I was whole-heartedly researching sea otters. I wanted to protect the sea otter, and I wanted to conserve the sea otter. After I joined Heirs To Our Ocean, the goal was to find a scientist or researcher focusing on the area of focus I have. Then I found Dr. Melissa Miller, who is a veterinarian and a sea otter pathologist.

Dr. Miller works with the Marine Wildlife Veterinary Care Research Center in Santa Cruz, and I was lucky enough to be able to do a necropsy on a sea otter with her. It was really cool. We found out the sea otter had died from a shark bite. Not from the shark bite itself, but from the bacterial infection that got into the shark bite after the otter was wounded. It was really a *fantastic* experience!!

Sea otters are important because they are a keystone species. They eat sea urchins and sea urchins eat kelp, so when the sea otter population goes down, the urchin population has no key predator. You could probably find another predator, but the population of the urchin's main predator has gone down, so the urchin populations increase.

They eat all the kelp and then create an urchin barren, which is basically a desert. You can look it up on your phone or whatever. It's really a desert of urchins. Kelp, along with the other main botanicals of the ocean, gives us 50–70% of our oxygen. So, we need our kelp and we need our sea otters.

Also, kelp absorbs vast amounts of carbon from our atmosphere to create its leafy structure, and it can absorb twelve times as much CO_2 when sea otters are keeping urchins in check. So, sea otters are very important.

The main source of sea otter mortality is land/sea pollution, including a parasite that comes from our wild and pet cats' poop. You probably know about this—*Toxoplasma gondii*. It's been

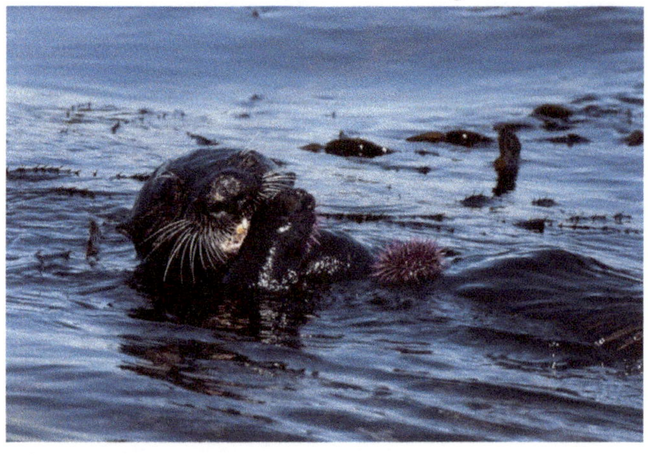

Sea otter feeding on sea urchin

getting into sea otters and it affects their brain, as does domoic acid, which comes from harmful algal blooms, which are being worsened by fertilizer runoff. Domoic acid accumulates in food sources eaten by sea otters. It causes them to have seizures and can result in death.

So, sea otters are affected by many threats.

DAKOTA PEEBLER

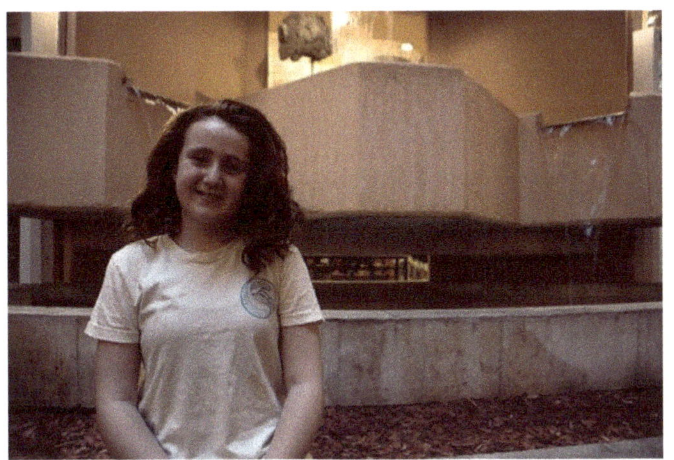

Dakota Peebler is a cofounder of Heirs To Our Ocean (H2OO), a group that started as seventeen homeschooled kids, ages ten to thirteen, from the San Francisco Bay Area who are taking the ocean crisis into their own hands. At the time of Dakota's interview, they were making a movie about human impacts on the oceans and how these impacts are affecting their generation and their health, as well as future generations and their health. The movie was also going to cover their journey and lead to making their movement a global one. As part of their efforts, they have been organizing beach cleanups, meeting with legislators, going to protests and anywhere else they can have a positive effect on our oceans.

Each child in H2OO has a specialty area. At the time of our interview, Dakota had two specialties in the project. The first was sea otters, which are a keystone species in the marine ecosystem. Dakota had been researching sea otters for four years, so she was eager to be able to research them further and study them whole-heartedly through this project.

Her second area of specialization was in Palau, where she focused on Palau's endangered species, and especially on helping create marine sanctuaries for their protection. Dakota came naturally to this. Her mother, April Peebler, was working in Palau with environmental law regarding sharks, and Dakota became increasingly interested in studying and working on behalf of the Palauan endangered species.

Dakota was born in the San Francisco Bay Area and grew up in San Mateo. She was eleven at the time of our interview and is homeschooled. She originally came to Monterey Bay to visit the Monterey Bay Aquarium with her family. They enjoyed it so much they kept going back and fell in love with Monterey Bay.

Today, as a young adult, she is also a junior board member and Assistant Program Coordinator for Heirs To Our Ocean. She has been able to organize and help prepare youth to talk to congresspeople through policy advocacy retreats and one-on-one consultations. She also creates her own art and educational tools through sustainable and reconstructed fashion, and engages the public through social media, networking and public speaking engagements.

The Story of Elwood: An Otterly Happy Ending

Michelle Staedler

(Date of Interview: 7/12/18)

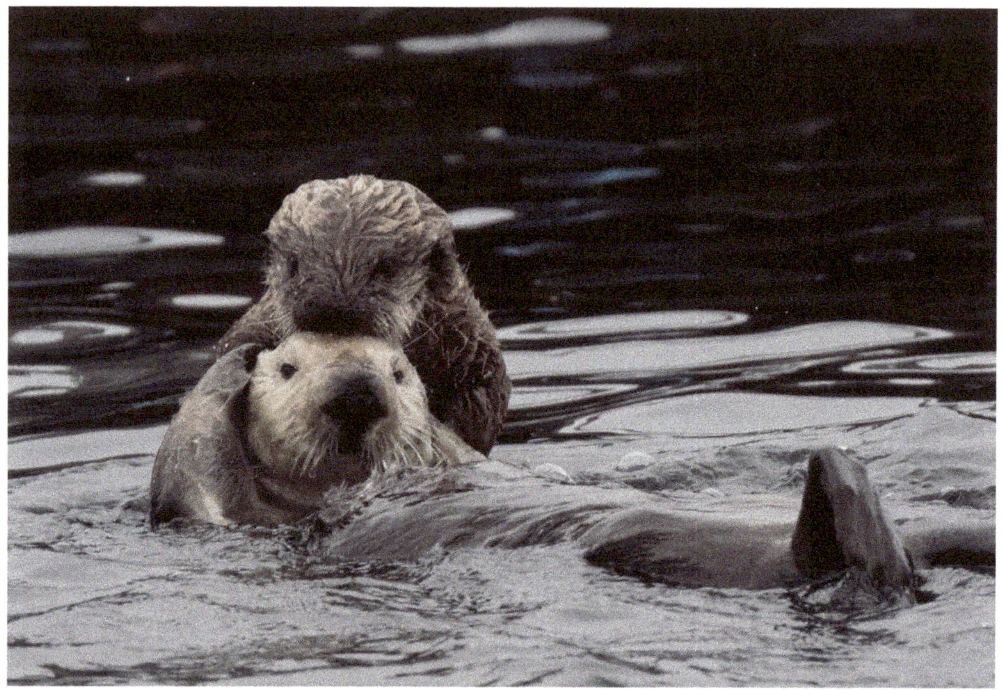

Southern sea otter mother and pup

So, one of my favorite stories with sea otters is about the time we were out doing sea otter captures. That always involves quite a few people. We have divers that go underwater using rebreathers[5] instead of scuba gear. And we have a Wilson Trap[6] that was designed by someone named Paul Wilson at the California Department of Fish and Wildlife; it's a special little basket we use to catch otters in.

We were out catching otters so we could tag them, identify them later on and record their different behaviors for a specific research project. While we were out there, on one of the days we saw this female swimming around at Lovers Point, and she had a pup, but the pup was dead. We were concerned about that, and were trying to figure out what to do about it.

---

[5] Closed-circuit SCUBA that produces no bubbles.

[6] The trap consists of a cone-shaped, aluminum frame that supports a net bag.

I think this was on a Monday and on Saturday we had rescued a little male pup up in Santa Cruz. We were trying to get him to settle into the Monterey Bay Aquarium and get used to our treatment and care without a mom. And, of course, he was having nothing to do with it. He was screaming at the top of his lungs. He was vocalizing. And we were trying to comfort him—put him on a waterbed, doing things that we would do back then that we don't do now.

Eventually, it became clear that it wasn't really working. So, when we found the female carrying the dead pup around Lovers Point, I connected with one of the staff that was working with that orphaned otter, and said, "Hey, I've got a really cool idea! Let's see if we can put that otter pup with this mom and see if she can actually raise him, because she's just primed to raise a pup and he's just primed to find a mom." The orphan pup was, of course, much bigger than the one that mom had lost, because that one was lost pretty soon after birth.

So, we said, ok, we'll try it. It was late in the afternoon. We launched one of our small research boats. We put the otter in a boat, in a little dog kennel that we usually use. He was vocalizing at the *top* of his lungs, just screaming and screaming. He was not happy with the situation. We motored out with the boat down to Lovers Point, and we sat there for a while, because a lot of times when females lose a pup, they will spend a bit of time vocalizing to try to reunite with the pup. They'll wait for a response from the pup. When the pup doesn't respond, they'll continue to vocalize.

When we brought the orphan out there, he started to vocalize and she actually heard him, and called back. So we were able to locate her, and found her just swimming around. Actually, I take that back a little bit, because we did catch her earlier at one point, and the reason we caught her was that the veterinarian at the time, Dr. Tom Williams, wanted to get a look at her pup to see if we could tell what had happened and the cause of death. So, we ended up catching her and letting her go, but we kept the dead pup.

So here she was, swimming around and vocalizing, as I mentioned, but when we got closer she got a little quieter. But as soon as the otter pup started to vocalize, she responded very quickly, and we knew exactly where she was. "So great, this is great!" We saw her kind of swimming toward the boat. We opened the kennel and put the little pup in the water, and wished him luck. You know, we were hoping she was gonna grab onto him. She swam over, but then kind of backed away, and he was lying there just screaming his heart out. He was not a happy camper.

Then she just went away—quite a distance away. It was already five o'clock in the afternoon, so we knew it was time. We were gonna have to go back in, but we weren't about to leave him out there in the wild, because we knew he wouldn't make it overnight. He kind of drifted away from us, and we were just sitting back hoping she would still come.

So now we're thinking—right, we need to go back. We'll pick him up and bring him in. We quietly motored our boat over there, and just when we got to him, she popped up from under the water, grabbed him and took off with him.

We were just sitting there like, "Oh my God, this is *awesome*!" It was, like, our first adoption of an otter pup in the wild. We didn't tag the female, but because we had spent a lot of time looking at her facial features—her nose, her muzzle— we kind of knew what she looked like. And he was a little… definitely a little bigger than she was, well, than her own pup had been. In that case, we were able to follow her for the next three months and actually watch her raise him, probably even to wean successfully.

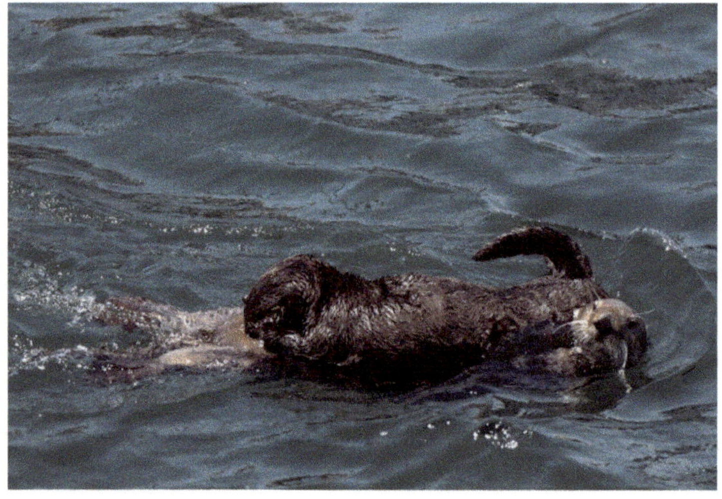

Nursing sea otter pup

That is one of my favorite heartwarming stories, to think about how we actually helped unite this mom and orphaned pup so they could go on and have a successful rearing, and hopefully be another happy otter story out there.

We named him. We don't actually name most of our wild otters, but occasionally we do, and he was called Elwood.

[See Michelle's bio after the following story.]

To the Rescue

Michelle Staedler

(Date of Interview: 7/12/18)

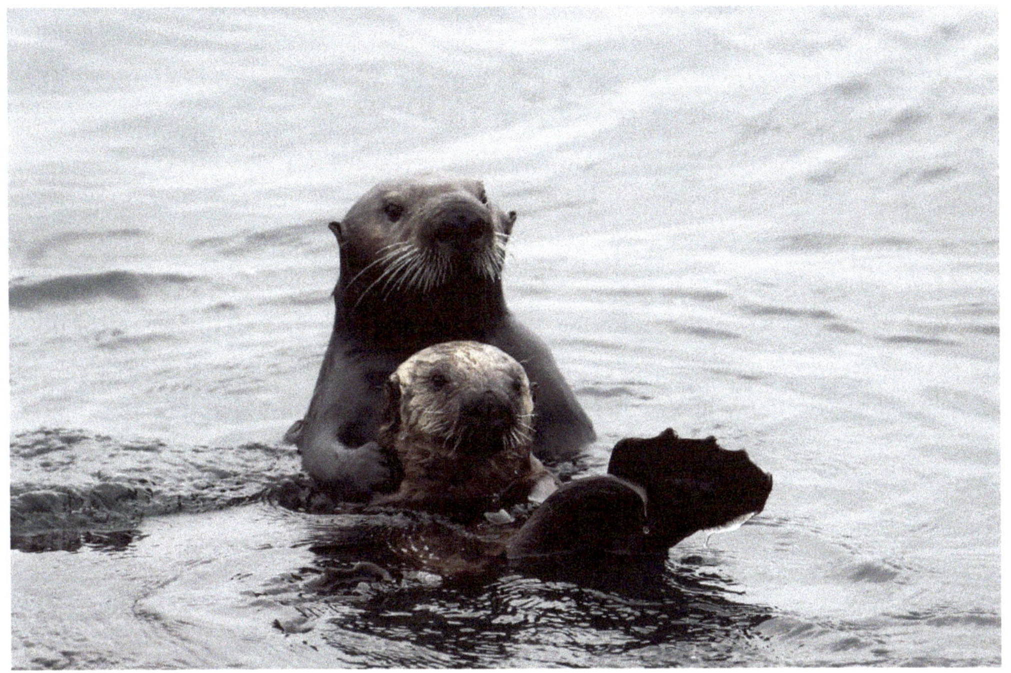

Southern sea otter mother and pup

Another story is about a kind of rescue situation, and this was in the really early days of the Monterey Bay Aquarium. Down Cannery Row they still have a lot of remnants of some of the old structures. And there was an art studio or something down the road, called Stohans, I believe; they were right on the water, and behind them and in the water was this big square remnant of some building. I don't even know what it was.

We got a call from them and they said they had been hearing an otter vocalizing, and they could see this female swimming all around. They wanted us to come and look at it because they didn't know what was going on.

Another woman named Julie Hymer and I went out to look, and we kind of surmised by going up in the building and looking out that there was a pup that had gotten stuck in this enclosed thing in the water and the mom was outside.

Well, what had happened is we had pretty big swells that day. I'm sure the mom was feeding and the pup may have been feeding with her, and a big swell came and kind of washed over, but as the swell receded the pup dropped into this big opening, and the mom, you know, was left without her pup. But she knew it was there somewhere. So, she kind of kept swimming around calling and calling.

So we went out and we had our wetsuits on. We had salmon nets in our hands, and we scaled the side of this thing, and I don't know how we did it, but we did. We climbed up, sat on the rim of the wall and looked down, and here's this little otter pup swimming around and he's vocalizing too. Well, we actually grabbed the dip net and tried to scoop up the pup—it was quite a ways down—and I think we were lucky enough that the tide was just right so we could still reach him.

So, we managed to reach him. I got him in my net and was very carefully trying to move him over to the side, then figured I'd lower him back down in the ocean, because by the time we got this done, the water was like ten feet below us and I didn't want to drop him off in the water. Well, I'm being so careful and I'm lifting, lifting, and he got his foot just on the edge of where I was sitting, and then he just propelled himself right up and out! And I'm like—oh no, he's going to hit the rocks. Something's gonna happen! But he propelled himself out down below, and his mom was waiting there. And right after he got out, she grabbed him and then swam away with him.

We made the front page of the *Monterey Herald*! It was really kind of fun, because everybody was watching this little sea otter rescue, which was probably one of the more unique rescues we've ever done.

MICHELLE STAEDLER

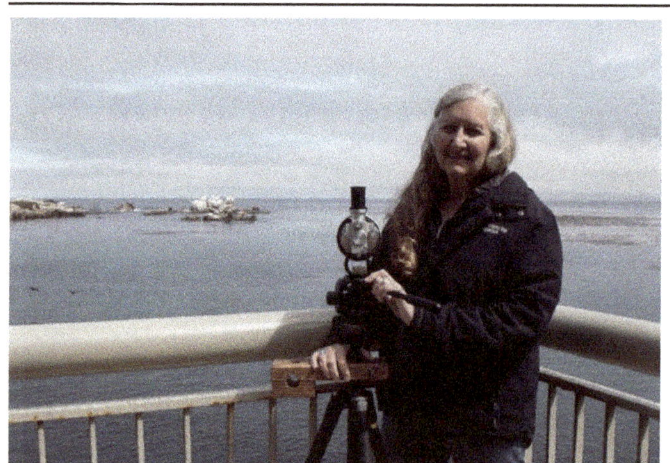

Michelle Staedler was the Sea Otter Program Manager at the Monterey Bay Aquarium, where she oversaw field research on wild otters at the time of her interview. The work is conducted in conjunction with aquarium partners University of California at Santa Cruz (UCSC), UC Davis, California Department of Fish and Wildlife, and the United States Geological Survey (USGS), among others. The research coalition has done a variety of projects over the years, and Michelle coordinated those projects with the different groups; she was also responsible for getting volunteers and staff to follow along and look at the animals and help collect the data.

Her work included overseeing the otter animal care component inside the aquarium. That included taking in rehab otters—otters of all ages—and caring for them, whether they're doing surrogacy with pups, raising the pups and returning them to the wild, or helping adults that need a little bit of R&R before they go back out into the wild. Michelle had a team of people that she oversaw for both of those components.

Michelle was born in Hartford, Connecticut and grew up outside of Hartford in Wethersfield, Connecticut, the next town south. She went to high school there and lived in Wethersfield for eighteen years until she wound up moving around and traveling. She eventually arrived in California to go to school at UCSC.

Always interested in tide pools and the ocean as a kid, Michelle applied to UCSC because it was close to the ocean and was a bit different in that courses were taken on a pass/fail basis with no grades. She focused on environmental studies, but was really interested in natural history and liked biology. However, she knew she wasn't going to be one of those people who sits behind a microscope and looks at things through the microscope all day.

She really loved the bigger picture: like going to an area and seeing all the different species that interact there. Understanding behavior was her main focus. Initially Michelle did some work on ground squirrels on campus. Then she worked on crab behavior—what they did underwater in tide pools. She was always interested in marine life, but there was a posting on campus looking for volunteers to help with a new sea otter research project, which led her in the direction of her lifelong career.

Michelle was familiar with sea otters, living in California, but having grown up on the East Coast, they were a new species to her. She would see them along the California coast and thought that it would be really cool to do some behavioral work on them. She volunteered with that project, which was conducted by Dr. Jim Estes and Dr. Marianne Riedman.

That was about the time that the Monterey Bay Aquarium started up. It opened to the public in 1984. Michelle started working for the aquarium in 1985 doing a research project studying individual sea otters. It was one of the first studies to look at otters as individuals, as opposed to studying them at a population level, where the researchers put tags on them to tell them apart. One thing led to another, and Michelle has been working with sea otters ever since.

Tag You're It! An Elite View
from the Whale's Perspective

Ari Friedlaender

(Date of Interview: 11/10/16)

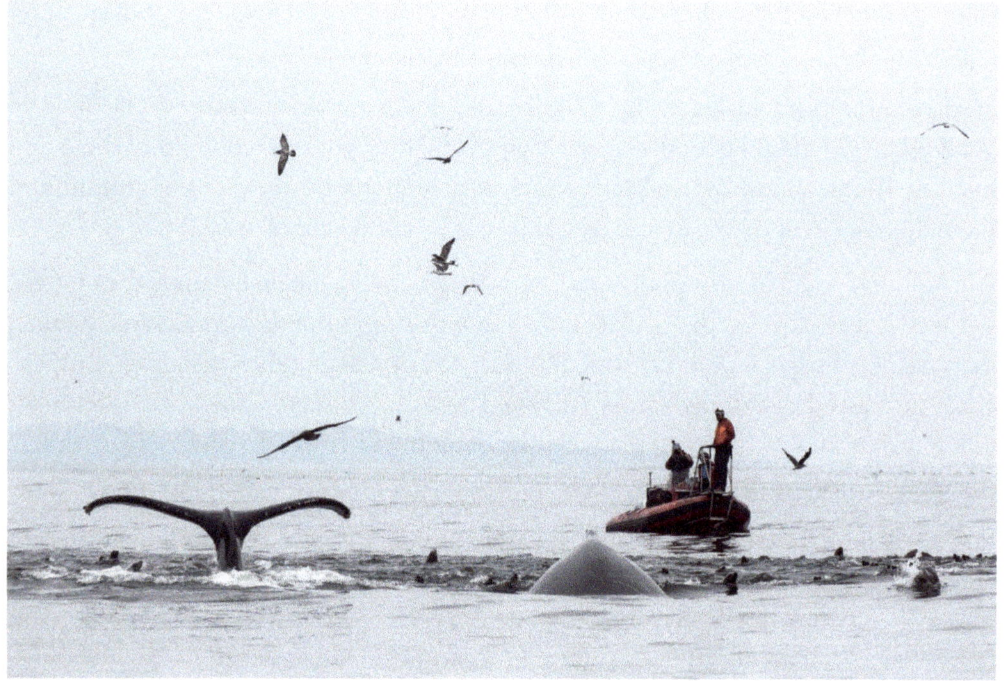

Tagging humpback whales

I think my most memorable experience on Monterey Bay happened maybe about five years ago. I and my colleagues Jeremy Goldbogen at Stanford and John Calambokidis from Cascadia Research had been developing new suction tags (shown on the next page) to put on whales, which measured the underwater movement of the animals and also included video. These tags allow us to see, from the animals' perspective, when they're feeding, what they're seeing, what their environment looks like. (*See* John's story, "I Felt a Little Sorry for the Anchovies" on p. 20.)

This happened on a day several years ago when there were a lot of humpback whales close in to shore. We knew there were a lot there, because Jeremy and I had gone out the day before and seen a whole bunch of animals. We called John that night and said, "OK, John, tomorrow morning let's meet at 7:30 at the boat ramp over at Moss Landing. We're gonna go out and deploy some tags." And John is a field guy who believes in a 'you start in the morning and you end when it's dark' kind of thing.

Jeremy and I hadn't really told him what the situation was like, about how many whales were around, so we get there in the morning and John is loaded for bear. You know, he's got enough food and water for several days. He's got a backpack full of stuff, and Jeremy and I just kind of show up in our shorts and t-shirts, and you know, our life jackets, and John, I think, may have been a little skeptical as to whether or not we were equipped well enough.

Well, we pulled out of the Moss Landing harbor in our small vessel and took a left to go through the jetty when we encountered our first whale. We were still in idle speed, and I didn't even have my tag pole ready or anything, so we passed that one up. By the time we got to the end of the jetty, there were two more whales.

At this point I was ready, so I said, "Well, John, why don't we go ahead and do this?" So, we put a tag on that whale's back right then and there. Then we moved about sixty feet, and there were two more whales. We put another tag on, and this repeated for the next, I'd say, about eight or ten minutes. 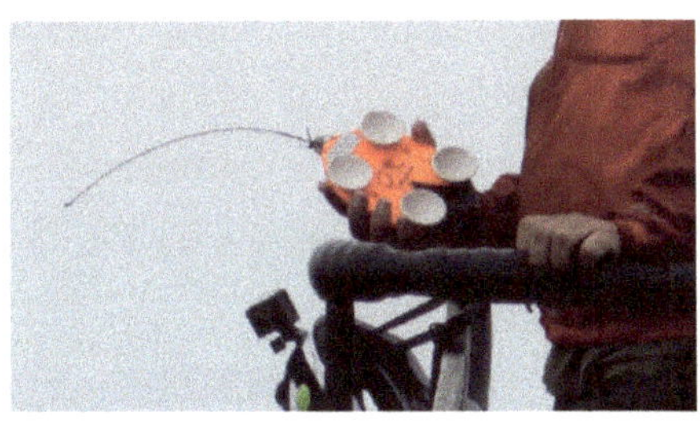 We put out all four of our tags in about twenty minutes. John never had the boat out of idle speed. Then we turned around and went back in.

It was about eight o'clock in the morning, and I could see John's brain just kind of short-circuiting with like, "Wait a minute, we're supposed to be out on the water all day. What just happened?" So, we went and each got a burrito—a nice breakfast burrito—and then we sat on the beach, and the whales were literally right there, off the beach in front of MBARI (Monterey Bay Aquarium Research Institute). We watched them go back and forth. You could see the tags on all the whales, and eventually one of the tags fell off. We could see it in the water. We waited half an hour, and it basically washed up right onshore in front of us.

It was one of the easiest days of science I've ever had! What was great about it was there were a lot of people around. There were a lot of whale watching boats. There were a lot of tourists. There were people on the beach, and we could talk to these people who were also seeing those animals right there about what our tags were doing.

Then when we got the tags back, the video was unbelievable! It was one of the first times we had seen, from the whale's perspective, what it looks like to feed in Monterey Bay. It was one of these events where there were birds diving into the water. There were sea lions all over the place. There were humpback whales everywhere. And you can actually see all that from the whale's perspective.

Each tag had a camera on both the front and the back, and we could see the school of anchovies, as the whale would come up from underneath the prey patch. You could see the fish sort of move around as the whale got close to the patch. As soon as the whale lunged, you could see diving birds—shearwaters—just hitting the water and grabbing fish right in front of the whale. Then there's a whole rat pack of sea lions back behind the whale, picking off the fish that kind of spilled out of the whale's mouth and may have been stunned by the whale.

We had this amazing view of how much life activity is going on under the surface, which we can't see from above. But from the whale's perspective, it's just happening all around. I mean it's like controlled chaos! To see all these animals interacting and feeding on the same thing in the same place at the same time kind of set the spark in our minds of, "Ok, there's a lot more going on here than we can tell just by being at the surface."

So, from a very simple morning, we got a pretty detailed and awesome, elite view of what this bay is like, and the richness of life that it promotes.

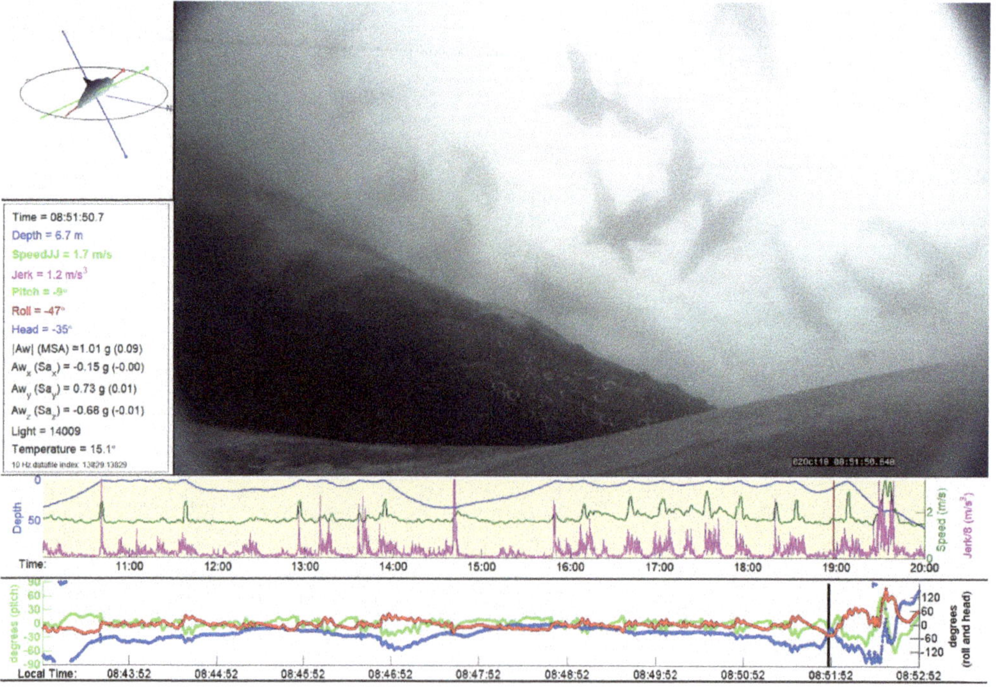

Humpback whales and sea lions © Friedlaender Lab for Bio-Telemetry & Behavioral Ecology, UCSC. Research conducted under NOAA/IACUC permits.

ARI FRIEDLAENDER

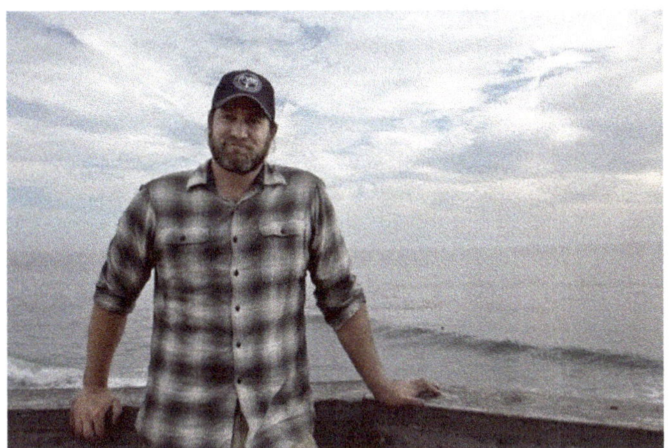

Ari Friedlaender is an Associate Professor and researcher at the University of California at Santa Cruz where he heads the Bio-Telemetry and Behavioral Ecology Laboratory. His previous lab was at Oregon State University. Ari is also a founder and one of the senior leadership members of the California Ocean Alliance, a nonprofit collaboration of scientists, educators and conservationists.

Most of Ari's research involves studying the foraging behavior of marine mammals and the impacts of human behavior on them. He and his colleagues study marine mammals in natural environments where they do what they do naturally, but he also does experimental work trying to understand the impacts of climate change, naval sonar and fishing gear on these animals.

Ari was born in New Haven, Connecticut. He grew up on the Connecticut coast, where whaling was a big part of the cultural history, but he was more into sharks as a little boy. Like most boys, Ari was into things that bite other things.

Ari knew he wanted to study marine biology when he was just three or four. His parents tell him that he asked them to join the Cousteau Society on his behalf when he was four, and they got a letter back saying he was the youngest member of the Cousteau Society.

Ari's academic background in marine science started in college. He originally went to school in Maine and then did his graduate work at Duke University in North Carolina. His undergrad advisor allowed him to study seals at the Mystic Aquarium in Mystic, Connecticut. Then he took a course in marine mammal biology at the Duke University Marine Lab in the summertime, which introduced him more broadly to marine mammals. At that point he met some of the mentors he would have later in life, like his master's and PhD adviser.

In his own words, Ari "ended up in the Monterey Bay area as a conscious choice to be in the best area to study a wide diversity of marine mammals in a pretty amazing environment close to a lot of places that do other research."

I Felt a Little Sorry for the Anchovies

John Calambokidis

(*Date of Interview*: 11/12/16)

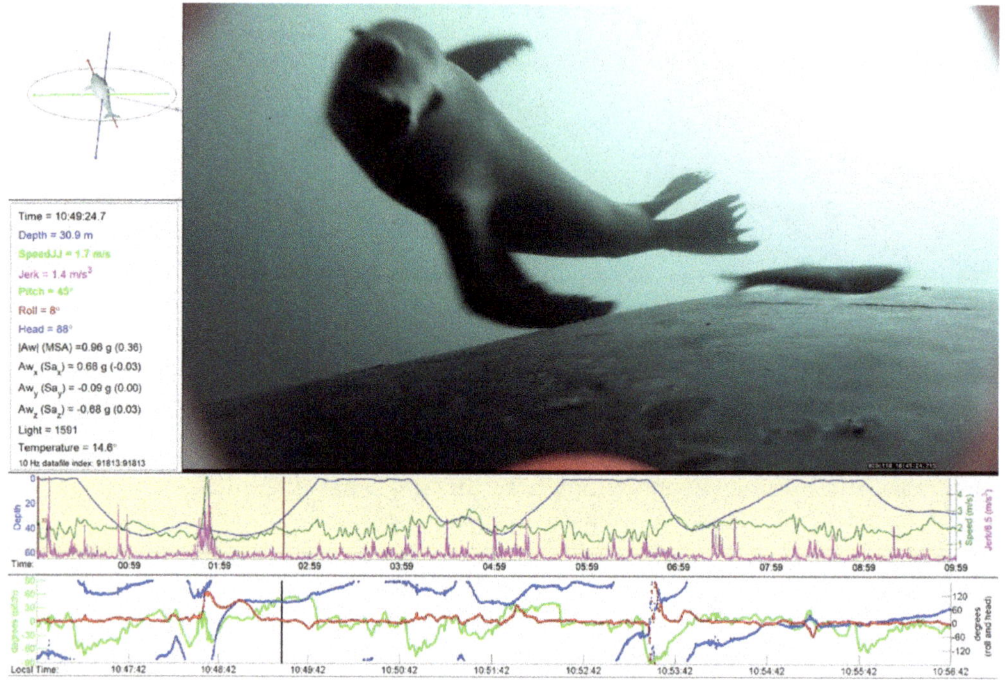

Humpback whale back, sea lion, and anchovy   © Friedlaender Lab for Bio-Telemetry & Behavioral Ecology, UCSC. Research conducted under NOAA/IACUC permits.

One of my favorite stories of working in Monterey Bay actually occurred just last fall. We'd been trying to study humpback whales and how they interact with other species and how they feed inside Monterey Bay. So to do that, we'd been working collaboratively with several other researchers—Jeremy Goldbogen at Stanford and Ari Friedlaender—deploying these suction-cup-attached video cameras. (*See* Ari's story, "Tag You're It: An Elite View from the Whale's Perspective" on p. 16.)

But on this one day, James Fallbush and I went out of Moss Landing, and we were looking for an area where we might have humpback whales feeding. And we found this dense group, as has become more and more common inside Monterey Bay, of humpback whales associated with lots of seabirds and a group of sea lions. We thought, well this is a really good opportunity. If we can get a video camera on one of these whales, we could get a sense of the sort of interactions that are occurring underwater between the different humpback whales, between the individuals, between them with their prey, and between them and all these other species that are present.

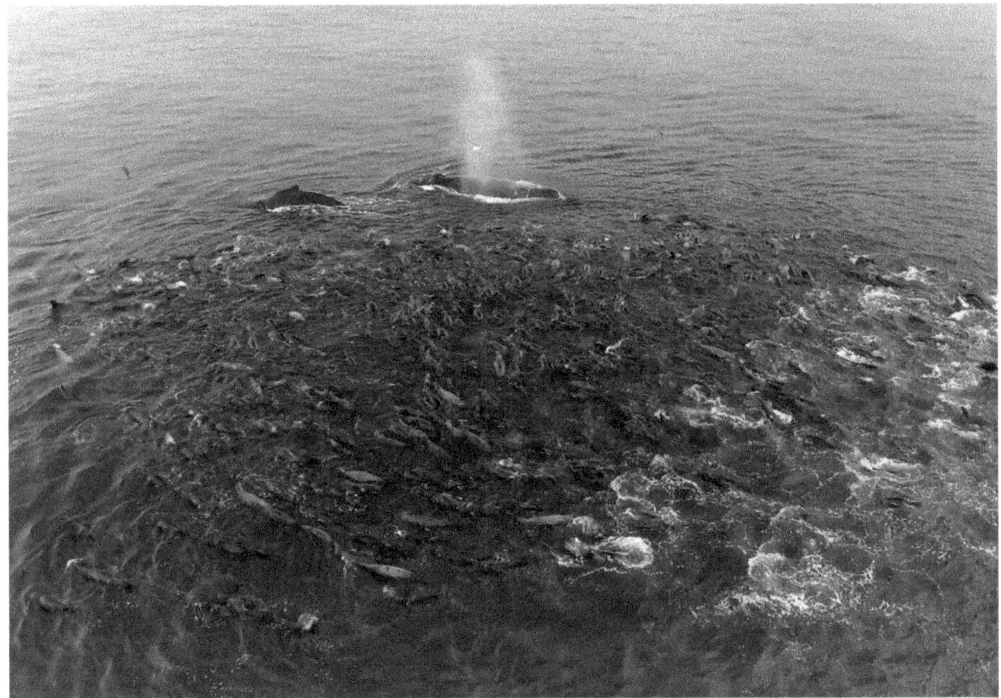

Humpbacks and sea lions feeding

But I was a little worried about how to approach the whales, who were surfacing more chaotically. We attach the camera with just a pole. I call it a long pole, but it's really only about ten feet long, so it's much less than the length of a whale, and with the whales coming up kind of unpredictably, how could we maneuver close enough, with these whales surfacing unexpectedly all around us?

I've deployed hundreds of these tags. I usually like to drive the boat and control where the boat is and have a little more predictable sense of where the whales are than in one of these aggregations. So we slowly eased into this group, which was about eight to ten whales feeding. I think we estimated about one to two hundred California sea lions were in the area, and many hundreds of seabirds.

We ended up getting a beautiful opportunity here where this whale wound up surfacing right in front of us, but not too close. And we were able to get the tag on the whale, then it dove down.

This particular tag had a video camera facing forward and backward, and when we got the video back, it was just incredible. I've studied whales for decades, and not really gotten a clear sense of what these whales do and how they interact under water. But the beauty of these tags has been that the cameras really open that up. The data they provide is fantastic, but the images kind of give you the ability to relate to what it's like to be a whale.

When the school of anchovies would come into view, it would look like a solid mass. It didn't look like individual fish. It was so concentrated and packed, it just looked like a wall. And you could clearly see in and see the whale lunge into it. And I think some of the most surprising things for me, that I'm still trying to process, were the interactions between the whales, and between the whales and some of the other species.

I think the thing that surprised me was that I was so used to thinking of humpback whales as cooperative feeders, and I think in many cases they are cooperating, but in this particular case it actually looked like they were kind of getting into each other's way. And that could be because maybe they hadn't quite worked out roles or routines, but you'd see the whale that we had a tag on, and it would be headed for a school of fish. And you'd think, "oh, he's got it lined up," and then all of a sudden you'd see another whale beat him to it, and he'd have to peel off to the side and not get a lunge in. It seemed like almost the majority of the time he was having to break off.

Now on the other hand, it was clear that the sea lions and the birds were benefiting tremendously by the humpback whale action. And it made me feel a little sorry for the anchovies, because the anchovies were kind of left with a lose/lose strategy. If they bunched up together tightly, that would be the way to avoid being picked off by the birds and sea lions, which mostly like to pick off prey one at a time. And so for that kind of predator, animals bunch together, making it hard to pick out one animal at a time. That's why schooling serves as a defense mechanism against many types of predators.

But the one type of predator that it doesn't work well for would be a predator that relies on them being tightly packed together, so it can engulf them in one bite. So here were the anchovies caught between a rock and a hard place, so to speak. If they bunched together tightly, the humpback whales could just take them in one mouthful. If they scattered or got broken up by the humpback whales feeding, then you could see—and I hadn't expected it, but—right in front of the camera would be these anchovies that got broken up from the school by the humpback whale lunging through them, and you'd have birds picking them off right in front of the camera as these individual anchovies were swimming by.

It was such a rich, dynamic scene. It kind of opened up that underwater world of how these animals were interacting with each other, and with other species, that I'd never quite been able to see before. And it was so dynamic, I felt a little sorry for the anchovies. I don't know, it seemed like there was no way out. It made me wonder, how do they survive this?

We ended up taking the first two minutes of that video, unedited, without making any changes, going just from the point of the first two minutes, and it's the most incredible thing to see. And when I get to show it to people, they're pretty amazed. Then I get to tell them this is the first two minutes of six hours of video, and we haven't tried to edit it yet.

So, I think that's been one of my most incredible experiences. It was really important to me to see this, because it also drove home a key point that was important at that time.

It was a time when there was also a purse seine [a large wall of netting deployed around an area or school of fish] fishery going for the anchovies. And what this video ended up showing—I mean, you can show data, you can make the point that the anchovies are the food of whales, and the sea lions and the dolphins and the birds are all dependent on it, but nothing drove that point home like this video. Just in that first two minutes you saw this group of a half dozen humpback whales and these hundreds of sea lions and hundreds of birds, all dependent on this school of anchovies. And then you imagine that school of anchovies being eliminated by fishing, and fishing that doesn't necessarily even yield a particularly high return. My understanding is that the fishermen get a very, very low price for the anchovies, and yet they are what fuels all this incredible wildlife.

JOHN CALAMBOKIDIS

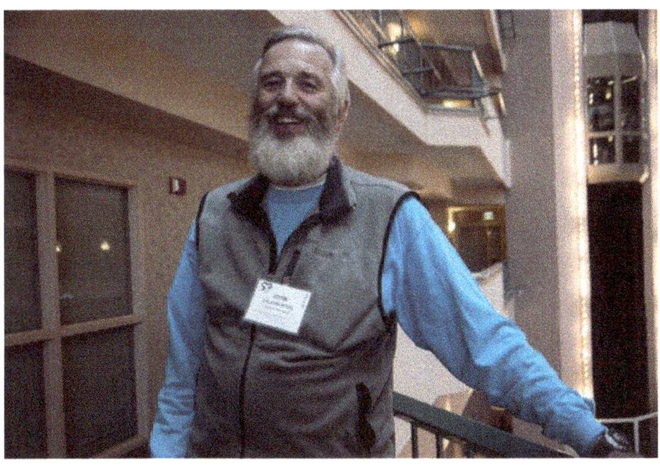

John Calambokidis is a research biologist at Cascadia Research, a non-profit organization dedicated to the study primarily of marine mammals, but also other animals, especially those they can help serve through protection and conservation. Cascadia Research is based in Olympia, Washington.

John was born in Cairo, Egypt to a Greek father and American mother who met in Egypt. He and his family came to this country when he was about ten years old. They lived on the East Coast, where John grew up. John came to the West Coast and Olympia, Washington to attend Evergreen State College in 1974 and has been on the West Coast ever since.

John got his Bachelor of Science degree at Evergreen, where he was introduced to research in his second year. He produced several papers from that project, then moved on to studying harbor seals, which also resulted in several scientific papers.

John started working for Cascadia Research in 1979 and notes that none of the founders had advanced degrees; all simply had Bachelor of Science or Bachelor of Arts degrees. Today the organization also has researchers with PhDs.

John's interest in marine mammals started early in his career. He was particularly interested in the effects of human activities and pollution on wildlife, especially pollutants like PCBs (polychlorinated biphenyls), which were recognized as a problem in the 1970s. John suspected they were having an impact on the marine environment.

He initially started studying harbor seals, which ate a lot of fish in Puget Sound, an area with lots of contamination. But John began to realize it was hard to study the effects of pollutants on these animals when we knew so little about their biology. Over time his studies started to get more into the basic biology of the animals. Then in the 1980s, he graduated to the big whales.

By 1986, after seeing his first whale, John was pretty hooked on blue whales. Something about their size, their beauty and their mystery captivated him, and he focused his research on large blue whales, humpback whales and gray whales.

The whales John studies move up and down the feeding grounds along the West Coast. One of the most productive areas runs from the bluffs of the Farallon Islands south to Monterey Bay. His focus has been on the Central California coast including Monterey Bay, as well as the Southern California bight. John notes that that region of the world is one of the best feeding grounds for blue whales. Monterey Bay is unique not only because of the abundance of wildlife there, but also because it is somewhat protected from weather, which provides a window for morning operations in the bay. Because of the ease of access, John can work there a greater proportion of the time, so he tends to focus his efforts there, instead of trying to get out to the Farallon Islands, where the weather may be problematic.

Where Oh Where Are the Blues?

David Cade

(Date of Interview: 10/27/17)

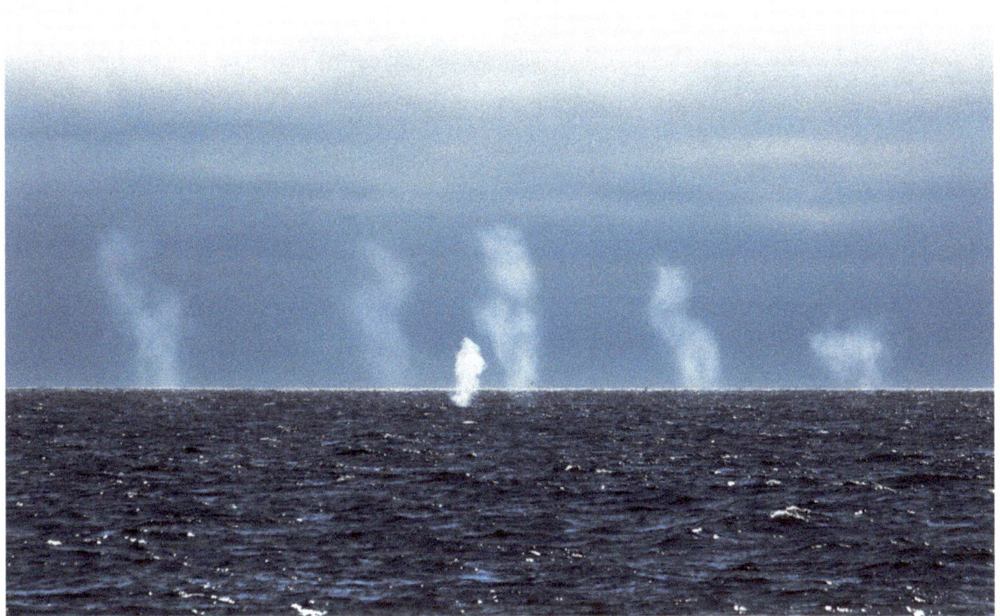

Blue whale blows

I have two stories I want to tell. The first one is about my first time diving in Monterey Bay. It really was spectacular. It was the first time I ever saw a sea otter while in the water. I used to be a high school teacher, and I took my students down to go diving off the breakwater. We saw sea otters foraging down there and diving birds going into the water. It really blew my students' minds. It's one of those things you can do to help generate interest in the ocean environment.

Well, now I study blue whales and humpback whales foraging in Monterey Bay and elsewhere in the world. The first time I ever started tagging blue whales in Monterey Bay was the summer of 2016. That was the year of the fires, the really big fires off Big Sur. In July there were a lot of blue whales up off the north shelf of the canyon, so we went out one day and there was smoke kind of drifting over the bay. It made all the particulates in the air really condense, so there was a lot of fog out on the water, too.

There we were trying to work with blue whales on this very foggy, but really calm, calm day. In order to find these whales, we would turn off the engines and listen for the blows. You could hear them, and we're going, "OK, we're driving down there," and we'd try to get to where we thought they were to put a tag on an animal.[7] You've got to get pretty close to tag, so we'd listen for the blow then drive in that direction. Then fifteen seconds later we'd stop again, and listen for the next one. We just kept doing that over and over. And finally we'd see the whale come up in front of us, and we'd pull up and put a tag on the animal. It turned out to be a pretty cool data set of these blue whales foraging in really dense, patchy prey conditions. That was a pretty cool experience.

Then this summer, we were down in Southern California to try to work with blue whales off the Channel Islands. But the wind out there was really rough. At some point after a few days of working down south, we called it and said, "We aren't going to work in Southern California. Let's go up to Monterey Bay, where we know the weather is better." We'd heard some reports of blue whales, though we were not quite sure what was going on, but we decided to give it a try.

So, we came up to Monterey Bay. We moved all our operations up here. It was like fifteen people—fifteen scientists—all moved up here, and we went out on the water. The first time we went out on a Sunday with just the small boats to see what we could find, and we found a few blue whales out along the mid-canyon/north-canyon edge. We found a couple of animals in pairs, so we put a couple of tags out, but we didn't see a lot of animals. We were trying to get drone images of these animals, too, so we could measure their sizes in relation to how they forage. We didn't get any images that day, but we did put the tags on.

The next day, we went out to recover the tags and look for more whales to work and to get drone images. We managed to find a tag floating. And what was really great was that, by the time we found the tag, because it had just come off about an hour before, the tag led us to an aggregation of probably twenty-five blue whales. Apparently, the animals had been foraging in the same place, all night long basically, and now we knew where they were hanging out.

So now we're out there with all the whales. We're trying to radio—we're in a separate boat—we're trying to radio our other boat, which is out there tagging a smaller group. "You guys gotta get over here. This is the place to be. Blue whales

---

[7] These are suction tags known as D-tags (see photo p. 17), which carry various instruments and are designed to fall off anywhere after four to twenty-four hours. They are placed on the back of the whale using a long pole. After they fall off, they can be retrieved by the scientists and the data downloaded.

popping up left and right. If you want to do drone flights of these animals, you can get pictures of the tag on the animal over here."

Well, we put another tag on. Then we were waiting for the big boat to come over to do the drone flight, so we could get a size estimate of the animal, just following this whale and trying to keep track of it. While we were doing that, we got to really know the animals' patterns—if you're out there long enough, you start to see patterns.

We were out there for probably two hours before the other folks came over, and we got a sense of the whales' behavior. So, when they surface, they're doing these U-shaped patterns and going back to the same spot. But sometimes when they're surfacing, they'll come up twelve minutes later a distance away in a different direction. We were just following them, following them, following them.

By the time the other boat got out there with the photogrammetry equipment so we could measure the size of the whales, we had it wired. "OK, guys, here's what you've got to do. Nine minutes exactly from when this animal goes down, you've got to go one hundred meters this direction, and then in nine minutes you've gotta launch that drone, and the whale will come up right next to you."

We were doing our best, and with animals you can never fully predict what they will do, but sure enough, they came up right underneath the drone the other boat had in the air. And we got these beautiful images of the tag on the animal. And because these whales were in pairs, now we had images of two animals—two really nice, clear measurements of them. But then we saw that the second animal didn't have a tag on it. Since we wanted to make sure we could maximize our data use, we had to do the tagging thing one more time. We had to predict again where the whales were going to come up so we could tag the other whale in this pair of blue whales, so we would have data on both of them. It worked out really well. It was just a really exciting day to be able to get the data we were looking for and try to understand these animals as well.

DAVID CADE

Dave Cade is a cetacean foraging ecologist who looks at interactions of blue whales, humpbacks and other rorqual whales with their prey. He is interested in how organisms group together in spatially and temporally restricted patches, and how predators can exploit these patches. At the time of his interview he was working in Ari Friedlander's lab at the Joseph M. Long Marine Laboratory at the University of California at Santa Cruz studying how minke whales and humpback whales forage on Antarctic krill resources in the same environment.

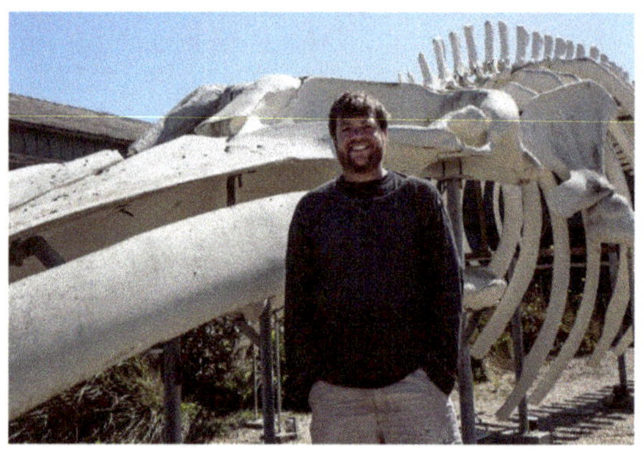

He earned his PhD in Biology working in the Goldbogen Lab at Stanford University's Hopkins Marine Station in Pacific Grove, California. Dave's doctoral studies focused on how different foraging conditions affect the dynamics of rorqual feeding, or more precisely, the foraging efficiency of baleen whales. He is currently a postdoctoral researcher in the Goldbogen Lab.

Dave was born on the East Coast outside of Washington, DC, but moved to Portland, Oregon when his father was transferred for work. Dave did most of his growing up in Portland, then moved to the San Francisco Bay Area in 2004, where he finished high school. He then attended Oregon State University, where he got his master's degree in science.

Dave had come to Monterey Bay to go whale watching when he lived in San Francisco, and like a lot of people, began to fall in love with the area. He recalls coming down one stormy day, and instead of going out whale watching, heading to the Monterey Bay Aquarium. He notes that it is as great an introduction to marine life as you can get. That day a great white shark was on exhibit in the open-ocean tank, and he was excited that he could watch all the animals interact.

Dave's love for Monterey Bay was also nourished by his experiences as a recreational diver. In his words, "The first time you see a cormorant diving through water, you're like, what is going on? The underwater environment is so crazy! Or the first time you see a marine mammal in the water." One day while diving, Dave saw sea lions, a harbor seal and a sea otter looking for little invertebrates. He said that was pretty great! He's always thought that Monterey Bay was one of the best places to dive and see and experience wildlife in the world.

While Dave came into his marine science work from a tangent based on his particular technical skill set as a math engineer, he's always had an interest in the marine world. Dave was working on his master's degree at Oregon State with Kelly Benoit-Bird doing active acoustic work looking at prey field concentrations. He was looking for a PhD opportunity and Jeremy Goldbogen was looking for someone to help him study the prey side of cetacean dynamics. David's quantitative math background enabled him to start studying the quantitative side of the prey capture work in the Goldbogen Lab. Now Dave does research affiliated with several institutions on projects all over the world.

This Is the Thing!—Blue Whales Are Incredibly Enormous!

Asha de Vos

(*Date of Interview*: 10/27/17)

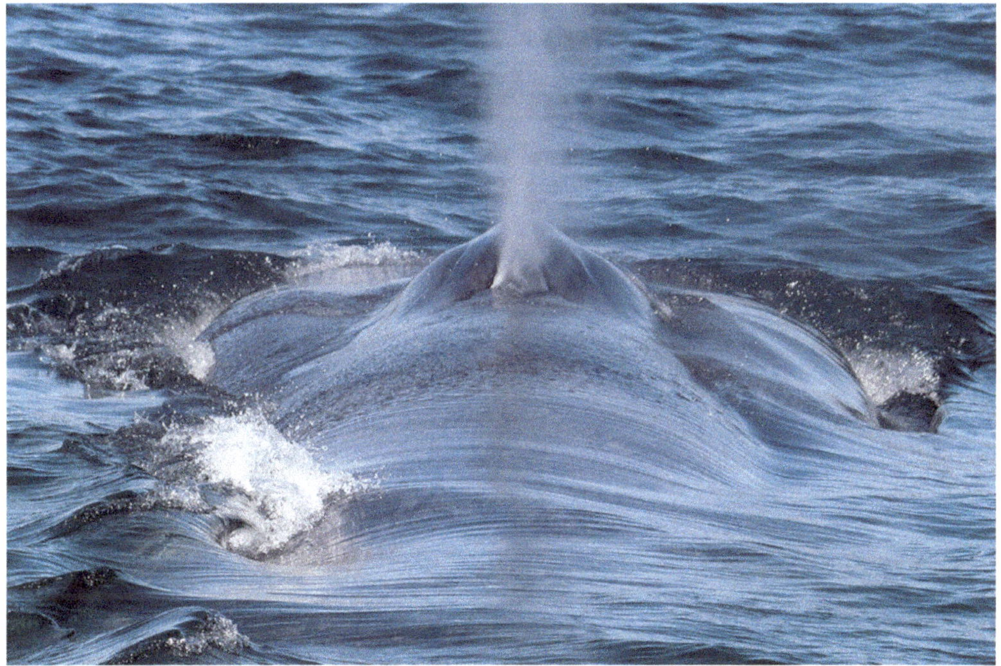

Head of blue whale

I had so many memorable experiences in the short time I was in the Monterey Bay area, I just think it's hard to *not* have memorable experiences there, because it's a very special place. But I would say for me the most exciting moment was when I was out on a whale watch boat and we were surrounded by all these humpback whales. It was incredible, right? And, of course, I'm standing on the boat like *super*excited, and the people—the tourists—were like, "Have you ever . . . ?" "You've never seen a whale before?" "Is this your first one?" And I'm like, "No, no, no, this is what I do for a living!" And the people are like, "Hmm, interesting."

But you know, to me, of course, it's always an incredible moment, where you have all these whales and you're trying to figure out how the heck this is going on, what are they doing under the water—all these questions that start popping up in your mind. So, I, of course—being an easily excitable person—make it quite easy to, you know, to have this explosive moment! But I think the most interesting encounter was this: we're watching these whales, and it's exciting, and people are superstoked, right? Because, they're saying, "Wow! Humpback whales! This is really amazing," and they're exclaiming how beautiful they are. And then on the other side of the boat up pops a blue whale!

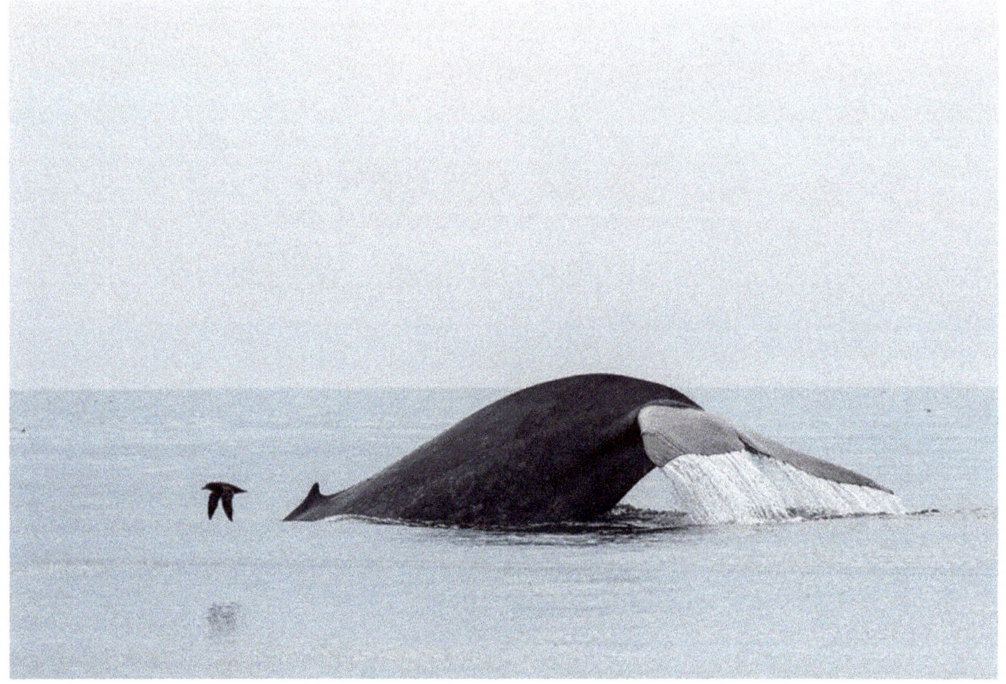

Blue whale fluke

I work with blue whales. I've seen many blue whales. Still, of course, I got excited. It was my first blue whale in Monterey Bay, and I was looking at it and thinking, "Wow, it's amazing!" Right? And for once I had, like, the sense of scale, because I have this blue whale right here, and then I'm seeing the humpbacks, too. I've seen these species separately, but here they were essentially together. And then it was superinteresting, because some of the people on the boat turned around, and a humpback whale popped up right next to the blue whale, and the people said, "Look, there's a dolphin there!!"

And me, I just turned around and said, "This is the thing! Blue whales are *incredibly enormous*! And they throw you off completely!" And the whale watchers' perspective, you know—that to me was so special, because I sit on small boats with these giant whales all the time, and I get that sense of perspective. But to see how huge and majestic and dominant they are in terms of their size in relation to the other large species in the ocean was a really, really special moment to me.

ASHA DE VOS

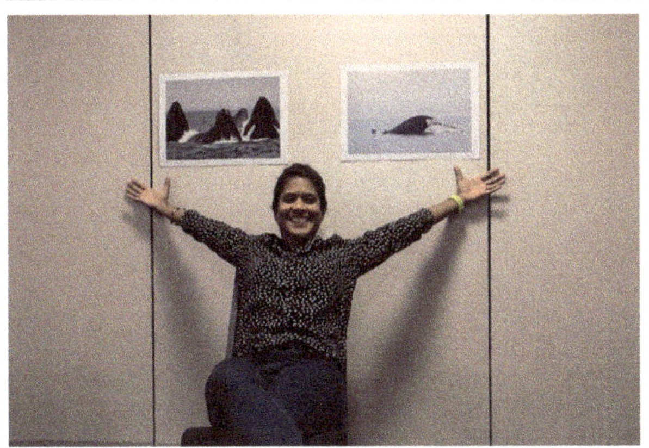

Asha de Vos is a Sri Lankan blue whale researcher and the founder of Oceanswell, Sri Lanka's first marine conservation, research and education organization. She was born in the island nation of Sri Lanka and grew up there. Unable to study marine biology in her home country, Asha left to study at the University of St. Andrews in Scotland, where she did her undergraduate work. She then got her master's degree at the University of Oxford in England, followed by her PhD at the University of Western Australia in Perth. Asha conducted her post-doc work at the University of California at Santa Cruz, which brought her to the Monterey Bay area in 2013.

Asha wanted to be an adventure scientist from the time she was six. Her parents gave her *National Geographic* magazines, which became her motivation to explore and adventure and seek out things that no one else had seen. Plus, Asha visualized herself in the magazine, a feat she has now accomplished! Also, while a child, she started swimming and developed a growing passion for the ocean. At the age of eighteen she decided she was going to do marine biology as her degree. Asha followed through, leaving Sri Lanka and engaging in her academic studies around the world.

After her extensive theoretical studies, she set out to get some fieldwork experience. She took off to New Zealand where she lived in a tent for six months and was involved in a variety of projects including working with Hector's dolphins and freshwater eels.

Asha then had the opportunity to get on a whale research vessel that was circumnavigating the globe. She got on board in the Maldives, and one day, while tracking sperm whales off the coast of Sri Lanka, she saw a very powerful, tall blow in the distance, clearly not a sperm whale. She got quite excited because she knew it was a blue whale.

The boat moved toward the whale, which turned out to be an aggregation of blue whales. She expected to see them mating, which is what one usually sees in warm waters, but that was not the case here. Instead of mating and babies, Asha saw whale poop, and it was that bright-red blue whale poop that started her on the trajectory of a blue whale career.

Asha realized that these whales had not read the same textbooks she had, which all

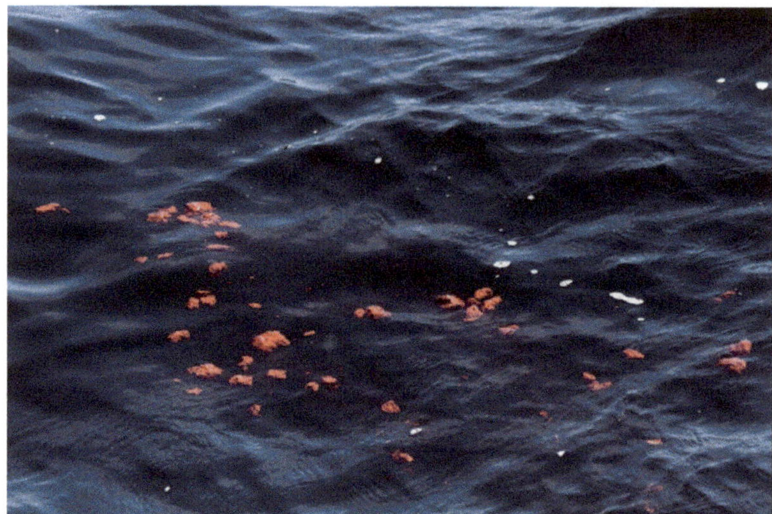

Bright-red blue whale poop

said that baleen whales migrate from cold water feeding areas to warm water breeding/calving grounds. Rather, the Sri Lankan blues were feeding in the warm tropical waters five degrees above the equator. This anomaly led Asha to pursue the answers to so many questions that arose regarding the uncharacteristic behavior of this population of whales.

After completing her postdoc work at the University of California at Santa Cruz, Asha returned to Sri Lanka where she has launched her own nonprofit called Oceanswell. Asha feels it is important to empower Sri Lankans with a local 'small but mighty' yet global voice. She wants people to realize it does not matter where you are, you can still be a powerful force for the oceans. Oceanswell's focus is on the next generation of ocean heroes, particularly diverse ocean heroes, including those from underrepresented nations who will conduct marine conservation research, and also engage others in conversations and storytelling about the magic of the world's oceans.

Asha sees training citizens of her own country as essential to creating opportunities for the young people, who will be able to carry on the work when she is gone. Asha visualizes creating an army of engaged, educated individuals to protect the oceans. She feels an obligation and responsibility to let people learn with her and join her on the adventure to create a collective voice, which can drive the change that is needed for ocean and marine protection.

The Whale That Couldn't Breach

Charley Peebler

(*Date of Interview*: 11/12/16)

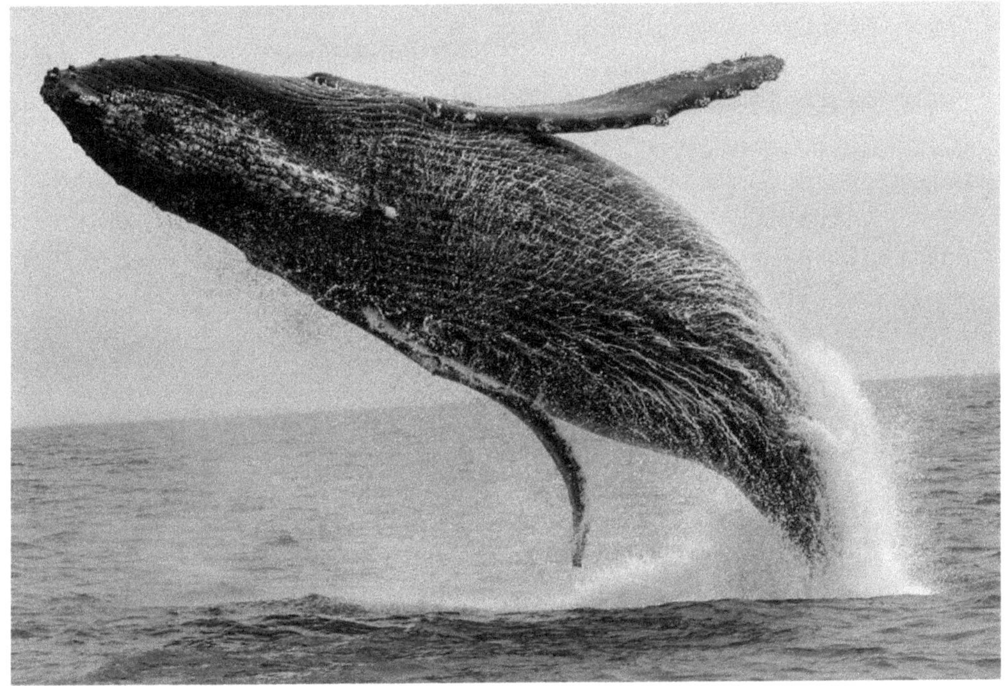

Breaching humpback whale

We were here in Monterey in April 2016. My family had rented a little beach house, and we'd go down to the beach. One day my mom said, "Oh my gosh, there's a whale outside!" So we all ran out down to the beach, and just started watching the whales. Then we saw a couple breaching! That was really awesome! And that was really memorable to me.

With Heirs To Our Ocean, I am now working on coral and on derelict fishing gear, and how derelict fishing gear affects whales and whale entanglements. But when I saw those humpback whales from the beach—where the whales were out breaching in the water, pretty close actually—I didn't think about how entanglements might affect them, because back then, Heirs To Our Ocean hadn't started. So I didn't really know anything about whale entanglement.

But now I realize that when I saw those whales out there, probably at least one of the whales in the pod had an entanglement on it, which makes me really sad, because that would mean it wasn't able to jump free like the other breaching whales. It's really horrible that it couldn't.

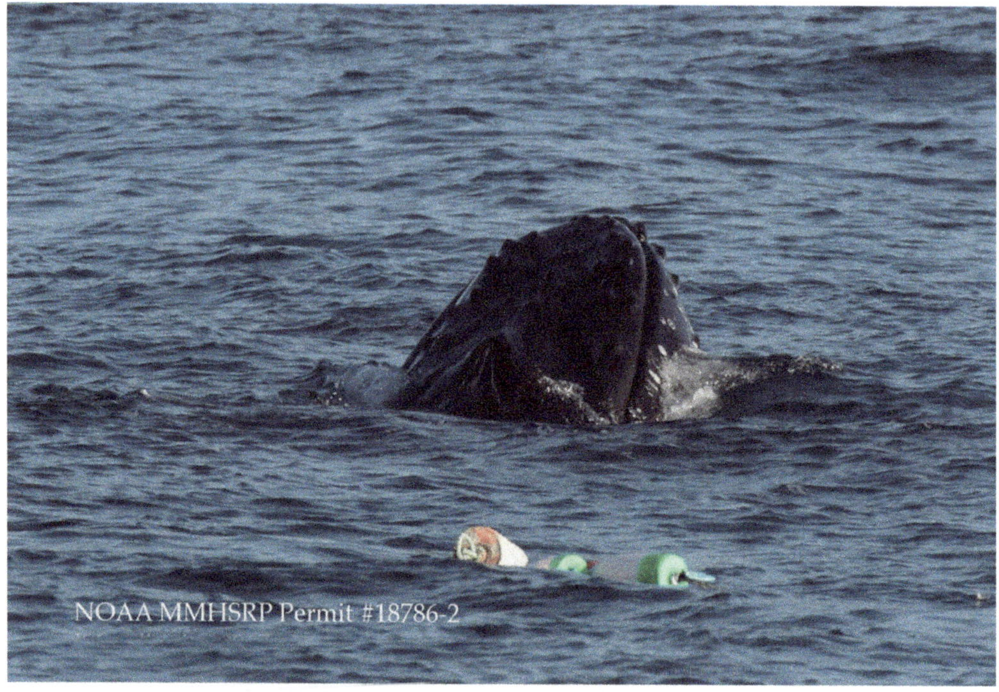

Entangled whale

Later I was interviewing Justin Viezbicke (NOAA West Coast [California] Marine Mammal Stranding Coordinator) at the Tiburon Marine Center, and it was incredible to learn how they disentangle a whale caught in fishing gear. It's really, really interesting to see the different types of tools, and the ropes, and the buoys, and everything, and how they detach the entangled gear from the whale. That was really interesting to me.

Then just talking with Mr. Viezbicke, one on one, was really amazing! It's incredible for a child my age to do this. But the only reason it's incredible is that nobody else ever does it, except for Heirs To Our Ocean. Or the occasional youth that stands up against a problem.

And so, it just makes me realize that I am really lucky to be able to see these beautiful creatures, these whales, and be able to talk intelligently about these issues. And I really want other kids to be able to do that too.

CHARLEY PEEBLER

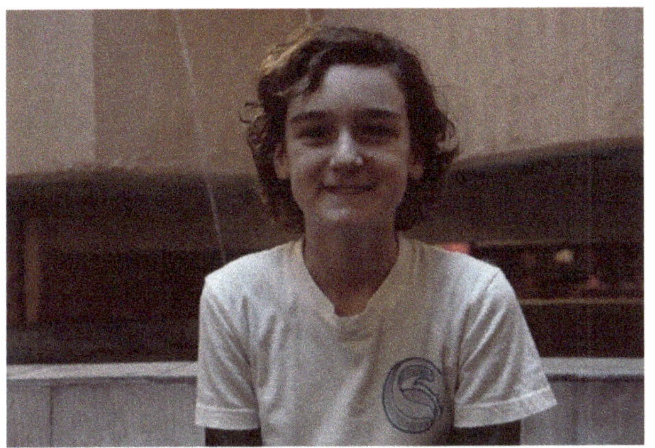

Charley Peebler is a cofounder, junior board member and assistant program coordinator of Heirs To Our Ocean (H2OO)[8]. At the time of our interview, Charley was one of seventeen kids ages ten to thirteen who were original members of Heirs To Our Ocean. The nonprofit organization describes itself this way: "Heirs To Our Ocean is empowering the next generation of leaders by connecting them in purpose, educating them on the intersection of the environmental and humanitarian crises they are inheriting, and cultivating essential skills to create innovative solutions and real-world change."

The members of Heirs To Our Ocean have worked on a full-length documentary film to show that human impact on our oceans is going to affect their generation and future generations. In addition, each member takes on one or two study topics of interest, which they pursue with the help of mentors. Charley's topics at the time of our interview were coral, and derelict fishing gear and how it affects whales.

Charley was born in the San Francisco Bay Area. At the time of our interview, they were twelve years old and had grown up in San Mateo, California. Their love of the oceans started early. As a young child, they watched *Dora the Explorer* and *Diego and His Adventures*, and those programs had a lot of marine life in their episodes. When Charley was five years old, the family went to the California Academy of Sciences and they really loved it. Charley and sister Dakota are both homeschooled, so they are able to continue to pursue their passion around the oceans and marine life.

Charley first came to Monterey Bay with the family to attend an open house at the Monterey Bay Aquarium. They continued to visit the area for Dakota's birthday, and with a cousin, and to stay in a house at the beach.

---

[8] Heirs To Our Ocean (H2OO) is an advocacy group founded by and led by youth. H2OO works to ensure youth are empowered, connected, educated and prepared to realize solutions to achieve a safer and healthier future. www.h2oo.org

The Saga of the Entangled Whale

Pieter Folkens

(Date of Interview: 11/12/16)

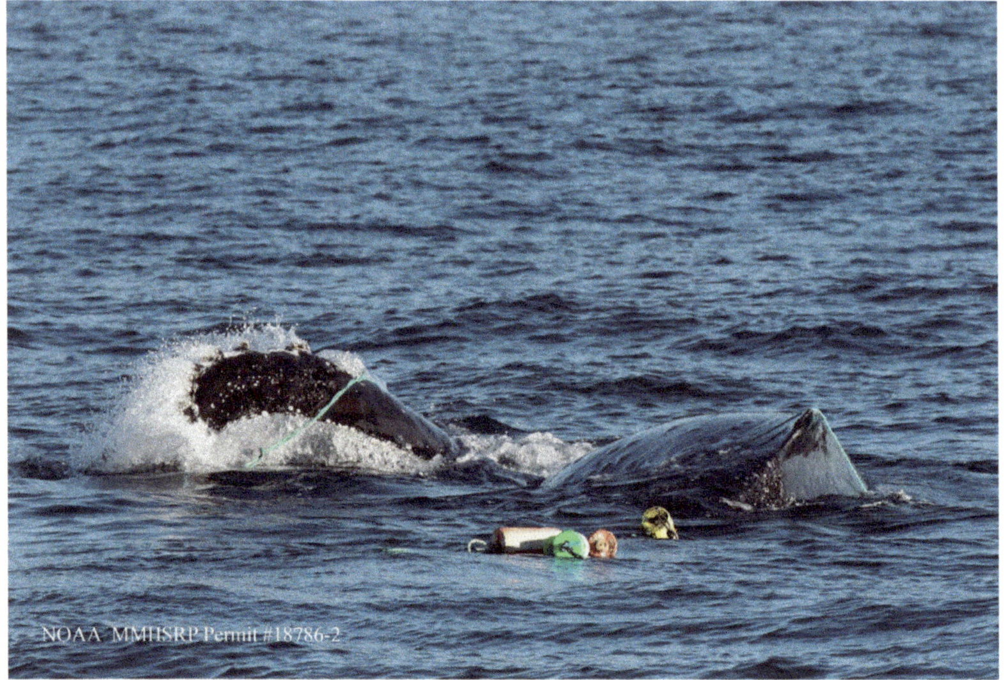

Entangled humpback whale

On July 3, in the late morning, a report came in of an entangled humpback whale that was near Monterey Bay. The initial team to go out from Marine Life Studies (MLS) was very good. There was a photographer on board by the name of Doug Croft, and we started to get the initial photographs of the entanglement. It looked to be a pretty serious entanglement, something that had gone on for a while. The rope had started to embed in the back of the animal. It was cutting into the mouth. The line clearly came over the head just behind the blowhole, in one side of the mouth, out the other side of the mouth, and then around a pectoral fin, and was dragging behind. The whale was clearly trying to get rid of the gear, but in that effort was just making the situation worse. We think it was dragging a lot of gear, and with the weight of that gear the animal was breaching, trying to get out of it. But it was simply cinching it up more and doing more damage.

The MLS folks saw and documented the whale, and we decided that we had to have a response. For the first phase of the response we wanted to get telemetry on the whale so we could keep track of where it was going. So we called for support from the Coast Guard—the motor lifeboat stationed there in Monterey. They agreed to come out because of how well documented the entanglement was. We had our Level III responder come on down to meet up with them and transfer some gear. So now the Coast Guard starts to come out.

Peggy Stap's crew from MLS is on the animal, watching it, and lo and behold, somebody in an open boat, with three adults and four kids, comes over to get a close look at the whale. This open boat with three adults—none of them wearing life jackets—plus three kids, come over because they want to have a little whale watch. As a result, they wrap their propeller in the gear trailing off the entangled animal. It starts to pull their boat backwards and they're taking on water over the transom. They go into panic mode, and start yelling for help.

Peggy calls the Coast Guard on Channel 16 saying, "We've got a situation where this whale is now hooked up to this private boat that's out there and the boat is now being towed backwards."

The Coast Guard is on the way with our gear, but now they immediately have to go back, get our equipment and our people off, because it's become an SAR mission—a search and rescue mission. They go back, take all our gear off their boat, and start to come back out. By that time the guys who got themselves hung up with the whale have reached over the back and gotten their boat disentangled, and have sped off, because they know the Coast Guard is coming out.

So we call off the SAR mission, and the Coast Guard has to go back to pick up the deployment gear and our crew, which is part of the deployment team. All this time Peggy's crew is standing by the animal and waiting, waiting for the disentanglement crew to come out. The situation was just snakebit from the start.

The Coast Guard finally comes out. By then it's starting to get dark; I believe it was getting foggy as well. But they were able to successfully deploy our buoy—that big orange thing that has the telemetry on it, by attaching it to the gear trailing off the whale. We planned on coming back the next day, and we got word the telemetry was working. All of our stations that had received the telemetry knew exactly where the whale was.

The next day, we get the whole team together again—Marine Life Studies, Alaska Whale Foundation, and sanctuary people—so we're all ready to go. The 'ping' is showing us that our whale is off of Point Sur—it's gone way down south. We've got to move all of our assets and go way down the coast and try to find the whale. With our Argos satellite tracking system, we have a delay. The way Argos works is when the whale comes up to the surface, if it stays at the surface long enough for the telemetry buoy to be floating at the surface and to be able to get a reading, it's got to happen at the same time there's a satellite passing overhead. If the surfacing and the satellite happen at the same time, we get an upload of the information on where the animal is. That information goes to, I think, some place in Africa or France, and then somebody at that end cleans up the data and posts it on the internet. We then go to our account and see where the animal is. So, there's this delay of twenty minutes or so before we get that. Meanwhile our whale is moving.

We're getting these fixes and we're getting a sense of where the animal is. To zero in on the animal we use a VHF antenna to find out where it is in that moment, as opposed to waiting twenty minutes for the Argos information. The problem with the VHF is that if you start getting a 'ping' it could be that direction or it could be exactly behind us. We're using two antennas. We're trying to triangulate, and we're having a heck of a time finding out where this animal is. And one of the confounding things is that there are a dozen blue whales down there. And there's fifty or sixty humpback whales. We stopped counting at that number—there were probably more. There were fin whales down there and all sorts of critters down there feeding.

So we're trying to locate a 'ping' coming off this whale, with all these other whales around, and you might have several of them surfacing at the same time. We've got two fairly substantial boats out there trying to find out where this dang thing went. Late in the afternoon we finally find the animal. We know exactly where it is. We get on it. We launch our cut boat and we go up on it[9]. In the boat are Jim Holme, Ryan Berger and I. We get up on the animal and we find out there's just this *immense* wad of crap underneath it. The gear wasn't just going around the mouth and around the flipper, but underneath it was all tangled and wrapped around with just literally hundreds of feet of line and buoys.

When we respond on these things we have attainable goals that we set for the time period we have. We don't say that we're going to go disentangle that animal no matter what. We make very defined goals. We're going to do this at this point, this at this point and so forth, and we do it in steps. What that does is it forces us to check our safety levels, our enthusiasm levels. When you're out in the cut boat, you have to be really even emotionally, because if somebody gets too excited, "WE'VE GOT TO SAVE THIS THING," you know you end up with a loss of situational awareness, and that's when you're going to end up with problems.

---

[9] 'Go up on it,' 'on it' or 'on the animal' means up close to it, even hanging onto the trailing gear.

We come back to report to everybody on the big boat, the Monterey Bay National Marine Sanctuary's R/V *Fulmar*. We're saying, "This is what we're seeing." But it's starting to get dark. Do we keep going or do we have to leave it and come back another day? Well, the two people in charge—Chris, who's the Master on *Fulmar*, and I—say, "You know, we've put so much effort into getting out here. We have all our safety stuff in gear." Holme and I, Chris, and Marshall—all of us— have had night operations training, so we know what we're doing. We've got reflectives all over the boat. And we say "You know what? We ought to give it another shot." Marshall offered me a headlamp, but I said, "I don't want that. I want to have all my peripheral vision." As long as we've got twilight I want to be able to see.

The goal was simply to get rid of the crap underneath the whale. We go out there and attach to it[10]. We're coming over the bow, and the whale is still pretty darn healthy, even though it wasn't very old and it was all tangled up. Boy, those puppies are strong! We're holding down on the animal on the bow so we can work ourselves up to it, so we can get to where all the crap is. After several attempts the animal dives, and it swamps our boat to where it just fills up with water. We were hoping to keep the animal at the surface, but when that happens, we have to let go, and then circle with the engines and get the water out, and then get back up on the animal.

Well, we finally get to advance our floats enough to where we can cut away all the crap, so that the only entanglement that is left involves the mouth, the flipper, one line that's loose and one line that has our telemetry buoy on it. At that point, we've taken off maybe two hundred pounds worth of crap. But we keep flotation on one line, hoping that the extra weight will pull the line through the mouth. Then we go home. It was the Fourth of July, and that was the second operational period.

As we're going home fireworks are going off and we're watching them in the distance. We had our fireworks for the Fourth of July. We get back to Monterey and the guys on the *Fulmar* allow us to stay overnight. The next morning we go out there again to find the whale. We've got the Argos system working, and we find the whale right away. We know exactly where it is. We go out there and we get on it. We're trying to figure out just what's left of the entanglement, so we start to do the more advanced analysis. In the second operational period it was too dark for us to get any pictures underwater. On this third operational period, we need to get a thorough understanding of exactly how severe the entanglement is. During the day,

---

[10] Attached (hanging on) via the line coming off the whale.

the animal has just been frustrating us, because it has been feeding while we've been trying to do that. It was also somewhat curious about what we were doing. We've got video in which we're on the animal, holding onto it. We move up onto the fluke. We've got our underwater camera on it, and the whale dives down and comes up, and you can see him looking at us. He just comes up and takes a look at us, and he rolls forward and keeps going.

We're attached to the whale at this time. By *attached* I mean we're holding on to what we call our working line, while the animal does what it's doing. Ryan is the point person. We're photographing from the *Fulmar*, and the whale starts to circle back onto our response boat and starts to lunge feed right at us. The animal's trying to be a whale, while we're trying to help him. The fact is that there's a line across its mouth and it's still dragging a bunch of crap. Mouth entanglements are the hardest ones to deal with, because the whale's not going to let us get up close to its head. We have a technique where we use Prusik[11] loops with flotation, so that we can work ourselves up close, because we know exactly where the danger zone is. We can control our approach right up to the edge of that danger zone and still be in a safe situation. There were a couple of times the whale actually tried to lash out at us and got us all wet, but we were still in the safe zone. We knew we were operating within our own defined parameters of safety. But this animal would just go down and come back up and feed, then do it all again.

Late in the operational period we decide that probably the best thing we can do is reduce the entanglement, hoping that there will only be a slight wrap around the right side of the whale. With the telemetry buoy on the other side, we hoped the gear would be loosened up so the weight of the buoy would pull it through by the next day. We've had several entanglements where just the presence of our telemetry buoy was enough to pull all the crap off. By now it's late. Chris calls around trying to find a place to park *Fulmar*. We're at Half Moon Bay at this point, which is a long way to get back to Monterey. The Harbor Master at Pillar Point gives us a place. We get in there around 9:00–9:30 pm or so, and Ryan, Holme, and I are just dead tired.

It's the end of the third operational period. We're done, and we're just kind of sitting in the salon looking like death warmed over, and Erin, who's part of the *Fulmar* crew, says, "All right, what do you guys want to eat?" And we're like "whatever." She goes off to Safeway to get us salads and burritos and sandwich makings and all sorts of stuff. Then we go to bed; we're dead tired, but wake up

---

[11] Prusik is a friction hitch or knot used to attach a loop of cord around a rope, so a Prusik loop is one made using Prusik knots.

refreshed. When you're dead tired like that, you sleep really hard, so you wake up feeling really well.

Next day we're starting our fourth operational period and we find the whale. We're starting to get really good at finding this guy really quickly. We immediately go out, find it, and we're on it. We attach to him, and we find that where we had made the cut had moved up on the whale about five or six feet. We're thinking, holy shitskies, that idea of using the flotation might be enough to pull the gear off. If it worked that much, perhaps hooking the boat to the whale will add more flotation to help pull it off. We take one of our buoys, and we hang it over the bow of the boat. For about the first hour, Ryan is holding on to it thinking that he'd hold on to the whale, and I say, "Ryan you're gonna be so tired here if you keep that up." Instead, with the buoy over the bow, I wedge it with my knee so that if the whale dives all we have to do is kick the buoy over and we'd be good to go. Now the animal is towing us along at 4½–5 knots. Not for ten minutes, not for half an hour, not for an hour, but for three or four hours! Just continually doing this! All right? When is this gonna be resolved? [*laughter*]

By now we've tried a number of techniques. We've even brought up the *Fulmar* to come up close to the whale to see if we can get it to move the other way. Imagine the situation: we have our boat attached to the whale and it's going in this direction. The entanglement is all on the right side of the head. What we want to have happen is we want the animal to move away, so that the line opens up leaving a gap from the animal, so we can then have a chance to go at it to cut the line farther forward.

I call *Fulmar* to come in closer and get off our quarter, hoping the noise of the *Fulmar* will cause the animal to move away from the *Fulmar*. That doesn't happen. What does the whale do? The whale turns into the *Fulmar* and crosses its bow to where our support crew on the *Fulmar* is looking over the front and they get a look at the whale, and they can see exactly what's going on. They can see the degree of entanglement. What had happened was, the line, as it was coming out of the left side of the mouth, was being pressed against one of the nares, or nostrils (blow holes) to the point where the nare had become very swollen, and the whale could breathe only out of one of the nares. Obviously, the situation was not going to resolve by itself. Over the next few hours Ryan and I discuss what we should do next. We decide what we need to do to give the whale the best chance is try to remove as much of the entanglement as we can. We'd already gotten rid of 95% of it, so we wanted to go that extra little bit where the only part that would still be on the whale was a wrap around the pec fin and what went through the mouth. Anything trailing would be cut off as close to the animal as we could.

And that's what we do. We hook up the knife to the pole, put the pole out thirty-five feet then walk[12] ourselves up as close to the whale as we think is safe. Before we do the cut, we want to make sure the whale isn't going to freak out at us. So, we do some sensitization in which we take the pole and tap it on the back to see what the reaction is. The first time we get a little bit of a buck. The second tap, the animal actually turns around and looks at us, "What is this?" Then we give it a while and touch it again to the point where the animal doesn't react at all. At that point, we figure we're safe to go ahead and make the cut. We move the knife up just above the pectoral fin and the line that is going over it. Well, the line actually goes under the pec and up over the back. We're able to get the knife underneath the line, pull it and we cut it! And the whale bolts.

All this while I think the slowest the whale has gone is 3½ knots. We're talking about ten hours on the water. We finally cut the whale free and it takes off. What we have done is give it the best chance for survival. Once there's no more drag on the line that's left, the line should start to relax. Through the healing process—you know when you get a splinter—the splinter kind of moves to the outside, and we hoped that would happen with the whale also. Because the animal was so strong when we left it, and because there was no more drag on it, we felt the entanglement would eventually resolve itself.

PIETER FOLKENS

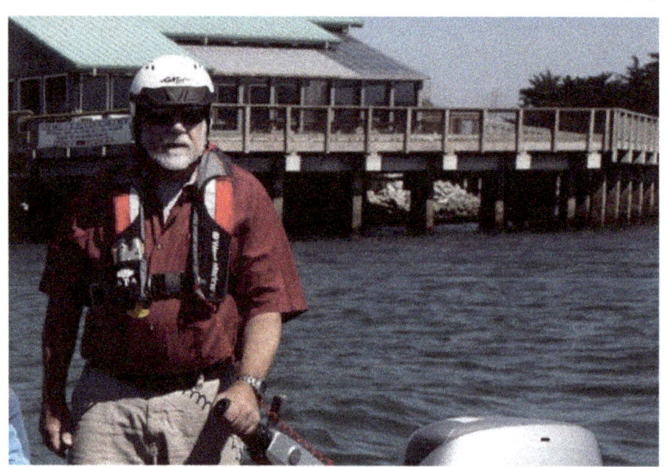

Pieter Folkens has been deeply involved in large-whale-disentanglement response since 1996. He's a Level 4, the highest-level person on the permit in Northern California. He got started with whale disentanglement in Alaska with the Alaska Whale Foundation. But the problem of entangled whales is very serious in the Monterey Bay area. Pieter also writes books, is involved in canine search and rescue, and is well known for his scientific illustrations, which have

---

[12] Slowly moved the boat closer.

appeared in multiple books and posters. His latest illustration project is *Marine Mammals of the World*, a highly detailed field guide.

Pieter was born in Bakersfield, California. He grew up 'all over,' living in several foreign countries, as well as spending a lot of time in Alaska and the High Sierra.

His initial introduction into the marine world and the Monterey Bay area came in the 1980s when Ken Norris requested that he come to Santa Cruz. Pieter then became Assistant Professor of Science Communications in the Division of Natural History at the University of California at Santa Cruz, which had a close affiliation with the Joseph M. Long Marine Laboratory.

Pieter's interest in marine mammals, however, came long before that. At the 'ripe old age of 8,' Pieter went on a field trip with his third-grade class. On that trip they discovered a fossil of a 13.5-million-year-old sperm whale. Pieter was so intrigued by the fossil that he got a bunch of friends together for his birthday the following summer and they traveled in a Volkswagen bus back to the same location where they had found the sperm whale fossil. He recounts that it was a small fossil, mostly skull parts and teeth. In 1979, Pieter went back to the site with the Natural History Museums of Los Angeles County and they did a more extensive, formal review of the marine mammal fossils in the Sharktooth Hill area, which is a well-known bone bed that covers a lot of California's Great Central Valley.

Along with Fred Sharpe, who became a Principal Investigator for the Alaska Whale Foundation a few years later, Pieter is one of the founders of the Alaska Whale Foundation, now in its twenty-eighth year, started in 1996. Pieter had met Fred in a backwater area and they got to talking. At that time, Pieter was a naturalist for Dolphin Charters and also a field agent for the National Marine Mammal Act. Turns out they both had similar thoughts about the color pattern of Pacific humpback whale pectoral fins, and the possible adaptation of the coloration as an aid to feeding. That collaboration led to Fred Sharpe's seminal work on cooperative bubble-net feeding, plus other behavioral discoveries about humpback whales in Southeast Alaska.

Good Things Come to Those Who Wait:
Tale of the White Dolphin

Katlyn Taylor

(*Date of Interview*: 10/1/19)

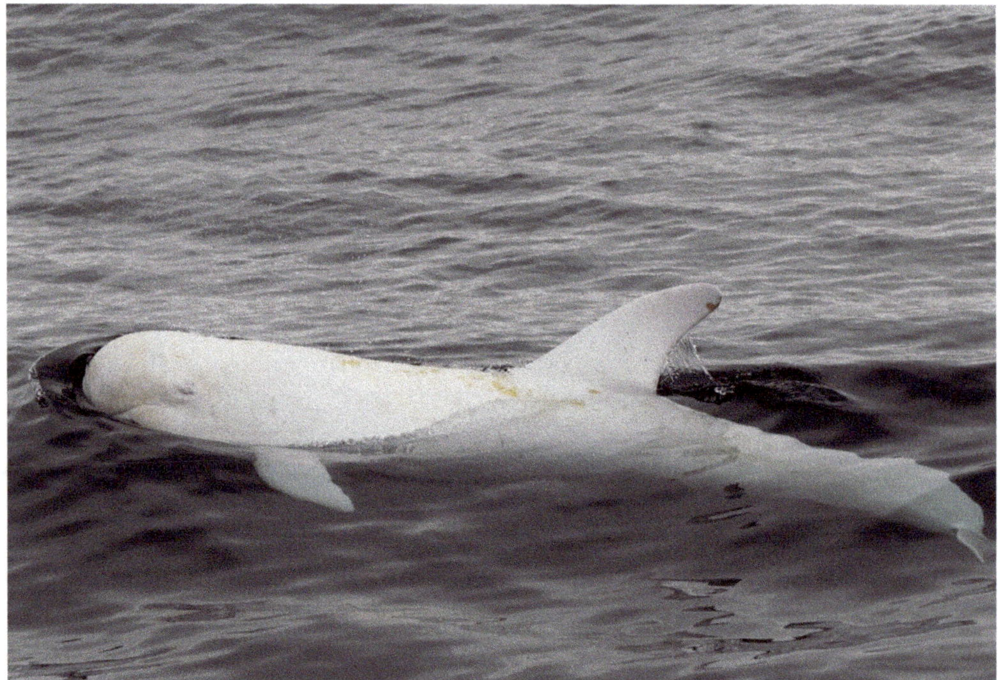

Casper

My most memorable wildlife encounter in Monterey Bay to date just happened. Yeah! I have worked in Monterey the entire sighting history of this all-white Risso's dolphin, and I had not seen it the entire five years I've worked here. I think the first sighting was like October 2014, and I got here in June of 2014. Then finally, this last week, *I saw it*!! [*laughter*]

I've been saying for like *months* to the captains, "I need to see this dolphin. I've not seen it." And they all forget. They're like, "Wait, wait, we've seen it a bunch of times." "I know, but I haven't, so, like, please help me!"

Well, we're headed out on a whale watch with Discovery Whale Watch. I was on the *Pacifica*, and we sent our other boat, the *Chubasco*, out at the same time. We came across this big group of Risso's, including Casper, which is what they've been calling the white dolphin. That name is up for debate, honestly, in my opinion[13]. But, anyway, its group has been around a lot. There've been four or five sightings in the last two months, which is pretty high, because the dolphin has only been sighted every six to eight months the rest of the time it's been around.

We had Risso's when we first went out on the 9:00 am whale watch, and it was really calm. And I was like, "Man, I really hope we find it. I really, *really* want to see it!!" So I was looking superhard! Every group of Risso's we had, I was looking, looking, looking. We didn't see it, but there were Risso's for miles—from just inside Point Pinos and out for at least three or four miles.

So, we kept kind of cruising along; we really wanted to find some humpbacks as well, because we can't just look at Risso's for forty-five minutes. Fine. I guess today's not the day.

But then the boat turns around. I'm outside on the deck, and I'm talking to passengers, and the boat does a 180. I run up to the wheelhouse, "Did they find it?!" And the captain, Rod, is like, "Come in here." And I'm like, "They've found it! *They've found it*! [*laughter*] I can't contain myself, and he says, "Calm down, I don't know, we're going to try." "*Thank you, thank you*!!!"

The *Chubasco* found it, and they waited for us to turn around and come back to them, so that I could see the little dolphin. We only got just a glimpse. I got three photos, but I was still just over the moon that I saw it. There was kind of a dark sky, with glassy, calm seas, so that

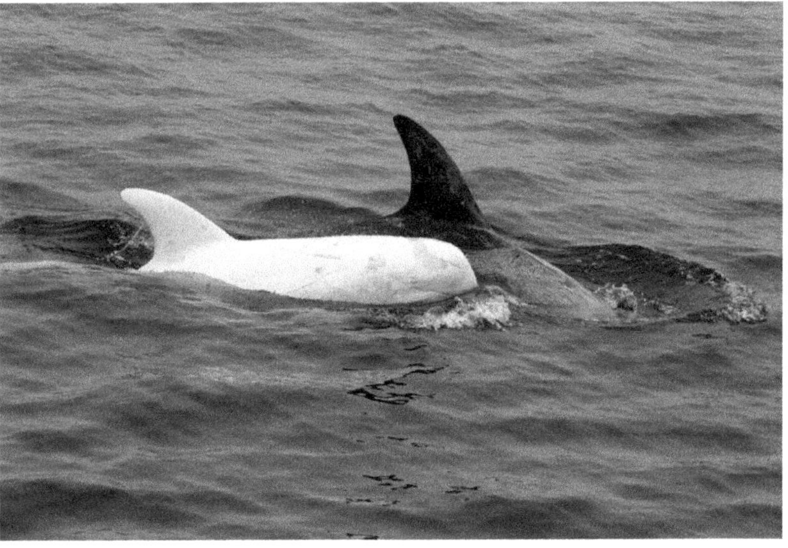

Risso's dolphins: Casper and friend   © Katlyn Taylor

little dolphin's just like this big white beacon sticking up out on the ocean.

And I was like, "YES, we saw it!" So then for me that was like trip *made*! Morning *made*! Well, we go out farther and have a great whale watch with humpbacks, and some nice looks at albatross, and then we're cruising back in, and

---

[13] Other names in use were 'Albert the Albino' and 'Lawn Chair.'

the Risso's are still there. There are still miles of Risso's. So, I'm like, "Hmm. I wonder if he's still there?" He or she. And I'm looking with the binoculars really closely, and then I find him/her! We go over there, and the captain gives us some extra time—an extra fifteen minutes—to spend with the dolphin, and it showed really well. It actually left mom for a while. A bunch of the adults, including its mom, kept traveling, and the little dolphin just stayed by the boat and circled around. And, *ach*, it was just so perfect! That was *incredible*!

Then all of a sudden toward the end of the sighting, the captain was like, "OK, we've got to go." And I was like, "All right," and I was telling the people, "We're getting our last looks at the dolphin," and other things like that on the microphone, and then the little white dolphin realized that all of the adults were gone and it had been by itself with the boat for a while, and just like, *'fwoooh,'* took off and caught up to the rest of the dolphins, which were already a quarter mile away.

So that was *really, really cool*. I'm *so glad* I got to see that. Good things come to those who wait.

KATLYN TAYLOR

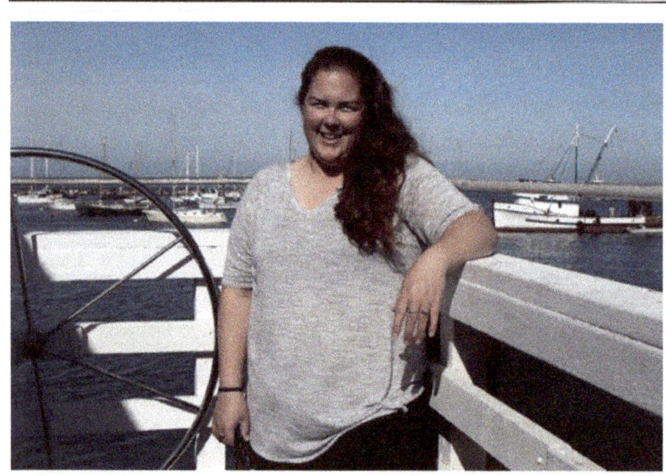

Katlyn Taylor is a marine biologist, guide and U.S. Coast Guard licensed captain. She has worked on ecotour vessels all over the United States, and in the polar regions since 2014. Katlyn coproduces *The Whalenerd's Podcast*, a show about whales, the oceans and more. She is the cocreator of *Wild Monterey Bay*, and is a three-time recipient of the Safina Center Junior Fellows Program. During her years in the Monterey area, she has worked as a naturalist and staff biologist for Discovery Whale Watch and Monterey Bay Whale Watch (MBWW) on Fisherman's Wharf, as a captain and naturalist for Blue Ocean Whale Watch in Moss Landing, and she was president of the Monterey Chapter of the American Cetacean Society.

Katlyn was born in Portland, Oregon and grew up in Oregon City, Oregon. She has always been interested in wildlife. As a child, she went to the Oregon Coast at least once a summer with her parents and sister. Her family bought tide pool books and taught themselves how to identify the creatures in the tide pools. Katlyn's parents are both educators and always provided her with the resources she needed to answer her questions about nature and with opportunities to experience it firsthand.

Katlyn attended Oregon State University (OSU), where she took a class about whales taught by Jim Sumich, renowned for his work with gray whales. Katlyn kept asking questions in class and Sumich kept saying, "Katlyn, science does not know the answer to your question!" So she decided to study marine biology. She graduated with a Bachelor in Science degree in Marine Biology and a Bachelor in Art in International Studies. While at OSU, she joined the Oregon Chapter of the American Cetacean Society and took the Naturalist class they offered.

In her final year of school, Katlyn volunteered with the Oregon State Parks Whale Watch Interpretation Program, which takes place all up and down the Oregon coast during the gray whale migration. In late 2013, her winter station sighted only one whale the whole rainy and foggy week. Four days later she and her parents drove down to Monterey. When they arrived, they parked at Point Pinos, and in the first hour they saw thirty gray whales. Katlyn realized the whales must have swum right by her post in Oregon, but she missed them all because of the poor visibility. She and her family then went whale watching, and Katlyn decided she needed to figure out how to come back to the area. In March 2014, Katlyn drove down again with some friends for spring break. She went whale watching and chatted up some of the whale watch companies about a job. After graduation, she took an unpaid internship at MBWW.

A month into the internship Katlyn began working in the whale watch office to make ends meet and stay in Monterey. The following spring an opportunity to work on the boats came up, including working with a BBC film crew, and also doing research for Nancy Black, the owner of MBWW. She continued her work there for over two years until she was recruited to join Discovery Whale Watch. At MBWW Katlyn met "this person named Jodi," who invited her to work on *Wild Monterey Bay* with her. Katlyn said yes, and the rest is history.

Coral after Coral after Sponge in the Deep

Andrew DeVogelaere

(Date of Interview: 11/27/18)

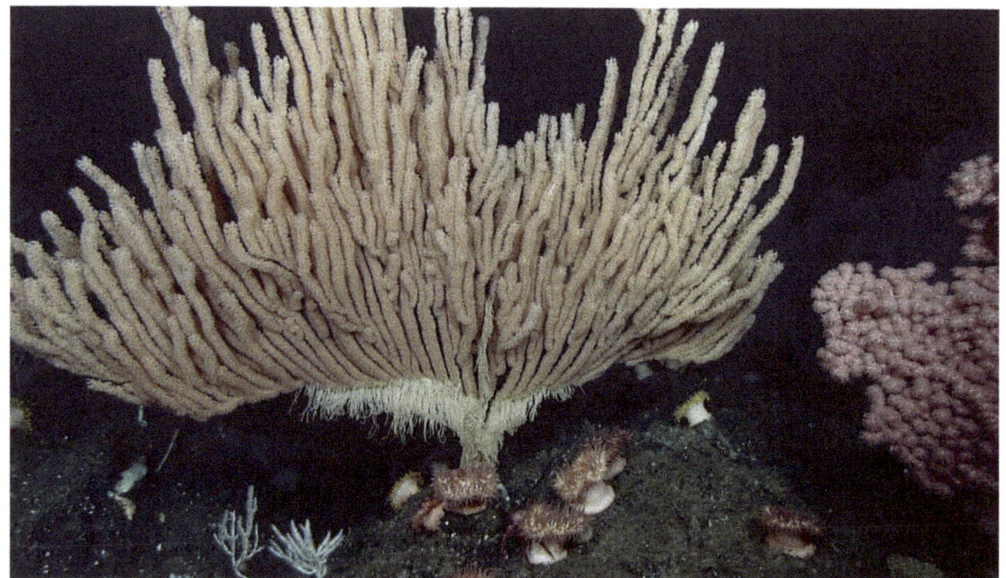

Bamboo coral   MBARI

When thinking about a great experience in Monterey Bay, I think about when I was younger and I wanted to become a marine scientist. I wanted to do things that were exciting, like going to interesting places, seeing beautiful things and making new discoveries.

Now when I look back, I think, "Wow! I got to do some of that, and I get to share that with other people." It's been very fulfilling, but I'm struggling a bit with what exactly is the special story that I'd like to tell here.

The first encounter that came to mind was drifting in a boat in Monterey Bay, and then having a humpback whale scratching itself on the bottom of the boat for about half an hour. That *was* pretty exciting!

Another dreamlike experience was diving off the Big Sur coast, scuba diving in the remote kelp forest. Usually around here when you're diving the visibility is not great. But I felt like I could see, you know, a hundred feet. I could see the individual kelp fronds, the harbor seals swimming through, and it was all crystal clear. I could also see my friends laying out their meter tapes to measure things. That was quite a beautiful experience.

But the story I want to tell now is one about a place called Sur Ridge. About thirty miles offshore of Point Sur there's a geological feature called Sur Ridge that is about eleven miles long and three miles wide. The shallowest spot is maybe 2300 feet, and then it goes down at the bottom to about 5000 feet deep.

My friend and colleague Jim Barry and I were on a cruise studying a lost shipping container just outside Monterey Bay. Miraculously, we finished our work early. And Jim said, "Wow, we've got an extra day. Hmm. That never happens." And then he said, "Why don't we go check out Sur Ridge? You're always talking about it. I know you want to go there. Nobody's been there to look at the biology." He said, "I've got some manuscripts I've got to work on, but we can check it out and see what we find there." We looked at a map and looked for the steepest ridge we could find, figuring that maybe we'd see some things at the top. It would be muddy along the sides, and hopefully we'd see some nice corals. Well, we headed out and finally got there.

Now we're with the ROV[14] pilots, sitting with the cameras, as the ROV

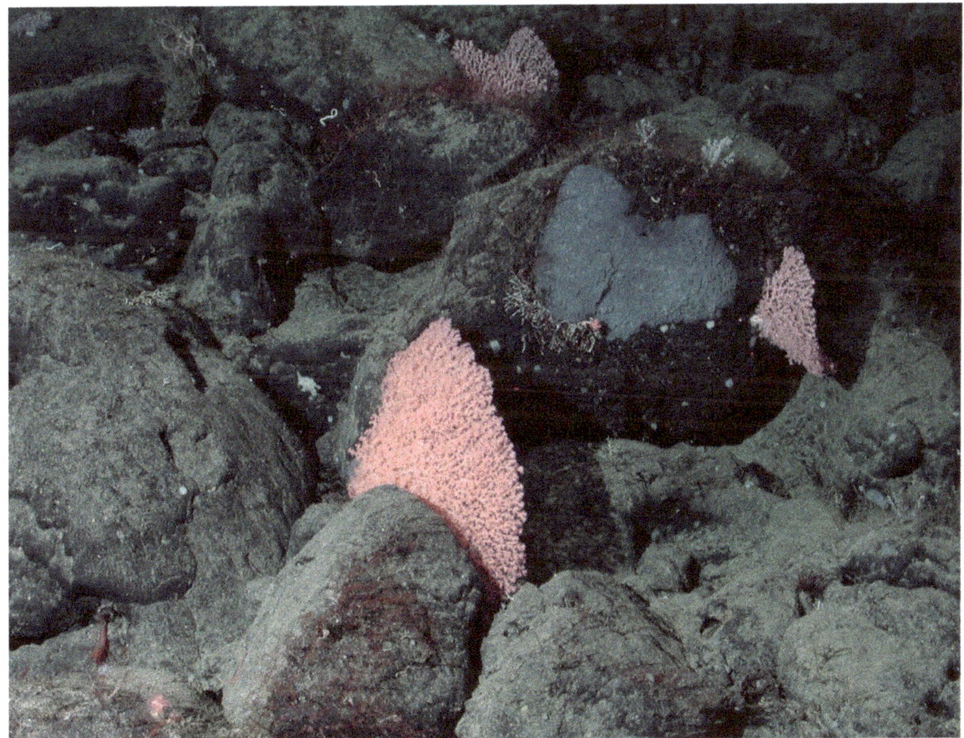

Corallium, *Precious coral*   MBARI

approaches slowly from the muddy floor up to Sur Ridge. Jim's kind of opening up

---

[14] Remotely operated vehicle. These are operated by specially trained pilots aboard the mother ship.

his computer working on some things, and as soon as we hit the bottom of Sur Ridge we see this *Corallium* on the screen: it's a beautiful, pink coral. It's called the Precious Coral. They make jewelry out of it. "Wow! That's a surprise!" We go a little bit farther and we see another pink coral, but this one is called *Sibogagorgia*! Then farther still, there are some bamboo corals. Jim now closes his computer, and he's starting to look. Even the pilots are getting excited, and the rest of the day we're just going up the side of the ridge, seeing coral after coral after sponge.

By the end of the day, we had been seeing corals all day long and everybody was really hyped up. The ROV pilots who are out there almost every day said, "Wow, we've never seen anything like this!"

So, not only is it beautiful out there, but you're sharing it with other people who are also excited, and yours are the first human eyes to see this particular place on the globe. Plus, you've found something that's really cool. And that still makes me feel excited. It's what you dream about doing when you're young and you want to be a marine biologist. On later trips at Sur Ridge, we were superlucky and saw a whale skeleton, an octopus garden, and chemosynthetic communities, where creatures such as giant tube worms with bacteria generate foodstuffs (sugars and amino acids) from inorganic compounds.

But one of the best parts is that you can get to Sur Ridge in four hours or so. It's closer than, say, the Davidson Seamount, which is also very special and where we've seen some similar things, but this site is both closer and shallower. There are a lot of corals, and we could visit it repeatedly and start doing studies there. So rather than just saying, "Oh, there's a cool coral" and moving on, we're like, "let's mark it, let's look at it through time, let's see what's eating it."

Then we also started doing studies on determining how old these things are. Some of them are a couple thousand years old, and that's pretty exciting. Then there's another scientist who says, "Let's use lasers to look at the particles moving around the corals and see how they're feeding." And then there's, "Well, what kind of currents do they need?" The Monterey Bay Aquarium was interested because they want to make an exhibit of corals, and what kind of currents do we need to keep these corals alive?

But for me, maybe the most exciting thing was that we're starting to develop—and we've been successful at developing—techniques for taking branches of corals and transplanting them, translocating them to other areas. And we're exploring how they do in terms of surviving and what's the best way to move them and bring them to the surface, plus what kind of substratum do we put them on, how do we package them in pots, and so on.

Because there are a lot of areas of the ocean that have been impacted by deep-sea trawling, oil spills or other human impacts, we're the first scientists developing ways to restore areas in the deep, not just by moving the coral, but by looking to see if they're making eggs or propagules that they can release.

So that's my exciting story about the deep sea. It's about discovery, about beauty, about learning, and it leads you to thinking about what a gorgeous place this is, what a special earth we have, and that we need to take care of it. Not just by translocating coral, but by sharing the information we've gleaned. We want to ensure that the next generation of marine scientists who are thinking, "What am I gonna do? I wanna discover some things!" will get excited. There are many areas of the ocean that won't be discovered for a long, long time. There are many places in the deep yet to be seen by human eyes. The next generation of marine scientists will be able to make amazing discoveries of their own and share them with everyone else, so that there's an even greater understanding of the ocean.

We need to lose some of the apathy around caring about the ocean that is present in a lot of society. We need to get people excited about our oceans and say, "Hey, we're connected, we should take care of them for the next generation, not just of scientists, but of human beings." So that's my story, and I'm sticking to it.

ANDREW DeVOGELAERE

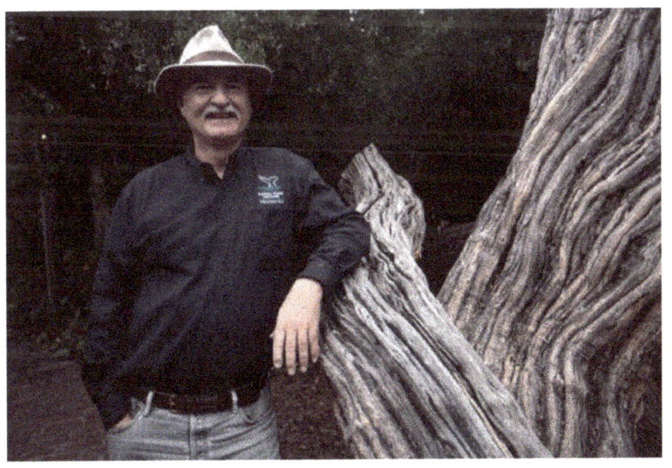

Andrew DeVogelaere is a Research Ecologist and the current SIMoN Program Director for the Monterey Bay National Marine Sanctuary. His position involves providing scientific information about the sanctuary to decision-makers, so they can make good, informed decisions and provide for ocean education. He is also tasked with understanding what's happening in the sanctuary ecosystems and monitoring change through time, particularly the health of the sanctuary and how it is changing.

Andrew has a small staff and a small budget, but he acknowledges having the brightest and best marine science collaborators here in Monterey Bay and, for that matter, anywhere else in the world. He says they're very bright, exciting people to be around, including the grad students, and they know more about this area of the ocean than is known about most places in the world.

Andrew was born in the San Francisco Bay Area. His dad was on the faculty of the University of California at Berkeley (UC Berkeley), so Andrew got to grow up in Berkeley and the Berkeley hills and experience all the good there was in that community.

He's been interested in marine biology since he was a kid, when he first became interested in marine and aquatic science while raising tropical fish, reading books and watching TV. And as he did with so many others, Jacques Cousteau made an impact on Andrew's young, impressionable mind.

In his youth, Andrew and all his friends had aquariums with freshwater fish. When he started his fish-breeding hobby he wasn't sure whether he wanted to get into freshwater biology or marine biology, but either way, the great visuals, photos and movies he saw during those early years inspired him to do something with his life he was passionate about. His parents were supportive and had always told him to do something he loved.

He decided to study marine biology as an undergrad, because of his love of fish and biology. Andrew attended UC Berkeley and was excited to declare his major as marine biology at the end of his second year. However, his advisor said don't do it, you'll never get a job, because his daughter had a marine biology degree and couldn't get a job. Andrew decided to take his parents' advice over his advisor's and followed through anyway.

After completing his undergraduate work at UC Berkeley, Andrew attended Moss Landing Marine Laboratories (MLML) on the shores of Monterey Bay, where he got his master's degree studying rocky shore ecology. He then propelled those studies into a PhD at the University of California at Santa Cruz.

While in school, Andrew did some consulting work for Kinnetic Laboratories in Santa Cruz looking at the impact of oil spills and associated rocky shore recovery rates. This background led him to a postdoctoral position at MLML, studying the effectiveness of different cleaning techniques after the *Exxon Valdez* oil spill in Prince William Sound, Alaska. At the same time, he worked as the first Research Coordinator for the Elkhorn Slough National Estuarine Research Reserve and served as an elected official as a Moss Landing Harbor Commissioner. In 1995 Andrew started at the Monterey Bay National Marine Sanctuary, where he continues his career to this day.

The Octopus' Garden

Chad King

"This looks like something Dr. Seuss created. It doesn't look real."

(Date of Interview: 11/12/19)

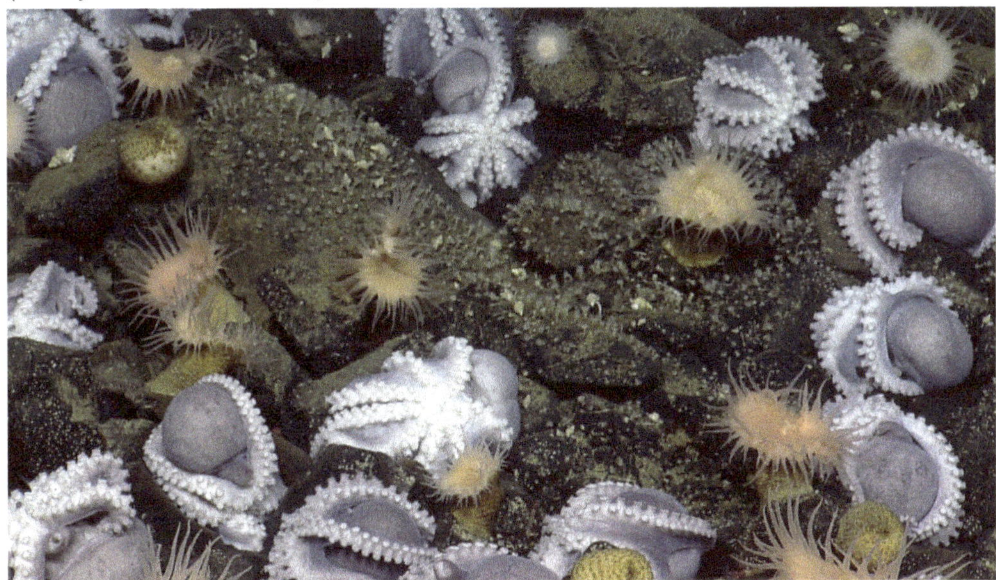

Nesting deep-sea pearl octopuses

© Chad King (OET/NOAA)

In 2018 we were tasked to go out on the exploration vessel *Nautilus*, which is run by Ocean Exploration Trust (OET); Dr. Bob Ballard, who discovered the *Titanic*, runs that outfit. OET and the Office of National Marine Sanctuaries had an agreement to use the vessel to go out, I think, over a three- or four-year period to visit different sanctuaries. OET does other things, too. In fact, Bob had just gotten back over the summer and that 2018 trip, when a big Amelia Earhart expedition had just aired on *National Geographic*. That's the same vessel we were using.

We went out in October 2018 to go to this extinct underwater volcano, called a seamount—Davidson Seamount—to look for corals and sponges in places that had not yet been explored. Kind of the apron of the mountain. This mountain is quite tall—almost 8000 feet—so it's like driving over Donner Summit in the Sierra Nevada, and it's twenty-six miles long, eight miles wide. We've explored a lot of the top of the seamount. We get these massive long-lived corals and sponges there, which is one of the reasons why this area was added to the Monterey Bay National Marine Sanctuary in 2008, to protect those corals. We were charged with going out to explore the flanks of the seamount, the foothills of the seamount, if you will, for corals and sponges, and near the end of our first dive, which was about thirty-five hours, we came across our special find.

These remotely operated vehicles (ROVs), like the one we used, can be in the water for quite some time. They don't require any bathroom breaks or food or anything like that. The humans in the mother ship up top, who were watching everything on monitors, comfortably with a cup of coffee, take four-hour shifts twice a day. And we stream everything live to the internet on nautiluslive.org, which is just incredible for bringing in other people.

We also have a science chat room, where we have experts that can be watching live as well, and they interact with us via private chat room to tell us the identity of an animal, or "hey, I would like a sample of this," or "hey, can you preserve it like that?" It really broadens the amount of expertise we can bring out with us. It's an incredible operation. It's just really eye-opening.

So the last hour of the dive, we came across this pocket. To see octopus down there is not unusual. Seeing one that's brooding, meaning taking care of its eggs, is also not unusual. But you see them just by themselves; they're solitary. We came across a pocket of about twenty brooding females, and we thought that was peculiar. They were in this little depression, at the top of a small ridge, and we decided to go and investigate.

When we landed we saw, as the camera stabilized, that the water was shimmering as it was coming out of the seafloor, much like you would see air shimmer off the pavement on a hot day. It created that oasis, shimmering effect. And we immediately thought, "this is warm water." This is big news! Nothing like that has ever been discovered around here. The fact that there were twenty octopus there, "Wow!" They're all lined up in this pool of warm water. Clearly, *clearly* they chose to be there. Why is that? Questions started flying through our heads. I'm thinking this is something new, but we're not cephalopod experts. We don't know if this has ever been discovered before. We're starting to fly through the area with the ROV and people are getting excited. So we decide the last forty-five minutes of the dive we'll go downslope to the east.

Then we just started running into pockets of hundreds of octopus. Well over a thousand in the duration of the dive. We landed in a couple of places, and every single place where there was a big aggregation, the water was shimmering, indicating there was warm water, most likely coming out of the seep. We couldn't measure it at the time since we didn't have access to a thermometer, but we were very excited. Not only that, but there are many other animals associated with these seeps, too—types of snails, shrimp, anemones, tubeworms, all sorts of stuff, so clearly there's a community dynamic going on here, too. And the questions were just piling up in our heads.

As it turns out, this is only the second such octopus association—brooding octopus associated with warm water—ever found in the world. But at the other location there were only 106 such individuals. Here we had well over a thousand that we counted within an hour. So we knew this was a *big* deal!

Unfortunately, the ROV had some technical problems. We had thought we were coming back for a second dive right away there, but we didn't wind up coming back. So it was very, very disappointing and depressing, but still very exciting that we discovered this within the last hour we were out, because we could have easily missed it. It was pure luck running into this.

Fast-forward to March of 2019, about five or six months after the original expedition, and the BBC had a week-long television event going on called *Blue Planet Live*. They were going to be broadcasting from several locations around the world, and one of them they wanted to broadcast from was this octopus garden.

They invited me along, and I physically got to get into a submarine and dive down deep. Now this is 3200 meters, which is more than 10,000 feet—more than two miles under the surface of the ocean. It took an hour and a half just to get down there, and that was going fast. It was probably one of the most incredible experiences of my life in terms of my job and what I've been able to do. I've scuba dived up and down the Big Sur coast, I've traveled to a few places here and there, but to actually be in a submarine, like Jacques Cousteau, two miles deep in the cold, dark water of the Pacific Ocean, looking at these octopus moms that we'd just discovered, was a transcendent kind of experience. It was absolutely magnificent.

I got to do a second dive to the top of the seamount as well, where for the better part of the last fifteen years, I'd seen all these large, ten-foot-tall bubblegum corals, but on that second dive, I actually got to see them in three dimensions. I don't think people understand the difference between seeing them on a screen and being able to look out of a porthole and see a whole landscape, not just a screen. Then you get context, perspective, depth—you get all these things that the human eye can perceive that a television monitor and camera can't. Again, it's an experience I'll never forget.

We were able to measure the water temperature! We had been told it probably couldn't be warm, but indeed it was. It was almost 10 degrees Celsius, which is in the low 50s in Fahrenheit, but it's near freezing down there in the ambient surrounding seawater, just about 34 degrees Fahrenheit or 1.7 degrees

Celsius. So, wow, what is attracting the octopus moms to this area? Is it the warmth of the water? Is it something in the water? Is it that the water cleans off the rock and they can smell their eggs better? Again, question after question after question start piling up. That's what usually happens in science. Once you've answered one question, it generates ten more. It's this bifurcating tree of, you know, curiosity I guess.

We were able to come back for one short dive in August with MBARI (Monterey Bay Aquarium Research Institute), and we were able to collect a couple of octopus specimens and actually get them identified by some experts around the world. They confirmed them as *Muusoctopus robustus*. We also collected a lot of animals that live within the vent, and analysis is still going on there. But we're looking at isotopes to determine what they feed on. We also collected water for water chemistry, to look at all sorts of amazing things.

We had the most recent expedition in October 2019, back on the *Nautilus*. This is the vessel we originally used in 2018. This time we revisited the first octopus garden. We were able to measure more temperatures. We now have a watermark high of 10.4 degrees Celsius. So that's getting up there. That's almost the surface temperature of the ocean out here, when you go surfing or boogie boarding. That's getting quite warm for the deep sea. We left a lot of data loggers out there that we'll be retrieving next year at some point, probably next fall. This is great, because every time we measure oxygen and temperature, it's just a moment in time. We know it's 10.4 degrees right now. Well, how does that spot change day to day, week to week, month to month, tidally, yearly or whatever? We were able to leave loggers there that will constantly record these variables. So, when we go back, we can look at how these things change over time, which will answer a lot of questions about the system.

We also collected more water for water chemistry analysis. We collected a few more animals as well. I'm just really excited, because we also were able to visually survey this entire feature, and we saw quite a few more octopus. I have a feeling we're well over 2000 now, in terms of numbers. We just have to go back and count them all on the video, which is going to be a fun, tedious job. But we can crowdsource it. There've been plenty of volunteers willing to do it.

The second dive was to continue what we wanted to do last year until we stumbled on this octopus garden, and that was to look for corals and sponges. We did find some incredible sedimentary cliffs that were more than fifty meters tall and reminded me of scenes from an Indiana Jones movie, or the desert Southwest or the Grand Canyon. It was remarkable geology. Nothing too much in the way of corals and sponges, but a lot of interesting stuff we discovered.

Then we came across a whale fall[15] serendipitously, just like coming across an octopus garden last year, and that was another incredible find! It's estimated that only seventy-five whale falls have ever been documented—that people have come across. That includes whales that were purposefully sunk. Maybe they were beached whales, and researchers were able to take advantage of the opportunity to sink them in the ocean in order to see how the environment changes: how the ecology succeeds, from the scavengers that eat most of the flesh, to the bone-eating worms that embed within the bone, to when it becomes just a reef of bones in five to ten years, or whatever it may be. This carcass was estimated to be several months old, only five meters long—so relatively short—but still in the middle stages of scavenging, so even though most of the flesh was gone, the internal organs were there. A lot of blubber was still there. Octopus and all sorts of fishes and crustaceans were there, just consuming the remaining tissue.

The bones were covered with this fuzzy red and yellow 'hair.' That was the bone-eating worms, genus *Osedax*, which were discovered only in 2002 by MBARI. So we knew this was an exciting find, because it's rare to come across these worms. We know they are all around the world, but what makes them come and settle on bones, when these bones can be miles to dozens of miles apart? It's a very interesting process.

Over the course of our time there, we were able to collect some of the bones that had the worms in them, along with other animals that were present. Again, with the power of the live-streaming and science-chat the *Nautilus* has, we were able to get in touch with the bone-eating-worm experts while we were on-site. They were able to provide expert direction on what to collect and how to preserve it.

Since then, we have given them the samples. They collected them when we disembarked, and we already have confirmation of one new species of bone-eating worm. There may be several more, too, so I've been in contact with those scientists. They're over the moon about this. So are we. This is the power of the collaboration of science and technology.

I'm really excited to see what else will come out of this find. We've collected eDNA[16] water, to look at the DNA that's floating around in the water. From that we'll be able to identify a lot of things. We also gathered more samples of worms and crustaceans and other animals, to understand what drives this unique micro-

---

[15] When a whale carcass sinks to the ocean floor, typically to a greater depth than 1000'. The carcass often creates a complex ecosystem that feeds a variety of deep-sea species.

[16] Environmental DNA; tissue, feces, etc. shed by organisms into the water.

habitat. Whale fall is a huge input of carbon and food to the deep sea, which most of the time relies purely on marine 'snow'—just the particles of organic debris that constantly rain down but that are really small amounts of food.

Everything happens so slowly in the deep sea. Metabolism happens very slowly down there, which is one of the reasons we're still interested in the octopus garden, too, because another species of octopus has been found to take fifty-four months, or four and a half years, to brood their eggs. We don't know how long the species we found broods, but for example, the Giant Pacific octopus up in shallow waters takes only three months to brood. So we know that it takes longer in the deep, and maybe living in the warm water seeping out of the seamount speeds up the process. We don't know. These are some of the questions we want to try to answer.

In the last hour of this second dive, after the whale fall, I wanted to go up this volcanic cone, this bump on the seafloor. In previous cones we had not found any vented water, but I just kind of theorized that this is what they call a 'low-temperature ridge-flank hydrothermal system.' That's a mouthful. Essentially, warm water, ocean water, is going through rocky outcrops, maybe the seamount itself, traveling underneath all of the sediment that's been piling up over thousands and millions of years, getting slightly warmed by the earth's crust, and coming out in weak points. It's like a pressure differential, so it squeezes out of these little broken areas of rock. So the idea is to look for broken areas of rock, anything that's volcanic or crackling, you know—that kind of thing. That's a very scientific term. [*laughter*] Sure enough, we came across a second volcanic cone, and near the summit we found some venting water. Peculiarly, we did not find any octopus associated with this vent, but I had a feeling we would eventually find them, and then as we neared the summit, we started seeing lines and lines and lines of these octopus. It was just absolutely incredible.

So, in the last forty-five minutes or so of the dive, after the whale fall, we came up the cone and found this area of venting water. It was interesting that we didn't find any octopus associated with it. But it was shimmering. We measured it and it was at 5 degrees Celsius. We collected some water. But I instructed the pilots, "Let's just keep going. I know there's going to be octopus here, because there's venting water," and sure enough, at the summit, we found these lines of octopus by the hundreds. Just like a network of veins and arteries, all associated with the venting water coming out of this cone. We didn't do any more measurements, but we confirmed the presence of eggs in most of these places, and proceeded as fast as we could to visually survey as much as we could, because we needed to pull the ROV because of impending weather—a big swell was coming along the coast.

Regardless, even though we only saw the tip of the iceberg, or the tip of the cone, literally, we really want to come back to this place, and that's one of the plans for next year.

Overall, it's been an incredible experience being a part of three *Nautilus* dives, discovering two octopus gardens, a whale fall, going out with the BBC and diving in the *Alvin*[17]. These are things I could not even have dreamt of a year and a half ago. That's how quickly things happened. I think that's the power of exploration and why exploration still needs to occur.

I think a lot of people assume, "Oh there's been plenty of deep-sea research," and all that. No. Less than 5% of the seafloor has been accurately mapped, and less than 1% has been surveyed to any extent. If you think about it, we're on the slopes of this mountain, which is much larger than a small state like Rhode Island, and the equivalent of what we are doing is being dropped out of a helicopter with a big headlight, you know, or maybe being in a small car and we're just driving along. And we're trying to describe the entire area based on a couple of dozen hours of driving very slowly, about three miles an hour through a park, or through a street, or a neighborhood. I think people have to realize we're seeing such a small bit of the seafloor every time we explore. It's important information, but because we're exploring just a fraction of a percent, this is the kind of stuff that you come across only occasionally, and this is why exploration is so important.

Experts were telling me, "There can't be warm water coming out of here. We know this area." And sure enough it's warm! No one had any idea that octopus were here in the numbers associ-

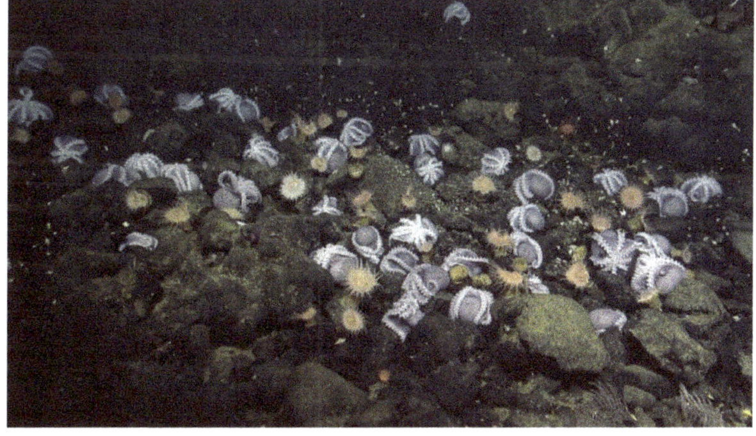

Octopus garden

© Chad King (OET/NOAA)

ated with warm water. No one knew of this whale fall here. We know they exist, but we don't know where they are. All of these are very serendipitous events, but they highlight the importance of exploration and why we need to continue to do it.

---

[17] A manned deep ocean research submersible vehicle, operated by Woods Hole Oceangraphic Institution.

CHAD KING

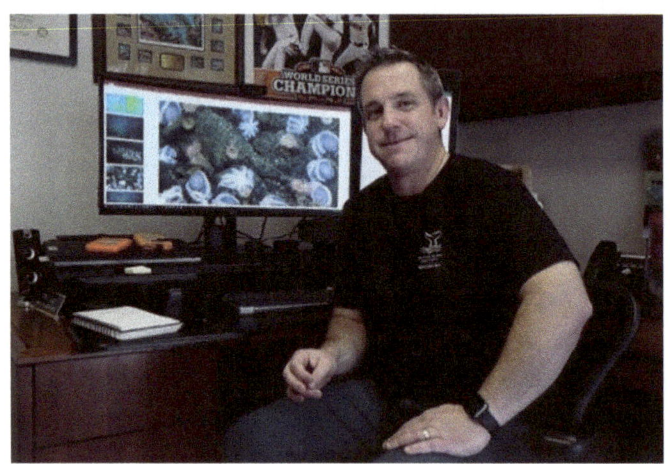

Chad King is a Research Specialist employed by the Monterey Bay National Marine Sanctuary, which operates under the auspices of NOAA. Chad notes that he and his colleagues are all given this generic job title, but perhaps it is appropriate as he feels he's a jack-of-all-trades, master-of-none, which he thoroughly and completely enjoys. Chad likes to dabble, be informed, experiment and learn about many of the disciplines and subjects within the field of marine science. He was hired to work with GIS (geographic information systems) making maps, doing cartography, and conducting spatial analysis, as well as doing research diving. Over the last four or five years, he's been put in charge of the sanctuary's deep-sea research. Even though deep-sea research is not his area of expertise—Chad's more of a 'Caltrans Director of Deep-Sea Research'—he says it's been great. He's very excited and pleased with this direction, as his team has been making all sorts of amazing discoveries!

Chad has been at the sanctuary now for more than seventeen years. During that time, he's created an app for Android and iPhones, which encapsulates all of the photos surrounding him in his office, and thousands more. There are now over 5000 photos available free online on a website the sanctuary staff have developed[18]. Chad also does video production, data analysis, writing papers, deep-sea research, and continues to work in kelp forest ecology. That's why he loves his job. There's something a little bit different each week or month.

Chad was born in Pinehurst, North Carolina. His dad was in the military, at Fort Bragg, California at that time. His family moved to San José, California when he was eight months old, so he considers himself a native Californian. As a kid Chad wanted to be a paleontologist, a marine biologist or a doctor. But when he was in elementary school, he had a very distinct fear of the ocean. Every time he went to the beach, he was unable to bring himself to go into the water past his waist. The

---

[18] https://montereybay.noaa.gov/materials/imagesvideo.html.

fear of the unknown was too strong, and he was scared of what might be out there. Not just sharks, but anything else.

However, Chad also had a natural curiosity for things and how they work. He figured one way to combat his fear was to understand it, so he started learning about the ocean. At that time the Discovery Channel was just starting, and Chad began studying Mutual of Omaha and Jacques Cousteau films. Then he fell in love with the concept of exploring the deep as well as coastal oceans.

Chad got his bachelor's degree in 1995. After getting this degree, Chad decided he wanted to go for his PhD. However, the professor he wanted to be sponsored by, John Pearse, was retiring the following year. So instead of school, Chad ended up taking a gap year and paying off his student loans. But one year quickly turned into four. Chad says it was easy to get used to the paycheck. The field he was in then was commercial real estate.

Chad had gotten a lot of encouragement to pursue what he loves, and he realized he wanted a professional degree. He was very interested in attending Moss Landing Marine Laboratories (MLML), applied there and got accepted working under Jonathan Geller, an invertebrate zoologist.

Chad came to Monterey in 1999 to begin his graduate work at MLML. He was then hired by the California Department of Fish and Game (CDFG, now CDFW) in Monterey and moved to the city of Monterey in 2000. In 2002, he got a job with the Monterey Bay National Marine Sanctuary. His childhood interest turned into his passion and he's stuck with it. Chad says, "I got lucky with my job." He's been able to scuba dive up and down the coast and around the world, and now he's doing some pretty exciting deep-sea research.

Black Tiger in the Bay

Lonny Lundsten

(*Date of Interview*: 12/12/18)

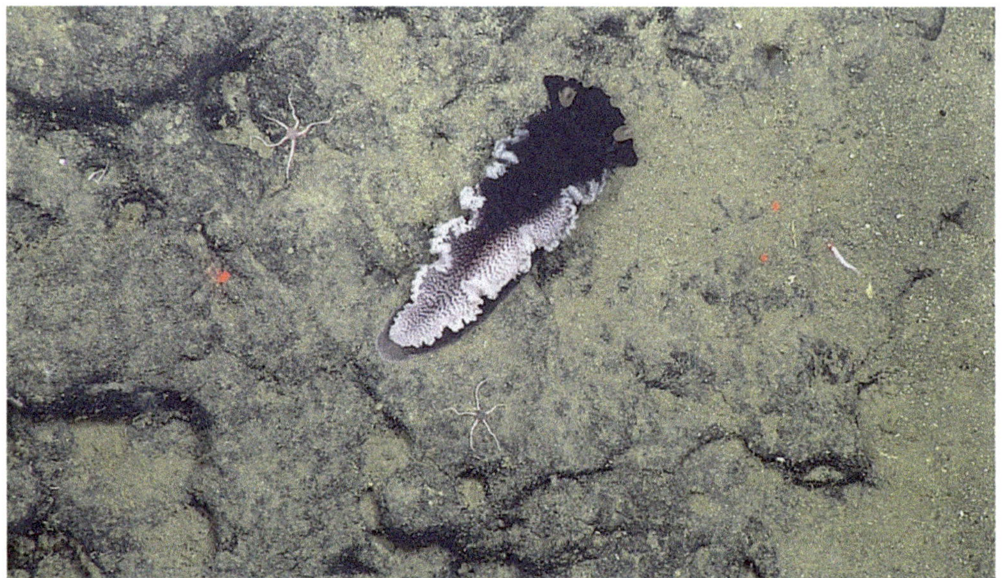

Tiger nudibranch MBARI (2016)

I have many memorable experiences of wildlife encounters in the Monterey Bay. Some of my favorites are these instances where I see an animal that we human beings have never seen before. One example is this Black Tiger nudibranch. This is a species that is new to science. We actually just recently published a paper on it.

We were diving with an ROV at Guide Seamount. An ROV is a remotely operated vehicle. It's a robot submarine. We were at about 1200 meters below the ocean surface, and we came across this relatively large nudibranch, which is a marine sea slug. And I'm familiar enough with the fauna out there at those depths that usually when I see something that I haven't seen before, there's a good chance that it's new to science. So we go in for a closer look. We did some filming, and I had a pretty good hunch that this *was* something that was new to science. We took some great video of it and we collected the animal. Then there's a formal process for describing it as a new species—a long process. We collected this animal in 2015, and in 2018 we published the paper describing it.

That type of encounter is one of my most favorite. I really enjoy seeing something that, first of all, nobody's ever seen before. That makes me feel as if I'm one of those Old World explorers seeing something that no other human has laid eyes on. It's pretty exciting, and recognizing that for what it is, is pretty special. And then to go through the process of describing it, creating videos and sharing that with the world is one of my favorite processes.

We've actually found many new species. One of the things I've been working on most often recently is carnivorous sponges. We've found a lot of new species even in our own backyard here in Monterey Bay. We'll do dives in the canyon, and we've found several new species of corals, several new species of carnivorous sponges, all new to science.

Monterey Bay is one of the most-well-studied ocean regions on the planet, probably the most well-studied deepwater habitat on the planet, and yet we're still finding species that are new to science. To me that is the most exciting thing about my job and about working here in Monterey Bay.

So back to the Black Tiger nudibranch. We were diving at Guide Seamount, which is a seamount just off of Davenport along the northern coastline of Central California. It's part of the Monterey Bay National Marine Sanctuary, and we were doing a survey to see what existed there. We had done some deeper dives on the seamount, but we really hadn't been to the summit. We didn't know what was there.

We go down and we see real dense populations of bamboo corals. These are a really interesting deepwater coral. They get quite big. They can be very long lived, and they are bioluminescent, which is just a cool, kind of fun fact about these animals. But we were exploring this region that was very densely populated with them, and as we're cruising with the ROV up a pretty steep wall, we see this large sea slug that I did not recognize. So we come in for a closer look. It looked similar to other species of *Tritonia* that we find here in Monterey Bay and along the West Coast of the United States, but the color, the rhinophores[19], and some other physical characteristics of the animal were much different than anything we'd seen before.

When we find something like that, we try to get as good a video and imagery as we can, and then we have to make a collection. We use a suction sampler on the ROV. It's basically like an underwater vacuum cleaner. We put this funnel up to the animal, suck it into a canister on the ROV, and then once it's collected, we preserve it and go through a formal process of describing it. We usually preserve the specimen right away. Most of them aren't going to survive, and you do need to

---

[19] Club or rod-shaped sense organs extending from the head of nudibranchs.

preserve them. You need to preserve the tissue to do all the analyses. For each type of species it's a different type of analysis.

Nudibranchs eat a variety of things. They mostly feed on things like corals and other Cnidaria[20]; that's their primary prey. Some do eat sponges, but they're mostly corallivores. We didn't see this one feeding, but we've seen other *Tritonia* feeding on corals. He was near a lot of coral, so I presume he's a coral feeder, but that's not known for sure. We could probably do some kind of gut content analysis, but when you have just one specimen you want to do the least amount of damage you possibly can. For nudibranchs you have to take out their ragula, which are their jaws and their teeth. So that's destructive as it is, but if we wanted to do a gut content analysis it would be even more destructive. If we had more than one, we'd probably do something like that.

But again, it's very exciting to be cruising along with the ROV in a relatively familiar habitat in a place where most of the organisms you're seeing you've seen before, and then all of a sudden, out of the blue, appears something you have not seen before. And it's a relatively large animal; it's a hand-sized animal. Most sea slugs are about the size of your pinky, and this was palm-sized, so pretty large. And just exciting! You know, to see that for the first time, it's *very, very cool.*

LONNY LUNDSTEN

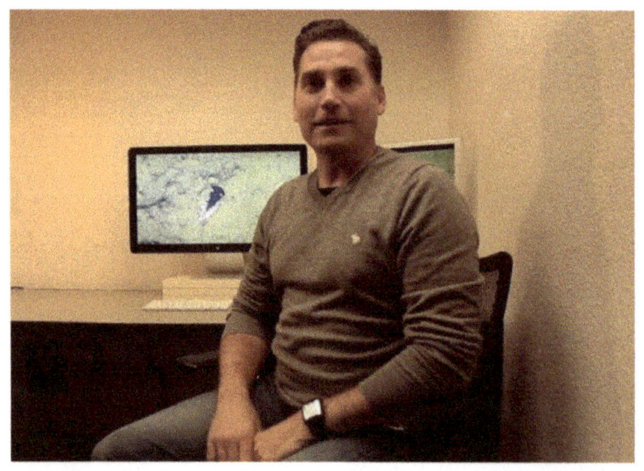

Lonny Lundsten's official title is Senior Research & Engineering Technician at the Monterey Bay Aquarium Research Institute (MBARI), but he wears a lot of hats. His primary job is analyzing video five hours a day. MBARI has several robotic submarines, which they deploy. One has the capability of diving down to 4000 meters and the robots have provided 25,000 hours' worth of video for MBARI's library. Every year, scientists are bringing in another 1000 hours or so. Lonny is one of five technicians who review all of the video footage, identifying species, geology and equipment that has been deployed. All of that info

---

[20] Type of aquatic invertebrates including hydroids, jellyfish, anemones and corals.

is put into a searchable database. The database tracks about 4500 different concepts and includes 6.5 million observations!

Lonny was born and grew up in Sacramento, California. After high school, he worked in his family's commercial print shop business for six years. The job entailed long hours, working in a hot factory, with fumes from printing ink and chemicals. The shop printed mostly magazines and such. But one day they did a trade with a dive shop to print little 8½ × 10″ pamphlets for them, and the trade was that two people could learn to dive. Lonny fell in love with scuba diving and the oceans and decided to see if he could make a living pursuing an interest in that.

The first thing that brought him to Monterey Bay was scuba diving and the Monterey Bay Aquarium. He was in his late twenties and fell in love with the area and decided to move here to pursue studies in marine science. Lonny went back to school at his local community college, then transferred to California State University, Monterey Bay (CSUMB) to complete his undergraduate work in marine science. As a senior, he started taking classes at Moss Landing Marine Laboratories (MLML). There he was exposed to the lab and the kind of work people were doing, and had great experiences working down in Baja California. After completing his undergraduate degree, Lonny attended MLML, where he earned his master's degree.

Lonny got a job at MBARI the summer before he started at MLML, working on seamounts off the coast of California, describing the ecology and biology of three seamounts. To complete his master's, Lonny reviewed 192 hours of video, which included 254 species and 140,000 observations that he used to describe the biology of those seamounts.

The bulk of Lonny's work is done in the lab, but he's typically out at sea six weeks a year. He's been to the Arctic twice, where he got to see a polar bear on the ice, and he's been in a submarine down to 2000′ at the Kermadec Arc, north of New Zealand.

In addition to video analysis, Lonny and his colleagues write scientific papers in which they describe species new to science. So far Lonny's highlight has been to describe fifteen such species. He also does all the social media for MBARI, plus video-related technology, including designing recording systems on MBARI's ships. He notes that you have to be prepared to be a jack-of-all-trades these days. In 2018, Lonny coauthored a paper that was published in December of that year that reported five new nudibranchs—two from Monterey Bay, one just south of the Gulf of California, one off the coast of Oregon, and the Black Tiger nudibranch from Guide Seamount just off of Davenport, California, in the Monterey Bay National Marine Sanctuary.

ROVing in Deep-Sea Canyons

Geoff Shester

(Date of Interview: 9/23/16)

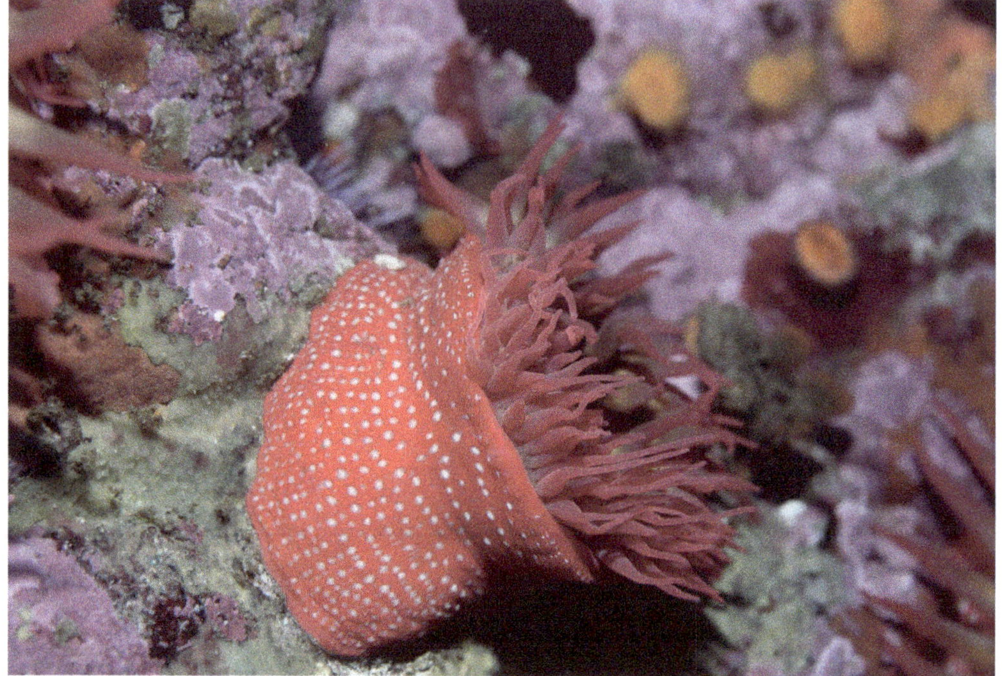

White-spotted rose anemone

© Steve Lonhart (OET/NOAA)

Ten years ago, Oceana helped secure some protections for seafloor habitats off the West Coast of the United States, and got over 135,000 square miles protected from bottom trawl fishing, which uses a type of fishing gear that drags on the seafloor. The purpose was to protect some of these deep-sea habitats. We discovered, in going through that policy process, that the most compelling information was video footage. Most of the seafloor had never before been seen by human eyes.

In scuba diving we go down maybe a couple hundred feet at most, and then we basically have a huge other planet down there. So, the idea is we can start providing more photos and images, and bring some of the dark, deep sea to the light of day and actually show this to policymakers. That can be a really effective tool to compel governments to protect some of these areas before they are damaged. Many deep-sea corals may be hundreds of thousands of years old, so if they are damaged, in many cases, it's really an irreversible impact. That's simply not something that can recover.

We learned about some of these corals and saw some of the footage that MBARI (Monterey Bay Aquarium Research Institute) was making in the deep-sea canyon in Monterey Bay. We didn't want to just wait for a bunch of other scientists or governments to try to go down there. We were like, "Can we do this ourselves?"

So, we worked with our office in Chile, which had actually hired an engineer who built remotely operated vehicles (ROVs) about the size of a beer cooler, and we had one shipped up all the way from Chile. They shipped it to the East Coast first, which was right around the time of the Deepwater Horizon oil spill. They used it out there.

Then we managed to get a sailboat, the *Derick M. Bayliss*. It was a research sailboat that normally just took tourists around on whale watch trips, but it had an A-frame, and so we were like, "Let's see if we can use this."[21]

Some of our staff drove the ROV across the country in a U-Haul. And the question became: could this work? Could we actually do it? Once it arrived, we got the ROV and loaded it up in the boat—took about a day or so to get it all set up to see if it would work.

So yeah, we were just learning how to use this thing. It reminds me of an old video game system. It has these little joysticks on it, and we're basically putting this thing out there and really feeling like we're astronauts. We're kind of going and exploring the depths, and it's amazing—it's like, it's right here, it's the backyard of all these people that live around Monterey Bay, all these people that come here to go whale watching. It's the perfect disguise; it's gorgeous! We have no idea what's down there!

And so having scuba dived for a while, I knew that the kelp forests were really an amazing ecosystem; that these undersea cathedrals that we have just right off Cannery Row in Monterey are some of the most spectacular spots I've ever been to. I've been around the world scuba diving, but then I go right here at home, and it's some of the most amazing stuff I've ever seen!! We were just thrilled to go down to some of these canyons.

We were able to learn about all of these places that had already been explored, but we really wanted to go to spots where no one had been yet. So, we got some amazing maps showing these big huge pinnacles and reefs and canyons.

---

[21] An A-frame, or gantry, is an overhead bridgelike structure that can support an ROV off the back of the boat, where it can be lowered and raised using a winch, rope and block without damage to the boat.

And we went out right off Point Pinos and all around the peninsula and basically tried to put this ROV in and see if we could even do it, and could we get footage of this stuff?

We started out and went to some of the shale beds and some of the reefs just right off the coast here, and got the ROV down. Once we could actually see the footage from this thing our minds were just blown! Right—I mean you've got huge reefs, teeming with life, you know, rockfish hiding in crevices, octopuses scurrying around. Some of the corals and sponges—they're just like bright pink and bright purple, with fish swimming around them, and it's just like, "Whoa!"

We started going deeper and deeper, down into Carmel Canyon. We're looking at vertical cliffs and every little hole had little eyes poking out. The more we would explore, the more we found fascinating things that you would never expect to see. Surprise after surprise! Just crazy tubeworms and sponges—we'd go over and see these things called Metridium anemones. They looked like gigantic cauliflowers. There'd be rocks just covered in hundreds and hundreds of these things.

Then we'd look a little closer and there's ling cod nestled inside there, hiding, and small little fish and small little snails. It's just like this fantastic, unimaginable ecosystem that's there that no one ever sees. It's pitch black down there, you've got these amazing things, and here we are with this spaceship, basically, going down with these big lights and getting this video for the first time.

It's great to now have the ability to show people what it looks like down there. A lot of people think, "oh well, it's just the shallow stuff and the deeper you go it's just gonna be a bunch of mud," but the deeper you go here, the more fantastic it is. And I think that's one of my favorite wildlife experiences where we just start seeing all these amazing critters and fish.

We discovered fish right off Point Lobos that no one even knew existed there. They thought that the farthest south they were was hundreds of miles to the north. And we're discovering species, improving the understanding, just real basic, of what species even live here. What species do we have? The fact that just going on a few dives you can actually see some of that stuff is just absolutely amazing.

One of my favorite dive sites is the Carmel Pinnacles, and we can dive down to the top of these pinnacles. The top is about eighty or ninety feet down. You can dive down there, but you can't stay down there very long and you can't go down a whole lot deeper. So, we went out there with the ROV into one of the newly protected marine reserves, and we brought the ROV lower and lower, deeper and deeper into the dark, down to the deep part of the pinnacles. Some of the walls, they're 100% covered, you can't even see rock, it's like a garden of living animals. They're covering the entire rock. There'd be these vertical walls hundreds of feet high covered in bright pink strawberry anemones and purple nudibranchs, and bright yellow sponges. And then beautiful corals, and big huge sea fans down there. It's an absolutely fantastic world, but we just get the smallest of glimpses.

The fact that we were able to acquire an ROV, drop it off the back of a sailboat right here in Monterey Bay and see things that nobody's seen before—I mean, that's *spectacular!*

GEOFF SHESTER

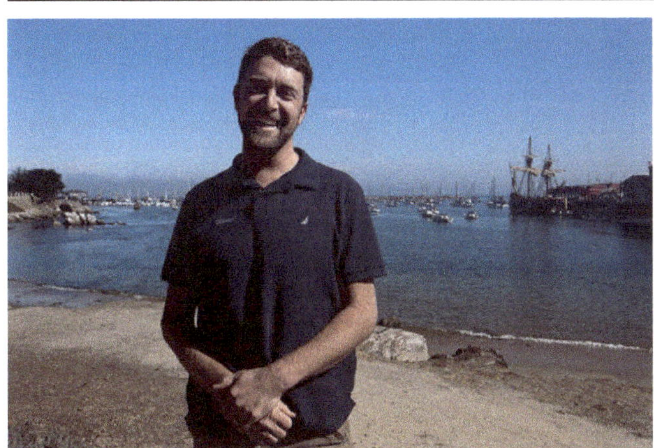

Geoff Shester is currently the California Campaign Director and Senior Scientist with the nonprofit organization, Oceana, based in Monterey, California. His work involves advocacy and marine policy, and he works with state and fishery management bodies to try to protect ocean habitat and reduce bycatch[22] in fisheries.

Geoff was born in Santa Monica, California and grew up in Carlsbad, California. He came to Santa Cruz on the north edge of Monterey Bay to go to school. He studied Environmental Studies and biology, and science and policy at the University of California at Santa Cruz. After graduating, Geoff started working at Oceana in Alaska in 2002, engaging in policy efforts to protect seaport habitats from overfishing and protect some coral reefs that had been recently discovered there.

After his Alaskan stint, Geoff decided to go back to school to get additional tools in order to be more effective. He knew that Stanford had a marine lab in Monterey and his wife was there. He enrolled in Stanford's PhD program, where he studied marine biology, population models, ecology, and the human dimension in sociology, and completed his doctorate. His focus was and is on maintaining fisheries while protecting habitats.

---

[22] Bycatch is the portion of a commercial fishing catch that consists of marine animals caught unintentionally.

Say What? Sei Whale!

Harry "Tinker" Neece

(Date of Interview: 8/9/16)

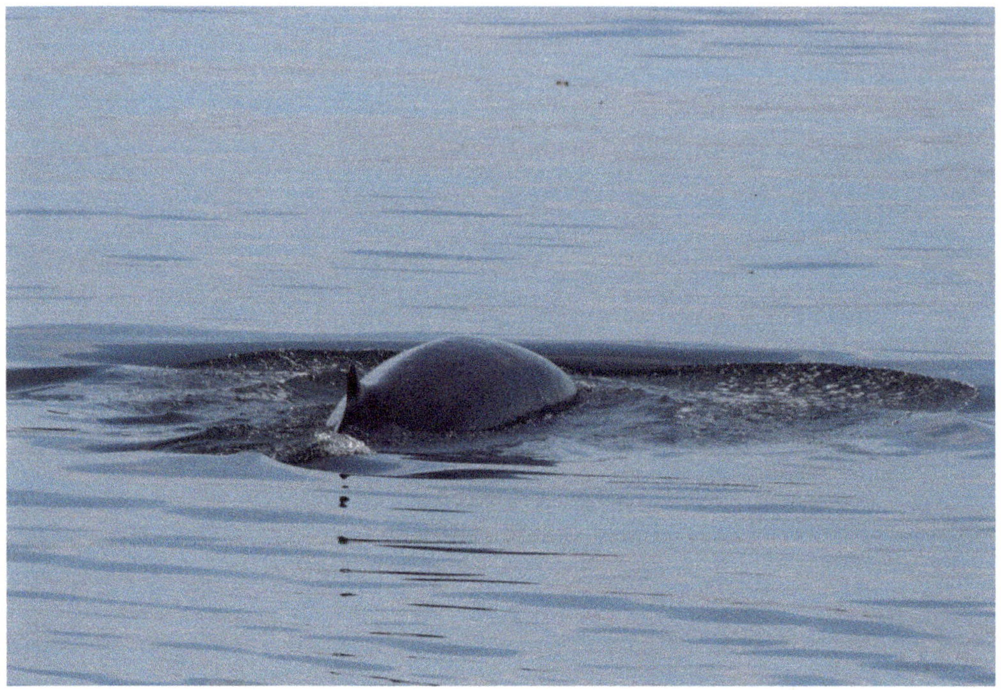

Sei whale   © Katlyn Taylor

Wildlife encounters. Well, the one we're referring to is the one with the sei whale, twenty-five miles southwest of Point Pinos on our way to the Monterey Canyon. After a good hour, hour and forty-five minutes of traveling, it began to be daylight and I spotted a blow at about our 2 o'clock position, 3 o'clock position, out to the west, traveling, and I had no concern about it. I mean, I knew there was a whale with plenty of time to pass. But lo and behold, less than five minutes later, I see an object in the water that's surfacing toward my boat, and it continued to surface under me until there was an encounter, a bump against the boat, a good little nudge that actually woke, shook up, quite a few people who were half asleep and said, "what was that, what was that?"

I looked out the opposite side of the boat and the whale just sort of continued on its way. Well, that's fairly unique. I never experienced anything like that. It was quite exhilarating! You know, because the fact is, *we just got hit by a whale!* Did we hit a whale or did he hit us? I was concerned, but it didn't appear that anything was hurt, or damaged, and that whale made the trip successful that day.

The following day, just about the same exact coordinates, crew members were hollering, "Hey, there's a whale back here! There's a whale back here!" I looked back toward the transom[23]. We're underway, cruising about twelve knots. We're not going full speed. Just cruising out. There's a whale making passes, porpoising back and forth across the stern of the boat. I look back, after it's been reported to me, and I see the whale make three passes behind the boat, from the left to the right. Port to starboard. Ok. Well. Then things quieted down. He left.

We're in the same location, so I assume that it's the same whale. That's an assumption—I don't know if it was the same whale. About a minute later, he's porpoising broadside on the port side, at 9 o'clock, *porpoising*! As if he were a dolphin right next to the boat, a 45-foot whale porpoising, less than ten feet away! Less than *ten feet away*! It was exciting! Traveling. He was racing us, is what he was doing. It was pretty, you know, what can we do with this whale? Is he mad at us from yesterday? Or is he playing with us? We don't have a clue! Actually, we think he was playing with us.

It was a sei whale. Beautiful animal. Beautiful animal. It was a very slender whale. Very contrasty head. It's hard to explain. Dark color edging on the back, around the top of the head. One time in my lifetime that it happened. Whether it will happen again remains to be seen.

HARRY "TINKER" NEECE

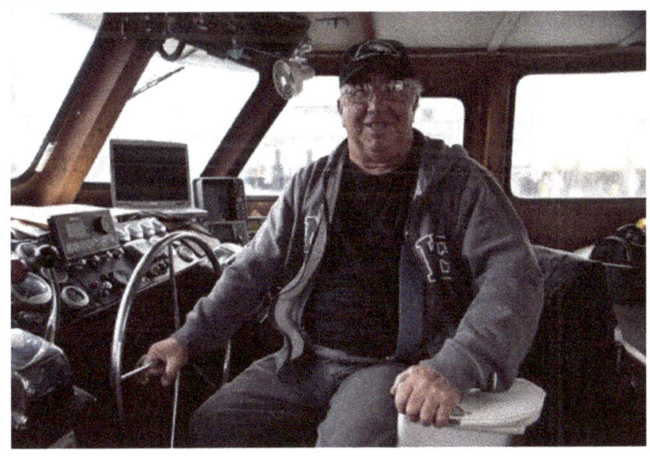

Captain Harry "Tinker" Neece was the operator of the vessel *Check Mate* for Chris' Fishing and Whale Watching at the time of his interview. Tinker (the name he's been known by since he was a child) was born in Salinas, California, but grew up in Seaside, California. His father was a deckhand, cleaning and maintaining boats in the Monterey harbor. His deckhand duties also involved cleaning fish for charter fishing passengers. Tinker helped his dad clean fish at an early age. He's been a boat captain for over fifty years. He used to split his time 50/50 running fishing trips and whale watch trips, though sometimes the two overlap. Now he has taken the helm of the *Star of Monterey* at Chris' and spends most of his time watching whales in Monterey Bay.

---

[23] The stern or back of the vessel.

The Whale That Rinsed Us Off

Jane McKenzie

(Date of Interview: 12/2/16)

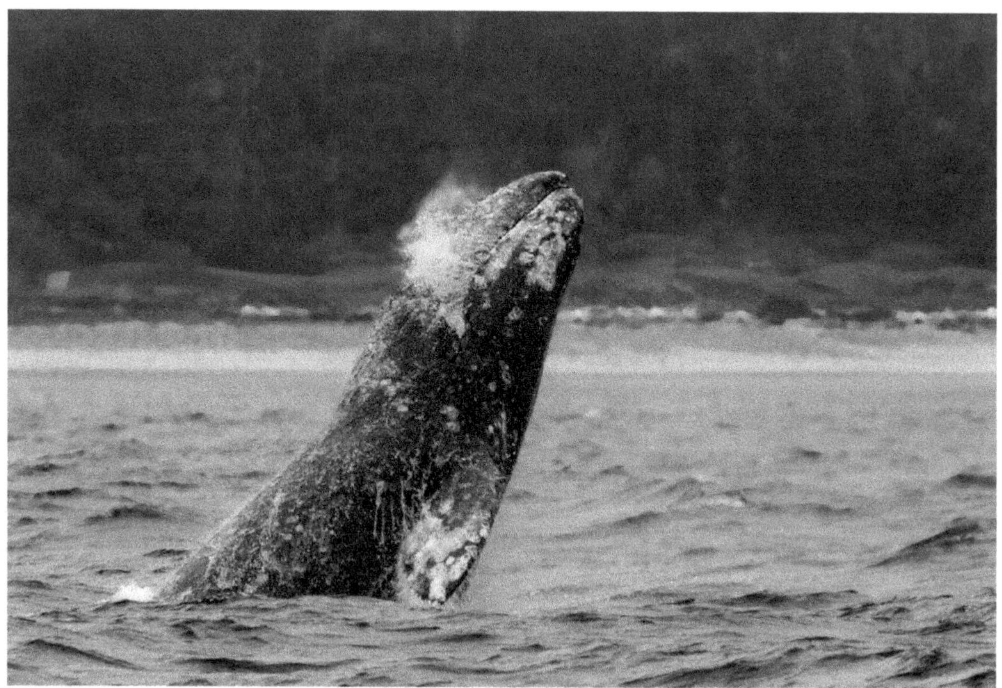

Breaching gray whale

I've been surfing any number of years in the Santa Cruz area and at different times we have different types of swells and different conditions and different things that happen. And usually when the north swells are coming in in the winter, it's a little different because they're bigger, you're out farther, it could be foggy—it could be any number of things. But you are farther out in the bay. I've got a little thing about sharks, so I don't like to be too way out there.

But this one particular day, I was out surfing with a friend of mine, Brenda Scott Rodgers. When it's big at the Lane[24], you paddle out and around the break—it's not at the point—you're paddling out and around the break. So, we were out there and there were a lot of people out, and, you know, people are catching waves and surfing past us, and pretty soon Brenda and I are out there. We each kinda

---

[24] Steamer Lane—world-renowned surf location off Lighthouse Point in Santa Cruz, California.

catch a wave in this one set, so we are paddling back out again together. And we're talking and not really paying attention.

Eventually we realized that we were the people farthest out on the water that day. There was nobody else, really, around us. We were just sitting there on our boards, and you know, fifteen, twenty feet apart and just chatting. And all of a sudden—it's really hard to even explain how it happened, because all of a sudden there was a whale in the air! And it was so close to us that when it came down, it splashed us. We got, like, rinsed, like, rolled off our boards. The thing that I so remember was, not only did it, like, take my breath away, but the eye of the whale— I swear it was *this* big! [*motions with hands*] And that whale had barnacles on it that seemed to be like six or eight inches around, all over the place! And I remember the coloring of its body and the smell of that whale breath and just being shocked to death.

We both got back on our boards and sat back up, and this was before leashes, this was before a lot of other equipment that we use today. And I remember that there was a lot of bull kelp out there, which is the kelp that is really long. It used to have this big bulb on it. And those things started popping up, because when the whale rinsed, or breached or whatever, and rinsed us off, I mean it was like the whole area came alive in a different way, and it was really pretty freaky.

But then I remember the kind of peacefulness that came with that, and the gift that that was for us from the universe. And how we just kind of sat in that moment and it was like life stood still for a while, though there was still a lot of sloshing and moving about. I wasn't sure where the whale went. We never saw that whale again in the next thirty minutes or so, but you really realized that you were in their playground. And that whale was doing something. I don't know if he was getting a bite to eat, or doing whatever, just checking things out, who knows. But it was…, I mean, that whale came down like twenty feet from me, and that's something. Even when I start talking about it now, I can almost feel the visceral part of how wild that was. I mean you're just right out there with them. I've never felt anything like that since.

In some ways there's many other parts to that, but it's really kind of led me to a life of—I think I have a heightened level of respect for what ocean animals are, what they do, how they go through their life, and what that must be like for them. You know, just to be able to jump out of the water. You know, did it see a surfer? I don't know. I don't know what it knew. Did it see that? I doubt it. But it was like this living creature just came by to say hi and he was *immense*! After some time, I remember looking over at Brenda, and going, "I'm getting out of here," because that scared the hell out of me, you know?—in a way… but in another way, it was a very spiritual kind of gift. So, I think we caught another wave then both went in, but every time I see Brenda now, we just kind of go, "remember the whale?" "Oh yeah, uh-huh." So that's my whale story.

JANE MCKENZIE

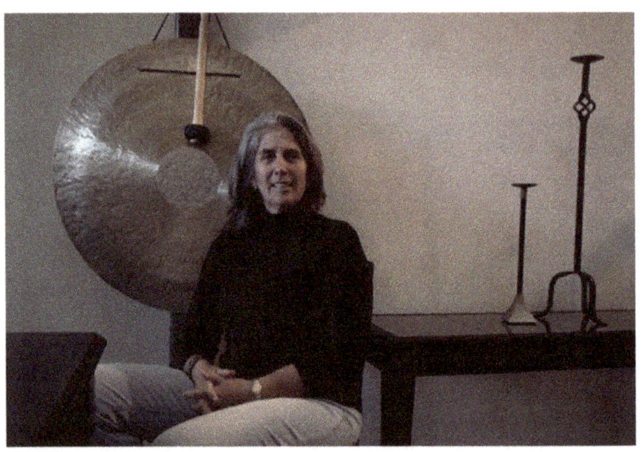

Jane McKenzie is a financial advisor in Santa Cruz, California, with an office not far from the ocean, where she regularly surfs.

When asked what work she does, Jane responds by saying she "provides real interesting and cool people with wealth management and investment strategies that work for them and their families."

Though Jane was born in Santa Monica, California, she moved with her family to Santa Cruz when she was just four weeks old. When she was eight years old her family moved to Hawaii, where they lived on a fifty-eight-foot Chris-Craft cabin cruiser for three years in the Ala Wai Yacht Harbor near Honolulu. Jane has lived her whole life along a coastline somewhere, splitting time between Santa Cruz and the Hawaiian island of Oahu.

She moved back to Santa Cruz as a preteen with her mom and sister. But she spent summers with her dad on Oahu. Jane started surfing there, back when there were 'real beach boys.' When she was just eight years old and weighed about sixty pounds, her father put her onto a ten-foot surfboard that weighed thirty pounds. Since then she hasn't looked back.

Jane is considered a pioneer of women's surfing in the cold waters of the Santa Cruz surf scene. Three gorgeous surfboards, including a classic redwood longboard, decorate the walls of her office. Tenacity and confidence were her calling cards, as Jane worked her way from Cowell's Cove beginner surf break, through Indicators into the lineup at Steamer Lane, traditionally the guys' 'turf' because of the big waves that break there during the winter months. Jane surfed the Lane when few women dared and soon garnered the respect of the surfing community.

Jane "The Lane" McKenzie, as she's known among her fellow surfers, is President and Team Captain of the Santa Cruz Longboard Union, where she gives back to the community that shares her passion and joy in riding the waves.

Fat Fin Shows Off His Prize

Kate Cummings

(*Date of Interview*: 9/7/16)

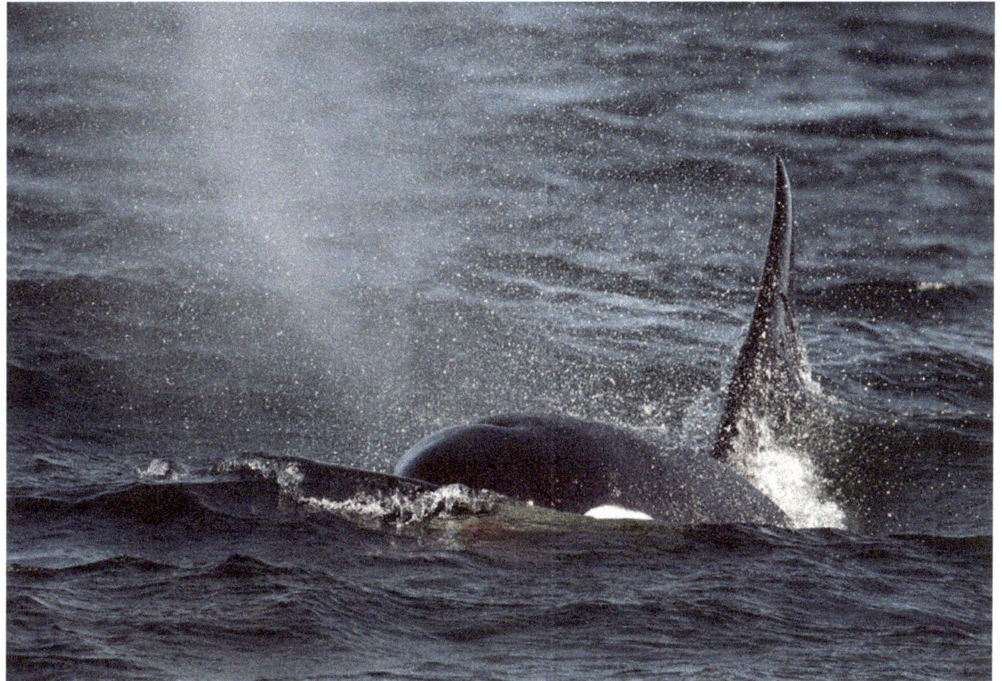

Fat Fin

It was 2011, the first year that Jim and I were running Blue Ocean Whale Watch. We came out of the harbor and had only gone maybe a couple of miles, and we see killer whales up ahead. We're getting closer and we stop and we're, like, 100–150 yards away, and we see that there's a male in the group. There's a male and a female and two offspring, the CA138s and Fat Fin. And we noticed, once we stopped, that Fat Fin totally changed direction and came toward the boat.

It was a beautiful day—June and hardly any wind, glassy and sunny. There are very few June days when it's nice and sunny like that. But Fat Fin came right next to us, stopped about five feet off our port side, and we looked down and he was carrying a carcass between his pectoral fins. It must have been an elephant seal—we couldn't really tell as they'd already skinned it. But it was a HUGE carcass—I didn't even know they could hold something between their pectoral fins.

I'm shouting on the PA to everyone, "Oh my gosh, he's coming over, he's showing us his carcass, it's *unbelievable*!!! And... as he released his pectoral fins, the carcass began to sink a little bit, and he went after it. Another whale watching boat was coming over to watch the killer whales, too, and we noticed that as that boat was approaching, Fat Fin turned and went right for them as well. He had been carrying the carcass all the way over to that boat to show them, too. I couldn't believe that he just wanted to show off what he'd caught!

The rest of the day, we sat in one spot, and this pod of killer whales just circled around the boat harassing northern fulmars, which was sad for the birds, but it was pretty amazing. The whales were kind of playing target practice with these birds all around our boat. The water was just so clear, and we could probably see fifteen feet down, so you could see the whole silhouette of the killer whales coming up next to the boat. It was just a very magical day.

[See Kate's bio after the following story.]

Boat Friendly and Mind Blowing!

K a t e   C u m m i n g s

(Date of Interview: 9/7/16)

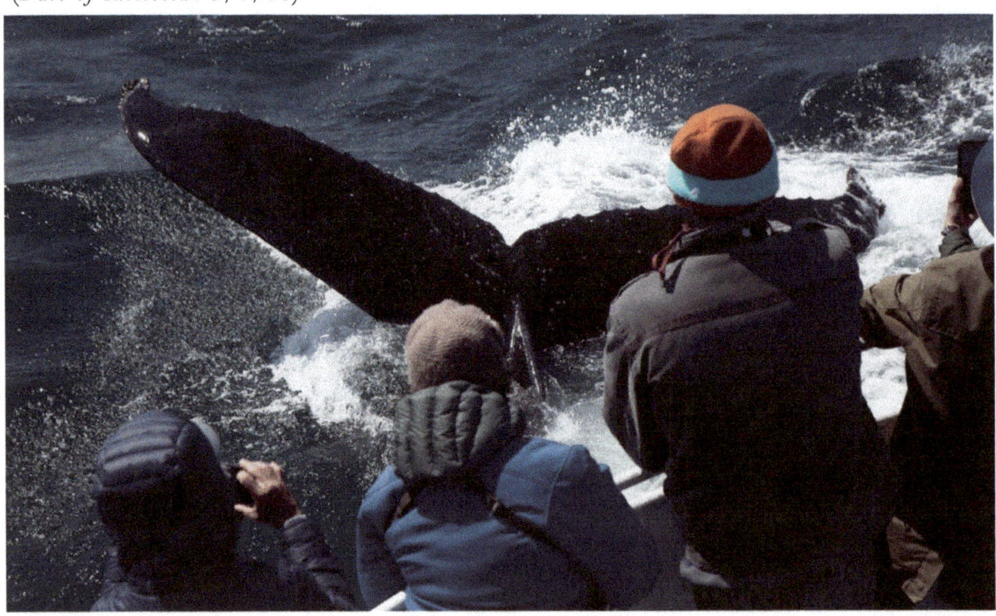

Tail of friendly humpback whale

Next story! This was when I was working on the whale watch boat *Sanctuary* for Sanctuary Cruises[25], so it must have been 2008. I was brand new to whale watching, so with every experience I was just overly excited, probably even more excited about it than the passengers were. We came out of the harbor, and we had one of the first friendly humpbacks I'd ever seen. *Sanctuary* is really low to the water. You can dip your toes in if you swing your leg around the side of the boat.

But this humpback came over to us and rolled all around and was just inches from the boat, looking up at people. It went right underneath us, and I could see its tail on the side I was on; the captain was looking through the door on the other side, and he could see its head out that side. And I'm freaking out and taking pictures of everything and shouting at passengers to look down at the fluke. The captain grabs my arm and pulls me over and says, "Don't say anything to anybody, but the whale is lifting the boat up right now!!!"

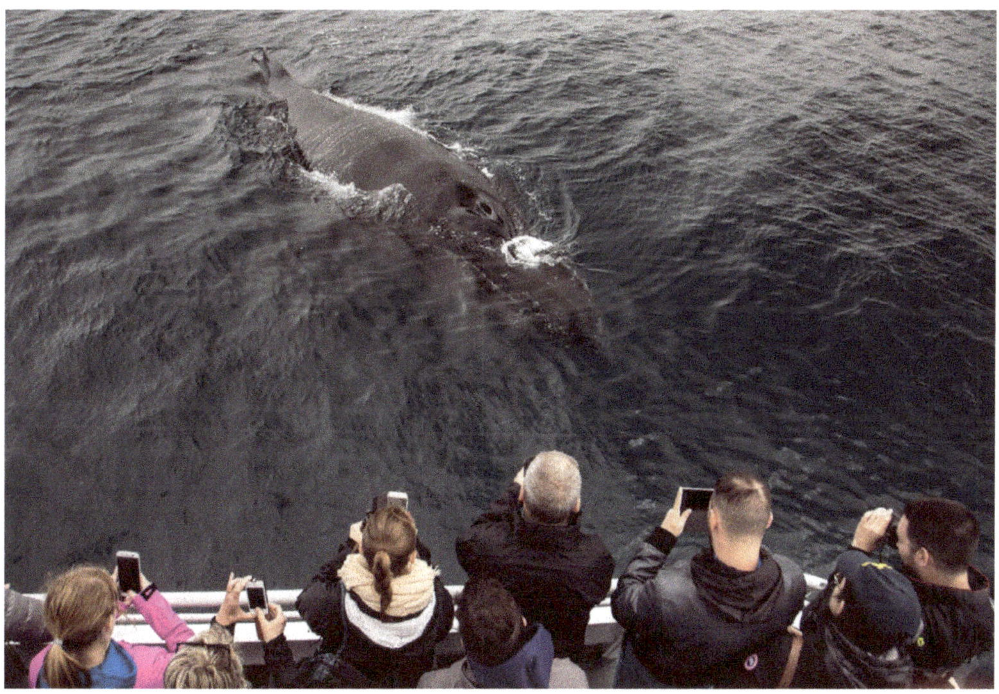

Friendly humpback approaches boat

I was like: "You shouldn't have told me!!! [*laughter*] I'm gonna freak out right now!" And once he told me, I could feel that the boat was moving and it wasn't just a wave or anything; the whale was actually supporting the boat on its back. Who knows if it was scratching its back or just messing with us? I don't know. But

---

25 A whale watch company out of Moss Landing, California.

it lasted a few moments and then the whale came out from under and started rolling around again in front of the passengers.

It was pretty cool. And the passengers were loving it! Happens anytime you've got a whale that's right underneath you, and it spouts right in people's faces. I love when people are holding their cameras over the side and the blowhole is right there and the whale just sprays right on their cameras.

KATE CUMMINGS

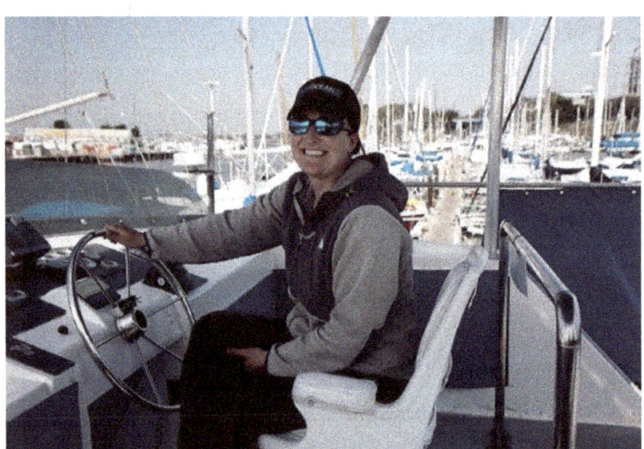

Kate Cummings is co-owner, captain and naturalist for Blue Ocean Whale Watch. She is also an excellent photographer, but when asked about her photography, Kate humbly replied, "I like taking pictures."

Kate was born in Santa Cruz, California but grew up largely in the San Francisco Bay Area. Her interest in whales started at the age of ten when the movie *Free Willy* came out. Initially her interest focused on killer whales, but soon it expanded to all whales. She said she even dreams about whales. Kate saw her first whale in Monterey Bay when she was eighteen on a whale watch trip with her mom.

Kate returned to Santa Cruz to attend the University of California at Santa Cruz (UCSC), where she studied sociology. While studying at UCSC, Kate met someone who worked as a deckhand and quickly decided that she had to do the same. Her first marine job was working out of Moss Landing as a deckhand on a whale watch boat, but she graduated to naturalist after a year, as she says, "because of being a big nerd." Most days you can still find her down at B dock in Moss Landing operating her daily whale watching tours.

One Close Pass after Another

Kate Spencer

(Date of Interview: 9/23/16*)*

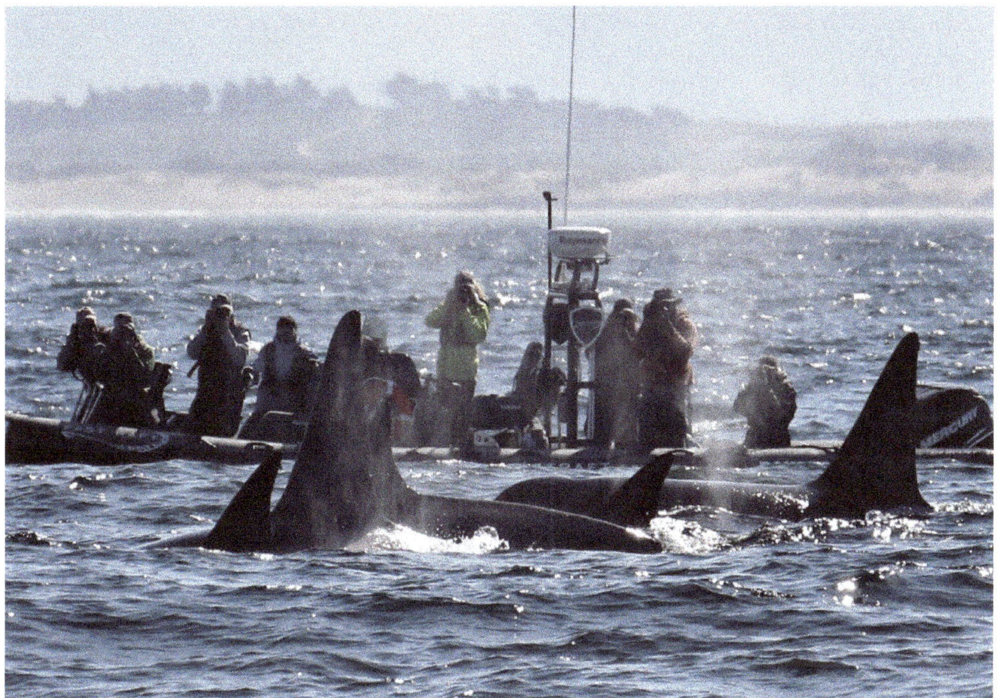

Transient killer whale family

I've had so many amazing wildlife encounters on Monterey Bay, starting with my first whale watch here. I went out and we saw a blue whale, which I didn't even know you could see near land. It turns out, of course, that they feed near land, but I didn't know that. I thought you had to go out into the middle of the Pacific Ocean to see a blue whale. And I saw a breaching humpback. It breached like thirty times, and I saw 2500 common dolphins that stayed with the boat for forty-five minutes. So I was immediately hooked by just sort of an average whale watch on Monterey Bay.

One of the most amazing things I've ever seen has actually happened several times—interactions between humpbacks and killer whales. I was the naturalist on a boat that found humpbacks following killer whales that were hunting a gray whale calf. The BBC, on a different boat, arrived later and filmed the rest of the encounter.

But I was on the boat that got there first, and we were watching eight humpbacks following this family of killer whales chasing a gray whale mother and calf. We were actually pretty far offshore. Those hunts typically happen near land, but this was out in the middle of the bay. And it was just *amazing*! The humpbacks were trumpeting and tail slashing in the general direction of the killer whales, even though they weren't getting right next to them that I ever saw.

This went on for hours. We were there for about an hour and a half. The other boat arrived and filmed it and stayed for several more hours. The action just went on and on as these killer whales finally killed the gray whale calf. And the humpbacks stuck around, I think even after the mother gray whale had left.

But just seeing that for the first time, humpbacks going after killer whales and being so obviously agitated, was pretty incredible. Most of the time they're just diving down to the food and they come up for air, then they dive back down. It's generally pretty calm. This time the humpbacks were staying at the surface and splashing and trumpeting all the time, and obviously following these killer whales as the whole hunt moved around. I've seen that a few times since, most notably on the small boat I run currently.

About a year and a half ago, maybe it was two years ago—it's still so fresh in my mind—we got out there on this glassy morning, and there was this huge raft of sea lions. And we spotted killer whales going after some of the sea lions. Most of the sea lions hadn't realized what was happening. There were also humpbacks feeding in the general area. When the killer whales started going after the sea lions, the sea lions started scattering in different directions. Whole groups of sea lions would swim away, then start coming back and they'd lift their heads looking like "what's going on?" Then the humpbacks started paying attention to the killer whales, and started sort of gathering around them. This kind of goes in slow motion for a long time. You have to be really patient and watch, because these dramas aren't necessarily all at a human pace. They're slower. Things happen under water, and then you see some of it at the surface, and then it disappears again.

But what happened over the course of this hour, was that these humpbacks just sort of gathered and were following the killer whales around as they were trying to hunt the sea lions. Then the sea lion groups would split and come back, sort of looking around. And why were these stupid sea lions looking around? It's because the killer whales already had a sea lion. The killer whales are trying to eat the sea lion and the humpbacks keep chasing them, giving them a hard time, and eventually *the whole thing went under our boat*!!

We had been sitting there at a very good, respectful, safe distance, with the engines off, making no noise, just watching, and then everything just turned toward us. And the hump-backs chased these killer whales, which ducked under the boat to come up on the other side. The humpbacks turned and one went over here and did this big tail slash over behind us and came up trumpeting. Another humpback was over there, and

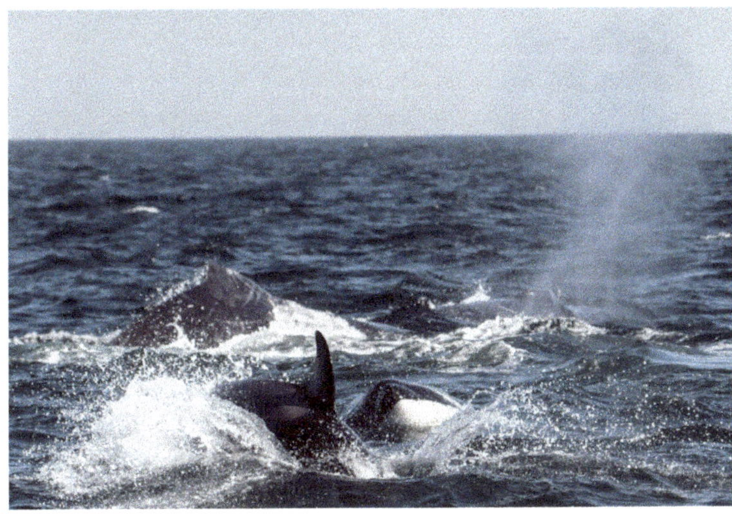

Humpbacks harass killer whales

the killer whales, a mom and a juvenile, were sort of regrouping over here. It was amazing to have that come toward us.

We know they knew where the boat was—I'm pretty sure. There was just enough water motion that I know they could hear us. And it seemed that the killer whales were actually using our boat as a screen, putting something between them and these big, 'bullying' humpbacks! Any time whales come close is incredible. And when you're on a small boat that's low to the water, you're *so close* when they come close. You get such an amazing sense of how big they are. And having this drama happen right under us! We yelled, "Oh, my gosh, I can't believe that just happened." It was so *exciting!*

I've had other experiences where whales have come up to check out the boat, not during interspecies interactions, but they've just come over to look. A whole family of killer whales will circle the boat and duck under and come up next to us. Others that come away from their group pop up next to the boat to look at us, then go back to the group. I've had a humpback come and spend fifteen minutes while the boat's sitting, just stationary in the water, the humpback just comes up next to us, disappears, rolls, comes up under the other side of the boat, barely touching us, looking. For fifteen minutes, just checking us out.

Those are really the encounters that stand out in my mind. Any time you get that curiosity or just are lucky enough to be the thing that's in the way that they want to use. Getting a close pass is always the most exciting thing.

KATE SPENCER

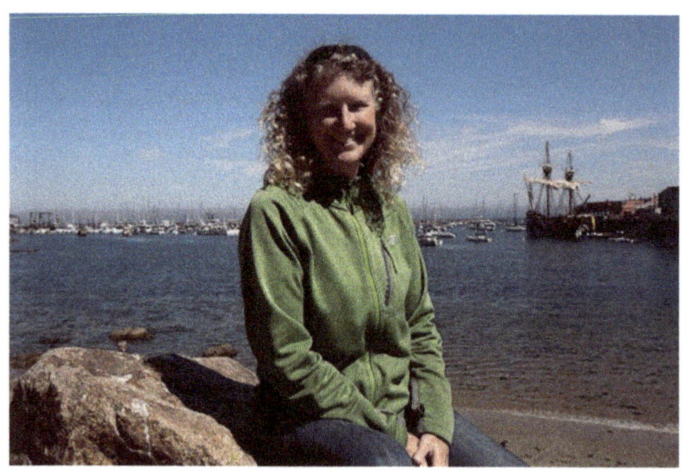

Kate Spencer currently owns, operates and is chief naturalist for Fast Raft Ocean Safaris, a small six-person RIB (rigid inflatable boat) whale watch operation. She runs trips primarily out of Moss Landing on Monterey Bay. She started leading whale watching tours on Monterey Bay as a naturalist in 2001 and began managing operations at Fast Raft in 2014.

Captain Kate was born in Washington, DC and grew up in nearby Arlington, Virginia. Her well-rounded liberal arts education included studies in biology, studio art and comparative religion. She holds a degree in organismal biology with a studio art minor from Smith College in Massachusetts.

After graduating, she worked at the Smithsonian National Museum of Natural History in Washington, DC as a scientific illustrator. Kate became very interested in tuna while preparing an exhibit illustration piece for the Smithsonian. She came to Monterey because of the Monterey Bay Aquarium and Stanford's nearby Hopkins Marine Station, and to learn more about these charismatic fish. Originally intending to work for three weeks, her stay soon stretched into five months. During that time Kate met a number of 'whale people' and signed up to go to Alaska to do whale research the following summer. There she participated in humpback whale field research with the Alaska Whale Foundation.

On her return to California in 2000, she got off the boat in San Francisco and has been in the Monterey area ever since. With Monterey as her base, Kate has shared her knowledge and used her skills in various whale-focused communities in both the Northern and Southern hemispheres. As a naturalist, Kate has guided small boat encounters with the friendly gray whales of Baja California, lectured on cruise ships in the Inside Passage, and driven Zodiacs on Antarctic tour expeditions.

Kate's photographic data was instrumental in helping build the Happywhale citizen science whale tracking site. She is also on the advisory board of California Whale Rescue and a first responder for entangled whales.

Humpback Bonanza

Ted Cheeseman

(Date of Interview: 9/14/16)

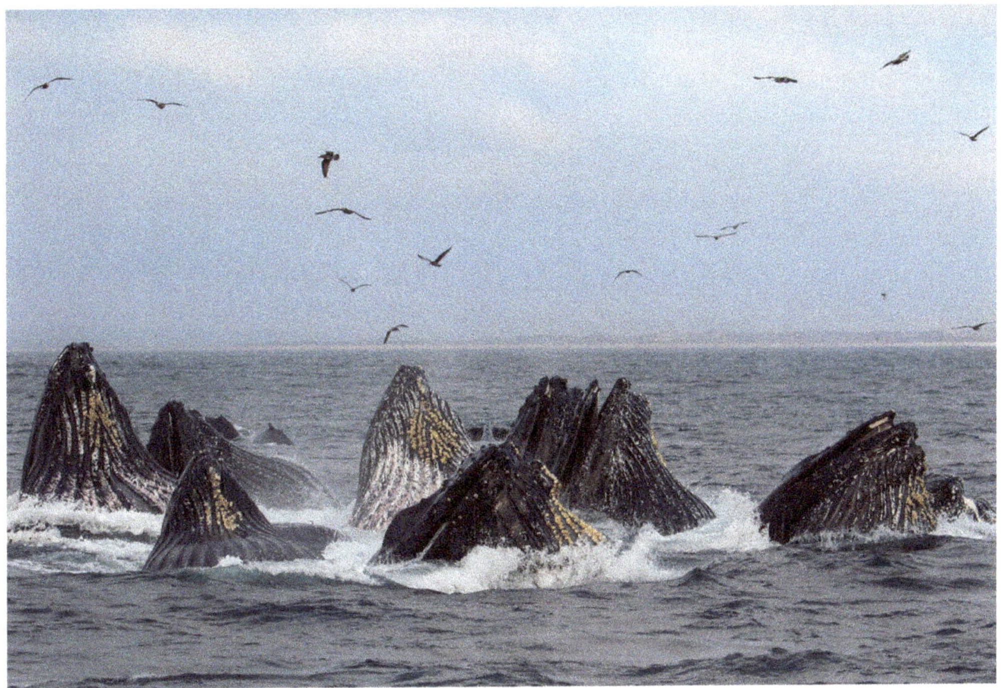

Lunge-feeding humpback whales

So yeah, a notable wildlife encounter on Monterey Bay. It's hard to pull out something so disproportionally memorable, because among whales it's all so grand. But not so long ago, on July 17 of this year, I was fortunate enough to be out. I'm actually not out on the water that much, but I was fortunate enough to be out that day, which was the day after a month of nonstop winds and kind of nasty conditions. And then there was this glorious day. As we traveled up toward Soquel Canyon, we just started seeing more and more and more whales, humpbacks particularly, but I also saw a blue whale.

And given the work that I've been doing on individual IDs with Happywhale[26], I was very focused on photographing flukes and identifying individuals and trying to figure out who we were seeing. So I was just shooting away.

---

[26] Happywhale was founded by Ted and is a web-based citizen science platform for sharing cetacean photo-ID images.

As a naturalist on the boat, I was trying to talk to people at the same time, announcing stuff.

Oftentimes what I will do is photograph a whale and then show people the fluke, particularly if we see one with killer whale rake marks and that kind of thing. But this day there wasn't time for that. Literally I didn't eat all day. Every time I turned to talk to someone, I felt like I was missing an encounter.

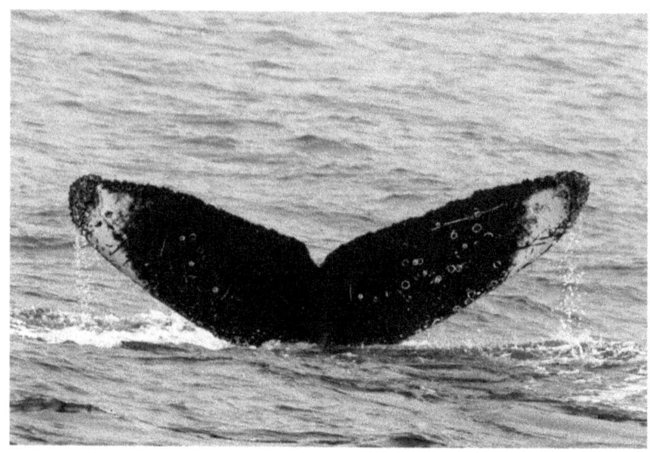

Snowy Owl, 239 sightings as of July 2024

So, my father, who co-led the trip, was the one talking most of the day, because he's a good talker, and I was doing the shooting.

It was hard to tell really, as it was, if we were seeing the same whales over and over again, because it was all happening so fast. There were whales all around. It was an eight-hour boat trip, and we pretty much took our time to get up toward the canyon. Probably from 9:30 am when we started to pull away from the harbor heading toward Moss Landing to 2 pm when we headed back down to Monterey, it was just nonstop whales, all the time, feeding all around us. And remarkably, blues mixed in with the humpbacks. There were humpbacks in groups of twos, fives, tens… so we realized it was quite an event while we were out there.

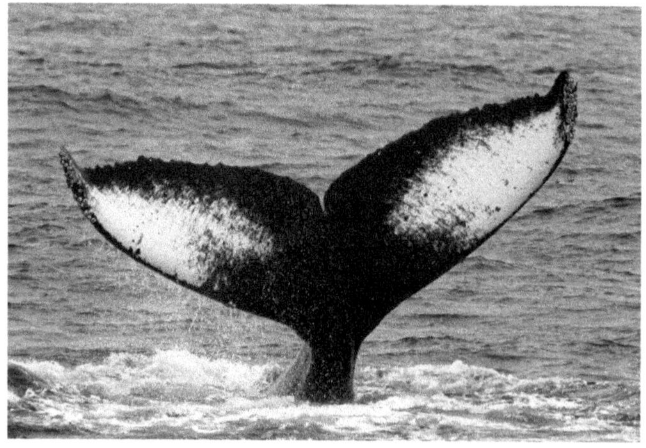

Female humpback whale Fran, the most popular and well-known whale in California. Fran's fluke photos were submitted to Happywhale 280 times— 271 of those taken in Monterey Bay. Fran was killed by a ship in 2022.

But, honestly, the specialness of it didn't strike us until afterwards, while I was looking through photos and happywhale.com and working with a couple of interns—University of California at Santa Cruz students. We started poring over the photos and dividing them up, divvying them up into individuals, and on our first pass, separating everything, we came up with potentially 140 individual humpbacks! Many of those, though, turned out to be the same whale sighted repeatedly throughout the day. But after poring through my photos, images from Kate Cummings, and images from a bunch of individual contributors, including Monterey Bay Whale Watch's images, and a few of Kate Spencer's photos, and with Jodi's photos—your photos—we came up with 102 individual, identifiable humpbacks. And there were a handful more where the fluke photos weren't high enough quality to really say anything definitive.

Having divided up the blue whales, we found there were at least ten different blue whales in there, too. What was particularly amazing to me is that over this last year we'd had a really high rate of resightings, but with those 102 humpbacks something was different. Over the past year we'd had an increasingly high resighting rate. When we started this project, it was something like a 30% resighting rate, and it had gone up from there, such that on any given day a whale in Monterey Bay had a 40–60% chance of being known to us.

On this particular day, something totally different happened—88% of the whales had not been seen, as far as we know, in Monterey Bay prior to that day that year!! This was based on looking at all of Kate Cummings' and Kate Spencer's whales from the year, and all the whales from Jodi—of your whales—that we'd done for the year.

So, my experience of the day was astounding! But the concept of the day that was most memorable to me is this—you have this wind event, which is generating upwelling, which is pulling the food to the surface and creating the incredible productivity of Monterey Bay. But what happened with the whales, you know, when the wind stopped, for whatever reason, it was like a dinner bell rang and the whales came in from offshore. The whales *came in*! One was a whale that hadn't been seen for twenty-six years, one of our longest-timed resightings for the Pacific Ocean—1987 to 2016!!

There was just this incredible abundance of whales, like a whole different population, and that to me, really makes me wonder if there's sort of a fabric of communication there among the whales. What's happening? What do they hear that has them suddenly just come streaming in, right there, superconcentrated around Soquel Canyon, all feeding?? And then they left!! They were done. A handful of those whales stuck around, but for the most part, most of them appeared to have left.

I'd love to know what that was all about, but just being able to witness it was very special.

TED CHEESEMAN

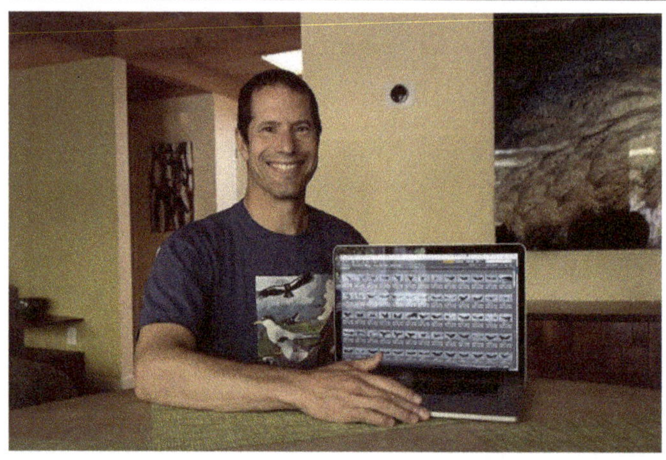

Ted Cheeseman is the founder and current manager of Happywhale, a citizen science fluke-matching program that utilizes facial recognition AI for fluke matching to try to better understand our whales through individual identification. Ted completed his PhD at Southern Cross University, NSW, Australia under the supervision of Dr. Phil Clapham, using data gathered from researchers and the public to better understand humpback whale distribution and survivorship across the North and South Pacific oceans.

Ted previously owned and operated Cheeseman's Ecology Safaris, a quality safari company started by his parents decades ago. Ted had worked in the company in various capacities prior to assuming a leadership position on the passing of both of his parents.

Ted was born in Mountain View, California, not very far from his current home, and grew up in the Santa Cruz Mountains. He's been moving closer to Monterey Bay ever since, in five-mile increments. If he ever gets rich enough, he plans to move the next seven blocks for an ocean view!

Ted got his master's degree in tropical terrestrial ecology from Duke University, but through working in Antarctica he became more ocean-focused. His father was a zoology professor with a passion for large terrestrial animals and marine mammals, and a love of animal behavior. Ted grew up hearing stories of elephant seals and their biology and behavior, among many other stories.

Ted went out on Monterey Bay frequently with his family when he was young, but always struggled with seasickness. However, he always liked being on the water more than he disliked being seasick. As an avid surfer, Ted manages to get out on Monterey Bay on a regular basis, and leads regular whale watch trips in the bay. He also leads expeditions to Antarctica and the Arctic, and tours to the Caribbean to swim with humpback whales.

My Whale Tale!

Deb Gillespie

(Date of Interview: 9/14/16)

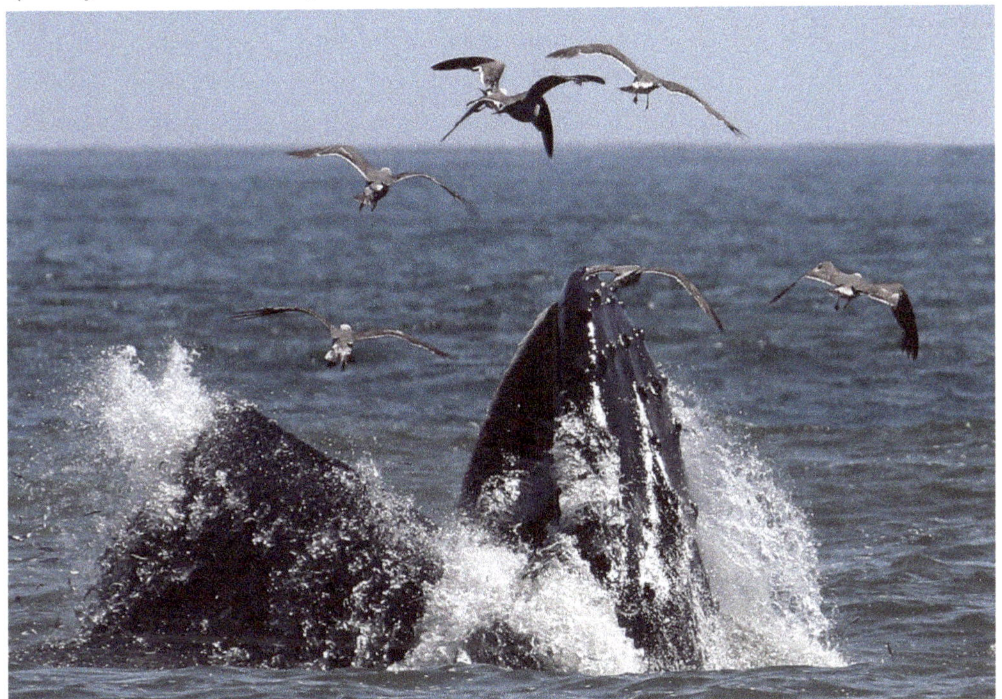

Lunge-feeding humpback whale

My most memorable wildlife encounter is definitely my encounter with the whales. I can tell you about it. Living near East Cliff Drive in Santa Cruz, I take a lot of walks by the ocean. And at that time, it was October 2013, there were a lot of whales pretty close to shore. They were just spectacular, and I was walking along the beach and watching them all the time. I did notice that some people were out in kayaks and on stand-up paddleboards and getting pretty nice close-up views of the whales.

I don't know, I just thought—I have never actually surfed before, I've not really gone out into the ocean—but I decided that I was gonna go out. I had a wetsuit and a short board, and I went out early in the morning because that's when I usually go for a walk. It was a full moon, and it was just a beautiful, beautiful morning. So I went out, like I said, pretty early, no breakfast, no beverage, nothing,

I just went out with no plan. I was on 38th Ave., and I paddled out. It was pretty far—I don't know how far as I'm not good with measurements.

And I didn't see anything. I was just like waiting and waiting and waiting, and still I didn't see anything. I was out there probably quite a while, *but* it was pretty exciting because I'd really never been in the ocean before—well like on a surfboard. After a while, the seals came right up to me. It was kind of scary, but I got used to them, and otters, and dolphins. Some dolphins swam right by me. I could hear them breathing, which was really exciting, and all the birds and sea lions were around. After a while I was ok with the sea lions. They'd come right up to me, just poke their heads up like they were little puppy dogs.

So anyway, I was hanging out there, and finally I saw some whale activity out by the Capitola wharf. At that point, I thought, "Well, maybe I'll head that way." I started paddling out a little bit, and then I said, "ah, it's just too far and they're not coming," so I was gonna turn around. Well, I was just basically turning around when I looked back one more time, and I saw the whales were actually coming my way. So, I just waited, and I waited for a while, and they were all under water.

Then all of a sudden, I could hear them, and I could see movement under the water, and then *there they were!* They surrounded my little surfboard, and there were probably four, maybe four or five. They were just right there and my arms and legs were just hanging off my surfboard, but I wasn't scared at all. I was just too amazed and excited to even think about being scared. And one of the whales came up with his full head and mouth opened up, and all the birds were flying around when his mouth opened, and that was *pretty cool!*

They were there for a little while, and then they started to leave. So, I started to leave, too. And at that point the sun was really, really bright, and I realized I hadn't had anything to eat or drink, and it had been hours, *and* I had to paddle all the way back. So, I started paddling and the sea lions were following me, which made me feel safe, but I was really losing strength, and I still had a long way to go.

I remember thinking to myself, well, if I die, that's ok. I just had this amazing experience. So, I just kept going and working my way through, but I ran out of energy. I was completely empty, but I started getting closer, and then there was a little bit of surf, so I caught a little surf and landed on the beach.

I don't know if anyone's seen the movie with Sandra Bullock where's she's out in space, and then she finally gets to land, and she's stumbling around, barely able to stand up. Well, that's exactly how I felt! I just couldn't get my bearings. And then I had to climb all the way up the stairs. Well, I climbed *up* the stairs, then at that point, I said, "I need water."

Should I go to the restroom, which was probably half a block away, or should I walk all the way home, which was probably five or ten minutes? Well, I decided to walk home. I just was in a daze, but I got home. I had to take off my wetsuit, and my fingers were numb. It was crazy! But I did it! I was really excited about it and I'll never forget it! And that's my whale tale!!

DEB GILLESPIE

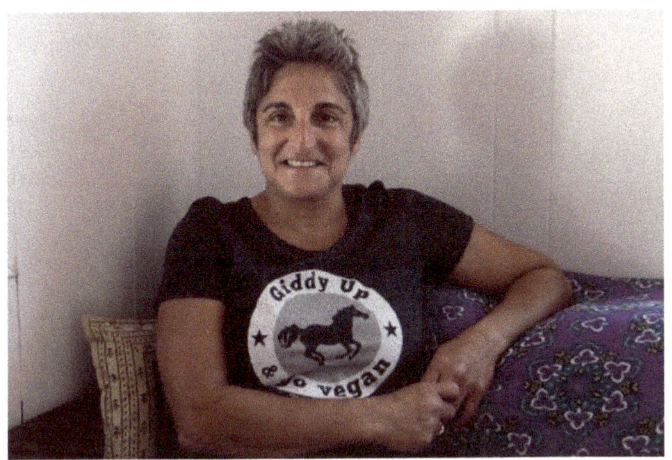

Deb Gillespie is a self-employed website administrator and social media marketer. She was born in Louisiana and grew up in Connecticut. She came to the Monterey Bay area around 2011–12, but lived part-time in British Columbia and part-time in Santa Cruz. She originally came to this area to visit her daughter, who had moved here, but Deb decided it was such a beautiful area, she would stay. Deb loves to kayak and previously lived on a boat in British Columbia, where she kayaked a lot. Deb got her Bachelor of Science in Business Management from the University of Phoenix.

We're Going to Die Now!

Tom Mustill

(*Date of Interview*: 6/4/19)

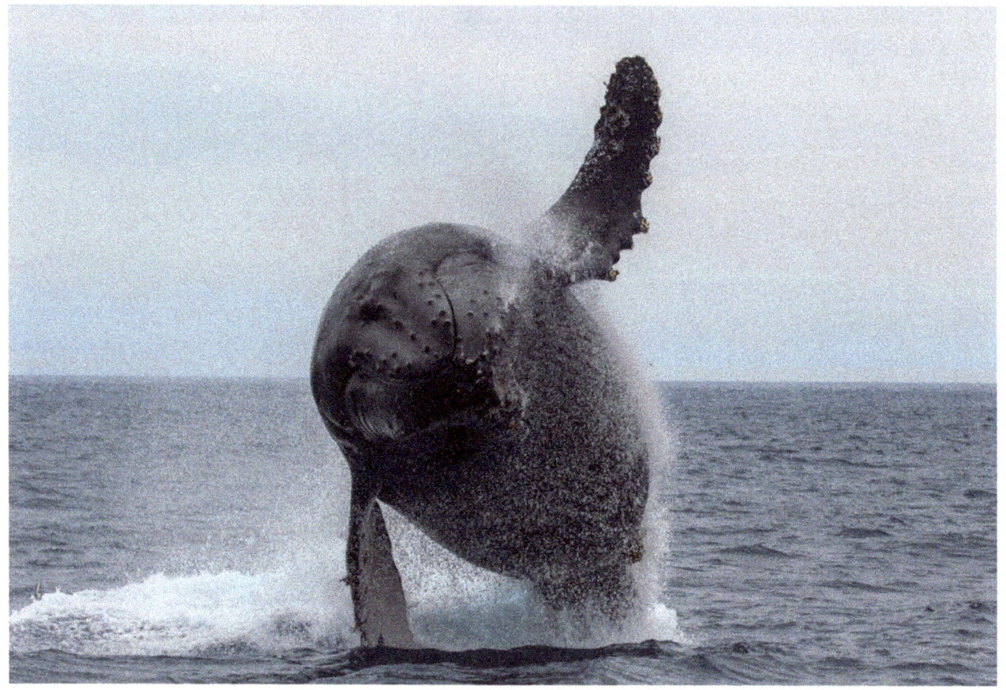

Breaching humpback whale

It was the 12th of September, 2015. I'd joined a group of tourists going on a kayak tour out of Moss Landing. It was cold and misty, and extremely still. I was in a two-person kayak with my friend Charlotte, and there were, I think, three or four other kayakers in the little group that went out with us, and there were a lot of other people in boats on the water already.

We paddled out of Moss Landing. As you may know, you go past the sea otters and harbor seals. Normally you have to paddle quite far out to see any sort of whale, if you're lucky enough to see one, but that day there were a lot of whales all around and very, very close. So close to shore that even, I think, a couple of stand-up paddle boarders had paddled out from Moss Landing.

I worked as an assistant on a whale watching boat in the Canary Islands when I was a teenager to make sure the boats didn't get too close to the whales and harass them. And as well as doing that, I was taking photographs of their fins for

ID, so I've seen a fair few whales before. Charlotte is an accountant, and she had never seen any whales before in her life.

Well, it was full on. I mean, when you're whale watching, you're supposed to keep, like, a distance, and our guide made that very clear. You don't harass the whales and you don't want to get hurt. That's ok when you can see where the whales are, but it's very difficult when there are suddenly whales arriving from different directions. You can't outrun a whale in a kayak. You can't move away from a whale that you can't see, if it's coming up to lunge feed underneath you.

So, we did our best to keep our distance, and I think we were pretty much ready to go back in. You know, we could smell the fishy, broccoli breath and it was wafting over us. Got some amazing looks, and it was a totally wonderful whale watch. We then turned back toward Moss Landing, and started paddling back to shore. We'd finished watching the feeding whales.

And then suddenly a humpback whale just came out of the water about two or three kayak lengths away from us and ahead of us. And I remember just sort of seeing the water—and it was so flat calm that day—and then just seeing the front of its snout just coming

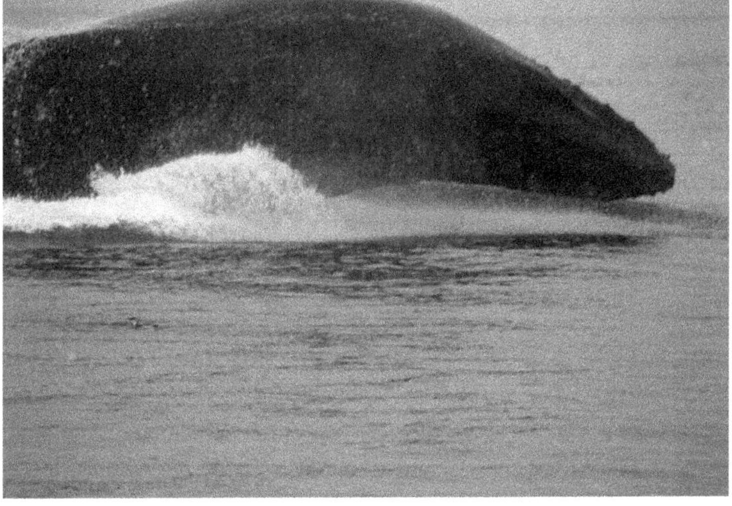

An adult humpback whale weighing over 30 tons breaches onto the kayak of Tom Mustill and Charlotte Kinloch in 2015. © Michael Sack (sanctuarycruises.com)

out, and it was like an elevator shooting up the side of a hotel or something. It moved so quickly, and it came from nowhere. And then it was above us.

And I remember thinking—the things I thought were very simple. There was no fear because it happened so quickly. One was, "Oh look, that's a whale. It's very close." And the second thing was, "Oh no, it's going to land on us!" And then I thought, "We're going to die now," because it was so big, and so inescapable. And I remember looking up at it and seeing it as it came down toward us. And I could see its ventral pleats. I could see the tubercles on its rostrum. I could see all the bumps on the leading edge of its pectoral fins. And just the level of detail was so strange, because you normally see that stuff through the water or quickly as it comes up and goes all back again.

It was just sort of looming at us. I can't remember what happened next. I've replayed the video of it. You can see two dots in the kayak in the video that a tourist shot. One of them gets really small, and that's me at the back of the kayak, farther away from the humpback. And I think I threw my paddle away and I just flipped the kayak to run away from the whale as much as I could. And the other one stays exactly the same height and that's Charlotte. And she was just transfixed looking up at it, and as we later learned, as it looked down on her. Because you can see in the video that it sticks its eyes farther out as it rotates.

And then, I was under water. I remember moving incredibly quickly under water. I love diving in the sea and swimming around, but I've never moved that fast. I didn't think it was possible to move that fast: that feeling of being in air, or being tumbled around, like if you jump off a cliff or something into the water, your stomach lurches, or when you go over a bump in a car. It was that sudden acceleration, but in water. And I remember it being very sort of white, and I'm thinking, "Oh, ok, I'm dead." I'm in shock. All my arms and legs are … so this is just the bit where I fade out, or the bit where it starts to hurt.

Strangely, I thought, I seem to still be conscious, and then I got spun around like a doll, like again, and I think that must have been as the tail moved, as the whale made off away from where we were. I had a life vest on, and then I could feel it sort of gently starting to pull me up, so I swam with that.

I remember it took—well, it felt like it took some time to get back to the surface. I think in retrospect what happened was that I turned the kayak, the whale's pectoral fin hit the nose of the kayak, and that pushed the kayak and us down under the water. But the impact shot us out of the kayak underneath the whale and the kayak, because we were pushed out of the kayak. We didn't have any bruises or cuts or anything.

We had our skirts on, and my feet were around the pedals of the rudder while we were in the kayak, and then I got back to the surface and I saw Charlotte's head bobbing around with a big grin, and I thought, that's impossible, she should be dead. And I just thought, and I knew, I had known that she was dead, because she was closer to the whale than I was.

And then she was alive and I was alive, and the kayak bobbed up and people came over, and we grabbed onto the kayak. And then a whale came along the surface, like straight toward us and just underneath us and fluked. Just next to us. And I was thinking, I know that whales aren't aggressive toward people. It's very rare for them to do something that might seem aggressive, but what's going on?

And then Kate Spencer sped over in her Fast Raft boat. I didn't know that was Kate Spencer. I thought this sexy black speedboat was the Police or Coast Guard coming to rescue us. We looked up at them and thought, "Brilliant, they're going to save us now." But they just kind of shouted and said, "Are you ok?" And all the tourists on the boat were taking lots of pictures. And there was Sanctuary Cruises' vessel on the other side of us, with like, you know, like the whole boat was leaning over as everyone was taking pictures. And we were floating in the water.

I don't think anyone realized that the whale had landed on top of us, apart from people in our kayak trip who had been looking at us, because we were away from where all the whales were feeding. So everybody else was looking to the side of us, back out to sea. Most of the video swings round to the side to catch the whale, and so I think most people just saw a splash, and then saw us bobbing in the water and thought, "Ah, they got knocked out of their kayak by the splash."

And we were in shock, sort of just grinning and shivering, and we thought, surely they're going to rescue us now. But actually they just asked us to get back in the kayak, and they tipped the water out, and they tied it to another one. We paddled back to shore.

And I kept saying to Charlotte, you know, "What the heck just happened, *expletive, expletive, expletive*? Like that was absolutely insane," and she just said, "Shut up, we're not talking about this until we're safely back on shore."

And we paddled, and I remember just seeing all these school children—there must have been like a school group who were also just paddling out of Moss Landing—and I'm saying, "A humpback just breached on us." I think they didn't understand what I said, and they just went like (gestures big smile and thumbs up), and I thought, "Oh no, no one's going to believe us," you know, because I didn't know somebody had filmed it.

I didn't think anyone had even seen it, apart from the guys who were with us. And they were really upset, because they had just been looking, and they'd seen us one moment, and then they'd seen a whale land on us, and we'd been gone. And there was just this white water, and they were, I think, the most upset, the people who had actually been on the surface.

Then we got out, and they gave us a cup of hot chocolate. And we got in our car and we drove home. We were staying at an Airbnb. Our friend Louise was in charge of renting it, and when we arrived she said, "you're late. We had to pack all your stuff for you. And if we don't move out soon, there's going to be a $25 late fee." We said, "A humpback whale just landed on us." And our friend Louise said, "Well that's fine, but if we don't get out of here soon, there's a $25 extra charge for the rental if we're late checking out."

So we both started to think, no one's ever going to believe us. They're going to think we're exaggerating, that we've made this up. Then all my friends in that group left, and I was going to go camping in Big Sur with another friend who lives in San Francisco and his parents. They drove up the road, and as I sat on the side of the road in Aptos, I said, "A humpback whale just breached on me," and they said, "Oh, that sounds strange."

And I said, "I'll show you." And I made them drive to Monterey Bay Kayaks, and I showed them the kayak. It had a dent in it, but the dent was not as impressive as you'd think a humpback jumping onto you would cause. I guess a piece of molded plastic is very hard to deform. And it *was* very bent, but I think my friend was imagining like a boat bent in two or something. So I think they didn't really believe me, or they thought I was exaggerating.

Then we went camping in Big Sur, and that night we stood overlooking the sea. I was having a beer, and my friend was having a beer, and he said to me, "There's a tarantula on your shoulder." And I said, "Oh, ha ha, there's a tarantula on *your* shoulder." And he said, "No mate, there's a tarantula on your shoulder." And I, still thinking he was joking, just went *"Ooh ew ah"* and just, like, went toward him, and he just backed off. And then I felt this, oh [*gesturing to his neck*], that does feel a bit strange there. So I whipped my shirt off and threw it on the ground. There were some other people at the campsite, and I think they just thought like, "Who's the weird guy who's drunk too much?"

This tarantula just scuttled out, and I thought, "What's going on today?" I just thought, "How can I describe any of this to anyone and have them believe me?"

Anyway, I'm there with my friend who was camping with his girlfriend at the time, and his parents, who hadn't met her before. I kept saying, "The humpback whale…," and trying to talk about it, and they're like, "That's very interesting Tom." "So, tell me (to the girlfriend), what do your parents do?" You know, it was very weird and very anticlimactic for such a dramatic thing.

And I remember lying awake and just sort of looking up in the tent, and still seeing that picture of this whale with all the water streaming off it, just sort of frozen there, and I remember thinking, "I must remember this. I'm never going to experience something like this again. I must freeze it in my head."

The next day we drove back to San Francisco, and I was Googling every second, you know, like 'whale,' 'humpback,' 'Monterey Bay,' in the hope that somebody had taken a photo or something. Then I saw this YouTube video. And, I was like, "Yes! People are going to believe me!"

By then 200,000 people had watched it, and then by the time I was getting on my flight the next day, I think a million people had watched it. So, I phoned my mom, and I was like, "Ah, you're gonna see this story; I'm fine, everything's ok," and then I got on the plane. And when I landed another couple of million people had watched it, and I had hundreds of missed calls on my phone. People were phoning my work—the BBC, previous employers, family, and Charlotte and I just got sort of swept up in it. And this video went viral and it became sort of a global news story.

There were cartoons of a whale jumping into a boat, in the British newspaper with the Prime Minister and his Chancellor of the Exchequer in a little boat, with the illustration of the opposition as a tiny whale about to land on them. It was totally bizarre!

And then we had almost a stranger experience of being part of the news cycle, which is really odd, because suddenly we were just being almost besieged by people. And you'd open up Facebook, and there are hundreds of people trying to get to you to ask us to talk about it. So we went to the BBC and told our story, and then it calmed down again, and life sort of went back to normal.

But my life couldn't really go back to normal, because I've always been interested in whales. My fiancée actually found a photo album of mine from a holiday to Canada I had as a child, and there were no family pictures in it. It's just postcards of killer whales that I'd collected. And I just thought, "I should follow this." And every time anything weird happened or anything unusual happened to a whale, all of my friends now thought of me as the whale guy, so they'd send it to me. And I got more and more drawn into whales.

Well, first I was astonished about how much you could learn about individual whales, and the identification of them—Happywhale and Cascadia and the work they've been doing for over twenty years.

And then I got interested in the people, in the disentanglement[27], the various disentanglement outfits, and the scientists, and the whale watchers. And I thought, "This is an amazing community." "Maybe I could make a film, about not just a person or a team, but a community who share an interest in an animal and use that as a way of showing the problems that those animals face, using my experience as a hook into that to get people interested with this dramatic moment, in a much bigger story about people who like whales, and about what's happening to whales. And so that's what I did.

---

[27] Efforts to disentangle whales that get wrapped up and caught in fishing gear.

TOM MUSTILL

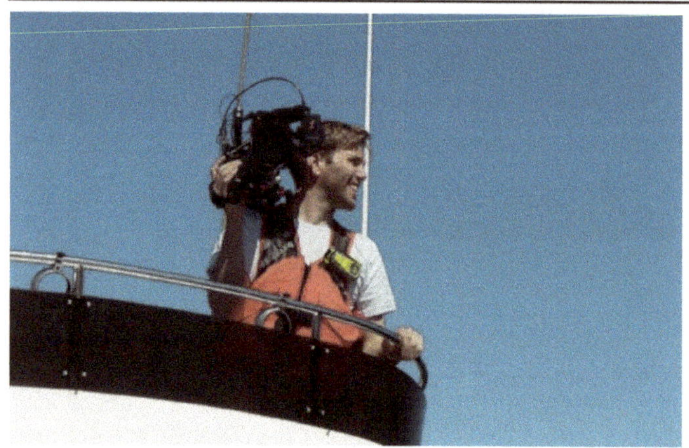

Courtesy Tom Mustill

Tom Mustill runs a small documentary film production company based in the United Kingdom. He pretty much does a little bit of everything, from finding a story, researching it, directing interviews, working with the film crew, sometimes ending up behind the camera, then working on editing and promotion as well. He wants to make sure the issues and people in his films benefit from the attention in a good way.

Born and raised in London, Tom calls himself a Londoner, a city boy at heart, though he's always loved the natural world and being outside. London continues to be his base as he travels to places with a lot more wildlife.

Tom first came to Monterey on holiday with a big bunch of friends. He had previously met Tierney Thys at a wildlife conference in Bristol, and she'd said if he was ever in town, he should come check out what she was doing. She was away during his first visit, but Tom met with her partner who is an engineer at MBARI (Monterey Bay Aquarium Research Institute) and showed him the ROVs they were designing. The two of them looked out the window and there, really close to shore, were humpbacks fluking and lunge feeding. Tierney's partner said Tom should really go whale watching to fully appreciate the whales, and the best way would be by kayak.

Tom phoned Monterey Bay Kayaks; they had two more places, so he reserved them, and that's where Tom's dramatic story with a whale begins. It was slightly ironic that it happened when he was on holiday, because obviously, he says, his job is to go and film animals, and he'd never had an encounter like that in his job.

Tom has always loved the sea, experiencing it as a surfer and free diver. He got a degree in Zoology at Cambridge University, where he studied marine ecology and ancient, underwater systems in the pre-Cambrian period, looking at fossil assemblages from 500 million years ago. When he was between school and university, he volunteered on a coral monitoring project in Fiji.

When he left Cambridge University, Tom was determined to become a conservation biologist. He worked in habitat restoration and management for a year or so. But then he thought he could have a better impact on the world and looking after natural systems by doing storytelling about conservation. The first big program he worked on was *Inside Nature's Giants*, which won a BAFTA and other awards.

That's how he met Joy Reidenberg. Tom had a whale they were going to dissect, and was told by a lion anatomy expert that they should call this American lady, because she knew all there was to know about the anatomy of whales. He phoned her up, wanting just a few tips, but she was so engaging and so knowledgeable the next thing he knew she was in Ireland heading out to the beach, taking charge of the entire dissection, explaining everything incredibly well, and she then became a permanent member of their team on the series.

Since then, Tom's been making films specifically in the area he's most interested in, which is where humans and the natural world meet—where humans and animals meet. Tom thinks audiences really respond to seeing other people in those stories. Makes them feel like they're part of that wonderful natural world they are seeing. As Tom says, if you show them stories about people who are doing impressive and inspiring things, and doing them well, it gives people hope and helps them feel things aren't all screwed up.

His last film project was *The Whale Detective* (PBS, January 2020), the true story that sprang from his epic kayak encounter with the breaching humpback, "We're Going to Die Now!"

Tom also published his first book, *How to Speak Whale: The Power and Wonder of Listening to Animals*, in 2022. It was selected as one of Amazon's "Best Books of the Year." In this engaging book he explores the work people are doing using new technologies to try and understand animal languages or communications.

Close Call in a Kayak

Joy Reidenberg

(*Date of Interview*: 10/27/17)

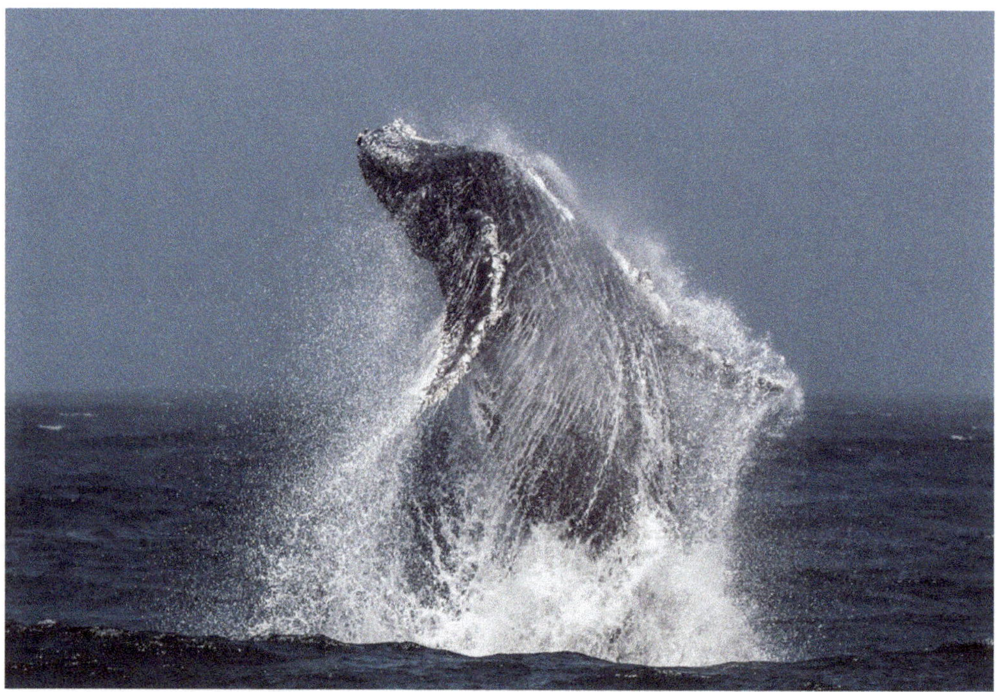

Breaching humpback whale

Now I will tell a story that didn't happen to me, but happened to a colleague of mine, while we were filming for *Big Blue Live*[28]. We (the *Big Blue Live* crew) were out in Monterey Bay, and I was there to talk about sea otter fur and humpback baleen, and all these other great things, all about anatomy. That was my role. At the same time this was all happening, there were people out on the water filming. One of the people who was out there was not involved with *Big Blue Live*, but was also out there at the same time all of this was happening. He was in a kayak with a friend.

He went out on the kayak to see humpbacks really close. But you know, you have a setback—a restriction on how close you're allowed to get. You can't get that close. He was properly obeying setbacks and was watching the pod that was

---

[28] A live television and online event celebrating some of the world's most amazing marine creatures converging off California's coast.

feeding. It was more than 200 yards away. And he and his friend were just lolling around; they weren't going anywhere, just sort of lolling around watching these pods feeding.

Then out of nowhere a humpback breached right in front of them, that they did not know was there. And it landed on their kayak and plunged the kayak down. The whole incident was caught on video by someone who was on one of the whale watching ships.

I didn't know this had happened at the time, but after I got back home I was communicating with my friend Tom—Tom Mustill. Tom is actually a filmmaker. He had directed some episodes that I had been in for another TV series, so he sent me an email saying, "I was in Monterey Bay when you were there filming, and guess what happened?" "I got breached on by a humpback whale!" "No, you're just joking me, aren't you?" "No, no, it really happened." Then he showed me this clip. I said, "Wait a minute." I'd seen this clip. It ran viral. Everybody had seen this clip. "That was you? No, you're just kidding me, right?" "No, it actually really was me." So, I thought, that's pretty bizarre. Well, I started looking at the clip a lot more closely, because my first impression was 'what an idiot, why were you so close to humpback whales?' But then he told me he wasn't close to the whales, this one came out of nowhere. They were very far from the whales they were watching.

I'm looking at this video clip, and I'm watching it frame by frame by frame by frame. And as I'm looking at it, I'm realizing that this humpback did not do a normal breach. Normally when humpbacks jump up, they jump up and they arc backwards because the head is so heavy. And the back of the head where the skull is is much heavier than the front, which is the throat, assuming there's no water in it when they're not feeding, ok? So as they arch up, they come out of the water, and they usually end up landing backwards on the back of their head.

This whale started to do that, but I think as it arched—and often they twist a little bit—it could see the kayak out of one eye. I think the whale was, like 'oh crap, I have to move, there's something in the way.' And it purposely turned in a way that was not consistent with how it was arching, and it didn't land on its back like it normally would. It ended up landing on its side. I think the whale purposely tried to avoid the kayak, because it saw the kayak at the last minute. It didn't know it was there when it was breaching. But it saw and really tried hard not to hit the kayak.

This whale was not trying to breach on top of my friend and his woman friend; this whale tried to avoid them. And it was only because it had to turn—you know, to bring the flippers around like when ice skaters make a twist, and they use their arms like this and they spin. The whale did that with its flippers and it made a spin, and one of the flippers hit the kayak and actually dented the front of the kayak. If the whale had actually not done that, the back of the skull, which is, you know, the size of a couch, ok? would have hit the kayak and probably would have killed Tom and his friend. But it didn't, so they lived. And they got plunged under, because as the whale hit, it sucked everything down with the pressures of pushing them down, but they popped up again and they were laughing. They couldn't believe they were that close to a humpback whale breaching. But they also didn't realize how close they were to death.

JOY REIDENBERG

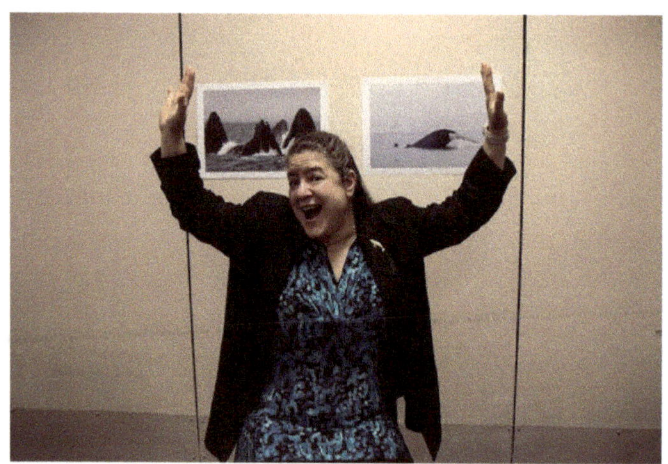

Joy Reidenberg is a professor at the Icahn School of Medicine at Mount Sinai in New York. She is a comparative anatomist, specializing in the vocal and breathing apparatus of mammals, particularly cetaceans—that is, whales, dolphins and porpoises. Joy acknowledges it is rather weird to be in the marine mammal field and be a medical school professor, but her interest in marine mammals really comes from being so excited about their adaptations and how they survive in such an unusual environment. Her goal is to try to understand these adaptations, bring the information back to the human condition and then remake those adaptations for treatment of human disease such as emphysema or cystic fibrosis. In addition, she hopes to develop protective devices to help deal with issues like decompression sickness for people who have to live and work in similarly unusual environments.

Joy was always interested in art, science and animals, but had no idea what she wanted to do for a career. Her father suggested she look in the phone book, which Joy actually did. It wasn't until she reached Veterinarian that she found something that piqued her interest. However, she went to intern briefly with a veterinarian and took preveterinary medicine in college, but decided the job was more that of a technician and did not involve the level of creativity and curiosity she wanted to bring to her life's work.

She attended Cornell University in Ithaca, New York, where she was in the College of Arts and Sciences, because she couldn't decide which to study! She earned her bachelor's degree there, and received her master's and doctorate (Biomedical Sciences: Anatomy) from the Mount Sinai School of Medicine Graduate Program in Biological Sciences.

It was the Chairman of the Department of Anatomy at vet school, who had a PhD, who told her to stop chasing the DVM, and go for a PhD—a degree in research. He gave her a job dissecting a giant jar of toadfish. Toadfish (croakers) were setting off underwater bombs, and scientists and the military wanted to know why.

Joy discovered that anatomy involved drawing, dissecting, learning and conveying information. She felt that science could be more creative than art. A scientist could ask any question and design the experiments. Anatomy was also very visual. It was a perfect career choice for Joy. As a teen, she had already been gutting fish, but didn't realize people would pay her to look at guts. At that time she had no idea that being an anatomist was a career.

She was born in Connecticut and currently works in New York City. She considers herself a Northeasterner, as she has only lived in three states—New York, New Jersey and Connecticut. However, she has visited Monterey Bay on multiple occasions and has been enthralled by her experiences there.

Joy initially came to Monterey Bay in 1989, the first time she attended a marine mammal conference—as a pregnant faculty member.

Educating the public outside of the academic setting seems to be a specialty of Joy's. In addition to *Big Blue Live*, she has appeared as a regular on *Inside Nature's Giants*, dissecting a variety of animals including a fin whale, sperm whale, elephant, camel, giant squid, great white shark, and leatherback sea turtle, and she starred in four episodes of PBS's *Sex in the Wild*. Joy is an engaging speaker and has also presented at scientific conferences including the international Society for Marine Mammalogy and the American Cetacean Society.

Taking a Whale Out to Sea

Monte Ash

(Date of Interview: 10/11/16)

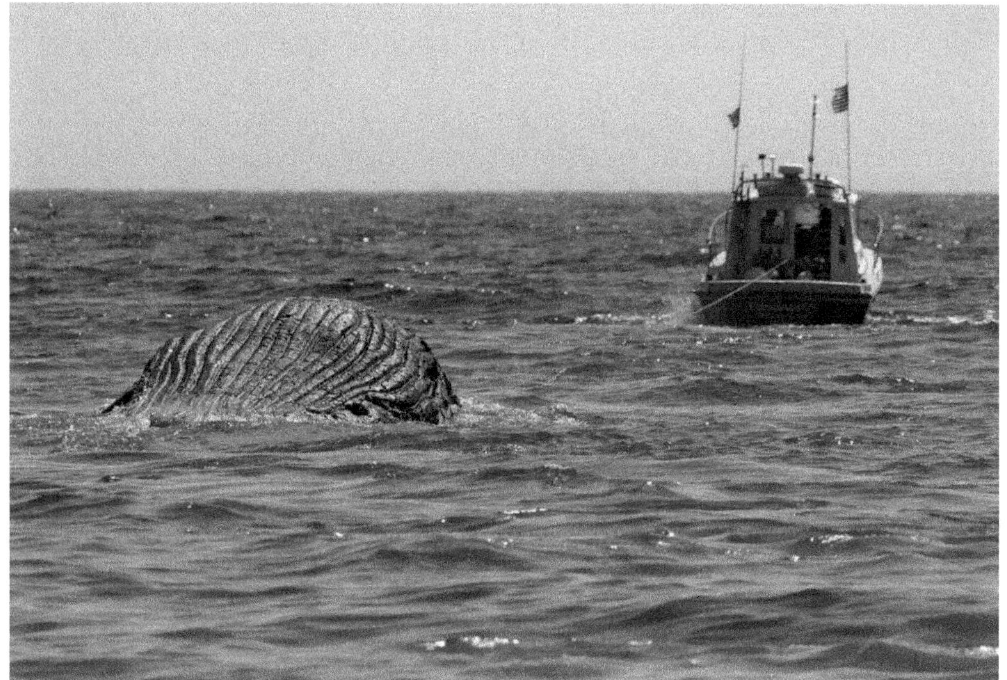

Humpback whale carcass being towed out to sea

Ok, let's talk about whales. So we'd been doing this job, towing boats, helping people out, for about a year, and I got a phone call from Justin Viezbicke[29] one day. Didn't know who he was—didn't have a clue—and he says, "I talked to your counterpart in Santa Barbara and he says that you're the new guy up in Santa Cruz, and there's a whale up in Half Moon Bay that's washed ashore, and the City of Half Moon Bay wants it removed. And your counterpart down here does a good job, so he says you'd do a good job, too. So we want you to go get it." And I said, "Wow! Ok."

Well, I called my counterpart in Santa Barbara and said, "What have you done to me?" [*laughter*] He said, "No, no, no, no problem. It's easy." He explained to us what to do, how to do it, what not to do, and things to be careful about. So I

---

[29] California Stranding Coordinator, Marine Mammal Health and Stranding Response Program, NOAA Fisheries.

got to know Justin pretty quickly over a period of two days. I got to know everybody in Half Moon Bay over a period of about twelve hours.

We got underway one morning with me and a deckhand, and my wife, who's the co-owner of the business. She drove up to Half Moon Bay with a swimmer, and we went from not knowing anything about towing whales off the beach to towing a whale off the beach in about eighteen hours. But with a lot of help from our friend down in Santa Barbara.

The first one we towed, probably close to a year and a half ago now, was a whale, a small humpback whale I believe, that was washed up right behind the campground in Half Moon Bay. That's why they wanted it removed, because it was gonna cause a health hazard. It was sitting on the beach. It stank. There were a lot of people that didn't want it there. It was kind of the height of camping season, and they wanted it removed. They've had other whales that washed up in Half Moon Bay that nobody cared about because it's just on a beach, so you let nature take its course, but this one they wanted gone.

The way it works is that Justin calls you and says, "There's a whale out there. I'm gonna coordinate with the entities that want it removed, and we'll get you out there as soon as we can, because people want it done right now." Right.

Well, we have to kind of plan our course, because we don't want to get there at low tide. We don't want to get there in bad weather. It's not delivering the mail, so it's something we want to kind of plan and give ourselves a good chance for success.

This first carcass towing we went on, we did a little bit of planning over that period of eighteen hours, and we kinda knew what we were doing when we got there. We put a beach crew on the beach and our boat out there just beyond the surf. Had a guy swim out from the beach and get the towline. We have a thousand feet of towline on the boat. We didn't have to put that much out, but he had to swim out and get it outside the surf line, then he towed it back in. He had the tow strap ready to go on the whale. And when I was out there on the boat waiting for him to swim back in, I noticed that there were a lot of people on the beach. There was a crowd of people, and they were all kind of starting to gather around my wife because she was the only one that had the red TowBoatU.S. t-shirt on, and she wasn't having it. She didn't want to have anything to do with them. She was concentrating on making sure to get that whale off the beach. There was a city manager and the assistant city manager, and there were police. And there were dogs and kids, because the campground is right there!

It was a big deal. There's a boat offshore, and there's this guy swimming a line in. That was probably the biggest event of the day, getting the line onto the whale, getting it strapped up. And it's the top of the tide and we decided there's enough water under the whale to pull it off the beach. I was kind of thinking we'd have to pull pretty hard, but as soon as we started pulling, the whale comes right off, and we start towing it out.

We get—I don't know—probably a half mile, or a mile off the beach in Half Moon Bay, and we call Justin, and say, "Justin, we got the whale. It's off the beach." He'd told us where he wanted it. He actually told us to take it to the west, to the most-western Farallon Island—I'm sure it has a name, that island. And he wanted us to go around the island, get upwind of the island and drop the whale off so it would wash up on the beach. So it would be in a place where nobody would be concerned, and where it wouldn't wash up back on the mainland. That's the one thing they did not want to have happen. When whales get removed, it takes a lot of time to do, and once I touch the whale and Justin has something to do with the whale, we kind of own the whale. To a certain extent we are responsible for its proper disposal.

He said, "Go out there, drop it off on this island, let me know when you're done." We had about a thirty-mile tow to get there. I didn't really know how long it was gonna take when we first started. I knew that we couldn't tow it like a boat. Boats are shaped like this [*gestures*], and go easy through the water. Whales aren't, especially when towed backwards, because that's where we attach—to the tail. We figured out we could go about three knots. [*laughter*] So do the math.

Ten hours: by the time we leave Half Moon Bay, this is the time it will take to get to this place in the Farallones—this magical island out there. So we had food with us, we had drinks. We knew that we were gonna be gone for a while, but not exactly how long. So we said, all right, set a course for this island. It was in the morning; we knew we'd get there at night, so we started kind of planning on what we were gonna do. How to get the whale close to the island, but not so close that we'd get wrecked on the island in the middle of the night. And we get to the point where we're just gonna—I know we're gonna—lose phone reception, because we're maybe six or seven or eight miles out, and I start getting texts from Justin, "Call me! Call me! Call me!" So I called him. He said, "That plan's not gonna work. Fish and Game[30] doesn't want the whale on the beach. They say that we'd have to get all kinds of permits, and they're not gonna allow it, because they don't have time to think about it enough. So we can't put it there."

---

[30] California Department of Fish and Game, now called California Department of Fish and Wildlife.

"OK. Where do we put it?" [*more laughter*] He says, "I picked another point for you. It's gonna be far enough out and in a different-enough current loop that the whale probably won't come back onshore." I say, "OK, where's that?" He says, "Fifteen miles west of that island." [*silence*] Fifteen miles, that's five more hours. [*laughter*] Ok. [*laughter*] "Right? Ok."

There's nothing we can do. There's this whale behind us, about 400 feet on the tow line, and we promised we were gonna put it on this island. And now we've got to promise we're gonna put it [*motions*]. We get out a chart, my GPS chart, and try to look at where to put it. We're gonna be five miles past the continental shelf, in a twenty-eight-foot boat, in the middle of the night, with a whale—a dead whale—attached to us. So, we just kind of settled in; decided we'd take shifts. I and another guy on the boat decided we'd take shifts driving, so we could sleep. For the biggest part of the journey going out though, it was daylight. So as we were going out, lots of things happened.

The first thing we were concerned about is that the course we had to take to go straight to where we wanted to be crossed all the shipping lanes that were going into San Francisco. So we've got a shipping lane that goes this way. And we've got one that goes out. As we approached, we could see—it wasn't quite dark yet, but there were a lot of ships. And ships in the shipping lane go ten to twenty knots. And we were poking along at three knots with 500 feet of line and a dead whale off the back.

We had to pick our way through the shipping lanes and make sure we weren't gonna get in the way of any big ships. We had to plan to give 'em a call and let 'em know that we were there if we got close to them. Fortunately, it was kind of one of these things that a ship went by, then we went here, then another went this way just as we were getting ready to go in that shipping lane. One went by and we went through and another one came by, and we were able to kind of weave our way through about four or five ships as we're going through. Good to get through there so we didn't get hit!

As we got closer to the Farallones, we could start to see the islands while it was still daylight. We could see the shapes of the islands. And as we got out there, the water started changing. It went from kind of, you know how it is; it goes kind of brown, then green, then blue. Just as we got to the really, really blue water, where everything turned into what looked like tropical water, there was just this multitude of life that came up.

A pod of dolphins came by and purposely checked us out. They weren't quite sure what we were doing out there, but we were something they weren't expecting, weren't used to seeing. So a pod of dolphins came by and actually went under the boat. We think we saw some turn around and take another pass, and there were quite a few that kind of hung back and actually swam under the whale. I'm sure they were checking out why this whale was swimming backwards on the surface. And we could see all that happening around it.

They were there for maybe ten minutes kind of milling around, but we just kept on going straight and steady. We saw a pod of whales. I don't know that they knew what we were doing or were curious about it, but they were very close to it. We could see they were feeding. Coming up, going down. Coming up, going down, but right out from the back of the boat so close that I could take video and pictures of the whale we were towing and the whales behind us in the same frame. So we were just parading whales for a little while.

And I think probably the best thing, the funniest, most amusing to me anyway, was that about thirty sea lions showed up on scene. Sea lions are very curious, and these sea lions were freaking out. Because they saw us, and being sea lions that are habituated to humans and boats, they probably thought, "Hey, look, a fishing boat." They all came up to the boat and were popping their heads up and kind of trying to get a look over the side to see if we were fishing, or cutting bait, or throwing anything over the side they could eat. Once they figured out that we probably weren't gonna feed them, they noticed the whale. [*laughter*] And it was like a pack of dogs had just seen something they had never seen before. They all stopped and they all stood up as high as they could, like this with their noses in the air [*mimics standing sea lions*]. And they all stayed real stationary in a little area about fifty feet wide, and just watched like watching a parade, just real stiff as this whale floats by them. [*laughter*]

You could just see them, just completely shocked, these poor sea lions. The whale went by and you could see them, kind of, you know, look around to see if there was anything else weird. And a couple of them followed the whale for a while, and the rest of them just kind of slowly wandered off.

We had those three encounters maybe in an hour or two of each other, right out there just past the shipping lane. That was pretty cool! The rest of the time we didn't see anything. We saw the islands. We saw a lot of ships. And as it got dark, it got kind of weird, because then we knew we were out there all by ourselves. There were no other ships, no traffic, no animals, and no other boats at all, and we're still moving, moving, moving. We think we've probably got five or six hours to go to get to our destination.

Well, we finally got there! It was a very lonely place out there for us. We recorded where we put the whale. We got the whale loose from the towboat, which was a little bit ominous. As we were going out the current was a north current when we first started, and when we got out there, it was going west. And we were trying to find the end of our towline, so we could unhook it from the line we were gonna leave on the whale, so we didn't have to handle the whale and would be able to identify the whale as something that had been towed previously. At that moment, the whale caught up with us. Just out of the dark. We could see the shadow coming toward us. We knew it was the whale, but it was coming at us, and we couldn't get away because we had lines straggling, and as the whale came up it just kind of nudged the boat. But we got all our line back. Got the line we were gonna cut off the whale cut off. Took a few quick pictures to prove that we were there, and that we did what we had to do, and turned around and came back to Santa Cruz.

We were gone twenty-two hours—from the time we left Santa Cruz, all the way out and then back. That's the longest one we've had. That was a long, long ride. We covered forty-five miles to get that whale to a point that it would not come back to shore.

MONTE ASH

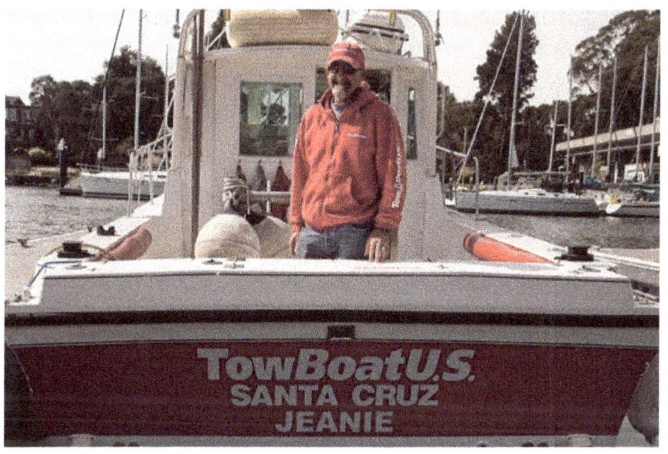

Captain Monte Ash is owner and president of TowBoatU.S. Santa Cruz, based in Santa Cruz, California. He's also the primary captain for the company, which operates in a fashion similar to a tow truck for members.

Monte was born in Kansas City, Kansas and grew up in both Wyoming and Kansas until he joined the Navy at age nineteen. His passion for water developed on the inland ponds, lakes and streams, where he spent his youth fishing. In Hawaii, he enjoyed being around the ocean. In the Navy, he spent six years operating a nuclear power plant on a submarine stationed in Pearl Harbor.

After leaving the Navy, he moved around quite a bit with his family while working for a power company as an industry executive and management professional. That stint included stays in Atlanta and Savannah, Georgia; Alabama; and Jamaica, until they finally settled in Las Vegas. His last position with that company landed him in Pittsburg, California. On retiring from that job, he took a year off, got his captain's license and affirmed that he wanted to be a professional boat captain. He purchased the twenty-year-old Vessel Assist Company, which was for sale at that time, and around 2010, he and his wife moved into the Santa Cruz Yacht Harbor, where they live aboard their spacious yacht docked next door to their two towboats.

Humpback Whales Running Interference

Alisa Schulman-Janiger

(*Date of Interview*: 11/6/16)

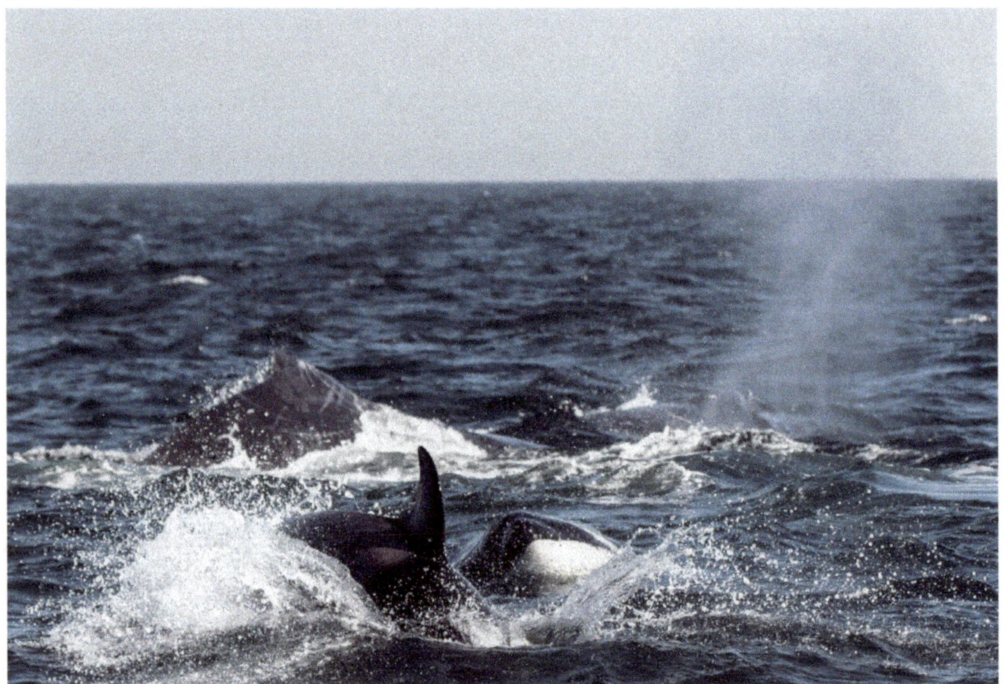

Humpback whales harassing killer whales

We happened to have the BBC out with us on a charter trip with Monterey Bay Whale Watch, on May 3, 2012. There were just three of us, Captain Nancy Black, deckhand Mike Merlo, and I, along with the BBC film crew. We were out looking for killer whales—the BBC really wanted to see killer whales—but they were interested in humpback whales, too. We'd been out that morning filming humpbacks, when we got a call at 12:05 pm from Captain John Mayer on the *Sea Wolf* that they had found killer whales attacking a gray whale mom and calf.

Naturally, we headed over there, because that's what the BBC folks wanted to see most, even though there were over one hundred humpback whales feeding in the bay, surface feeding on krill. The humpbacks were everywhere, and they were lunge feeding, a spectacle in itself. Plus, it was an amazing, flat calm, beautiful day.

It took us about half an hour to finally reach the *Sea Wolf*. When we arrived, we saw several killer whales going after a gray whale mother and calf. The calf was being pushed up into the air by the killer whales, and you could see blood from its mouth. There were also a couple of humpback whales in the mix. They were quite agitated—trumpet blowing and tail slashing. I took still pictures at first, trying to capture as much as I could to try to ID the animals.[31] Then I pulled out my video camera; 12:38 pm, three minutes after we had arrived, was the last time we ever saw the gray whale calf. That was the end. It had already died and sunk out of sight. Of course, the killer whales stayed there, and the gray whale mom stuck around for about fifteen more minutes. But what was really interesting was that a humpback whale was diving down with the gray whale mom. The mother would dive down where the calf had disappeared below, then that humpback would follow right after her. They would both be underwater, and it seemed to us they were looking for the calf. When that happened, the killer whales initially backed off, but then they came in, too. After about fifteen minutes the gray whale mom left and took off headed toward shore. We stayed expecting to watch the killer whales feeding. We had about ten killer whales there at the time, as well as several humpbacks.

We're documenting all this, along with the BBC, and the humpbacks are vocalizing. They're trumpet blowing, they're bellowing, and they're slashing their flippers and slashing their flukes. They're really loud and they're facing the killer whales and following them around. Then we saw a few other humpbacks in the area, and they came in, too. We stayed on the scene over a period of seven hours, and during that time the humpbacks never left. Instead, we saw more and more coming in. At one time, we counted as many as seven.

Later when I analyzed the photos, I realized we had at least sixteen different humpback whales, identified just by their flukes, plus additional humpbacks that didn't fluke. One individual was there for at least three and a half hours. The humpbacks that had moved into this area included several of the whales we'd seen in the morning, hours earlier and several miles away. There was a lot of food [anchovies] around, but it was very interesting that the humpbacks didn't feed. We observed only one humpback feeding bout the entire time during the seven hours we were there. That one time four whales came up really quickly in a feeding lunge, and then they went right back, side-by-side, touching each other, facing the killer whales, trumpeting, approaching them, following them around—really interesting interactions. It was a very long day and we finally headed back to the harbor, as it was so dark we could no longer see.

During the bulk of the time we were out there the killer whales were feeding on the calf. An oil slick spread, an indication that the whales were feeding on the calf blubber, and I noticed another group of killer whales around—Chop Fin or

---

[31] Humpback whales are identified by the coloration and scarring on the underside of their flukes. Killer whales are identified by their dorsal fins, the saddle patches on their backs and eye patches.

Stubby's group. The group Chop Fin hangs out with is a group we call Jagged. They were there. But Chop Fin wasn't at all involved in any part of the attack or the feeding. He kind of stayed off to the side. There was also one female killer whale who would go over with her mom and her siblings and hang out with Jagged's group for a while, then come back and feed. In fact, she seemed to do most of the active feeding.

And we had albatross. We had dozens of black-footed albatross around! Plus, we had black-vented shearwaters feeding on the blubber. It was a very noisy affair, and it took a lot just trying to record all these interesting interactions. We took notes, trying to keep tabs on which whale is feeding, who's interacting with the humpbacks, who is the new humpback arriving, and trying to recognize and ID a few of the known humpbacks while we were in the field.

The whole event was really astonishing! Not just because the humpbacks were interfering—or seemed to be trying to interfere—with the killer whales during the hunt, but even after the calf was dead for seven hours, the humpbacks stuck around. Some researchers like to say that's because the humpbacks were trying to stop the kill, because they were probably attacked themselves as a calf, or that they're trying to protect a calf, but there were no humpback calves around. Were they trying to protect a calf of another species? The ideas that are generally put forth just didn't quite make sense. The humpbacks seemed to be protecting the carcass. They didn't want the killer whales to have anything to do with the carcass at all. Whenever a killer whale would start feeding, then a humpback would begin trumpeting at it and slashing all over the place.

The whole day-long encounter was extraordinary. We'd been talking to Bob Pitman, a colleague who was pulling together accounts of humpback whales interfering with killer whales feeding on different species. We'd already contributed sightings and it was supposed to be the end of the period to collect sightings for the paper. But Bob said we needed to include this, as it was a unique encounter— seven hours with lots of humpbacks nonstop. When we left and it was dark, there were still multiple humpbacks in the area. They were just as boisterous as earlier in the day and still following the killer whales around, while the killer whales continued feeding on the carcass.

It was all quite amazing! And the event actually became a major focus for the scientific publication that came out in *Marine Mammal Science*, because it was the longest documented encounter of interaction between humpbacks and killer whales, and it involved the most individual humpback whales, too. Scientists often say that this behavior by humpback whales may be altruism. But when we talk about altruism, why in the world could they have been doing this? Hard to say, but it was fascinating, shocking and totally awesome!

ALISA SCHULMAN-JANIGER

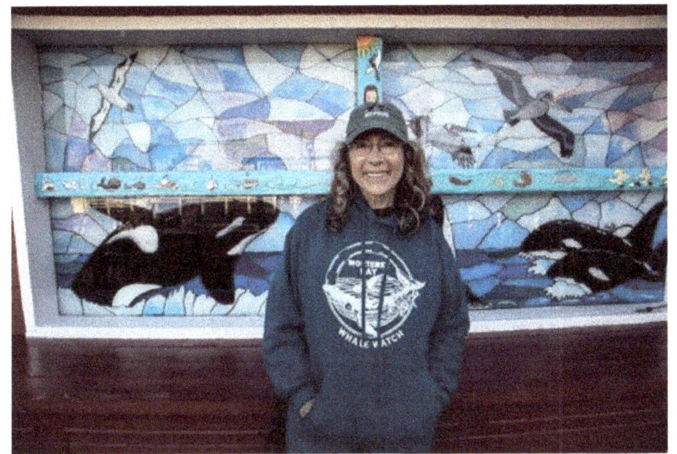

Alisa Schulman-Janiger is a marine biologist and the Census Director for the American Cetacean Society (ACS) Los Angeles Chapter's *Gray Whale Census and Behavior Project*, now in its forty-fifth year. Alisa is well known as a transient killer whale researcher with the California Killer Whale Project. She's also actively involved in humpback whale identification, and she teaches a naturalist class for the Los Angeles Chapter of ACS.

Alisa was born in Maywood, California and grew up mostly in Long Beach, California. She became interested in the oceans at age five when she saw her first grunion. Her kindergarten teacher brought an octopus to class in a glass jar and couldn't answer a question Alisa put to her. That defining moment led Alisa to decide to become an educator.

A marine biologist with a teaching credential, Alisa taught on boats for ten years, worked for the California Department of Fish and Game doing environmental reports, worked back East for two years studying humpback and right whales, and has been a naturalist for the past thirty years.

Simultaneously with her work on the gray whale census, Alisa spent twenty years teaching marine science in high school for the Los Angeles Unified School District. She retired as soon as she could to follow her passion spending time with whales and conducting whale research.

Whales are what brought Alisa to Monterey Bay—killer whales and humpback whales. She had previously gone to Monterey on vacation and for conferences, but when she got into killer whales in the early 1970s and early 1980s, there were more killer whales up here, with the most sightings in the Monterey Bay area. Alisa began to spend more time here primarily to learn about the killer whales of California. She has since become one of the top California transient killer whale experts.

Mystery Killer Whales

Nancy Black

(Date of Interview: 1/16/17)

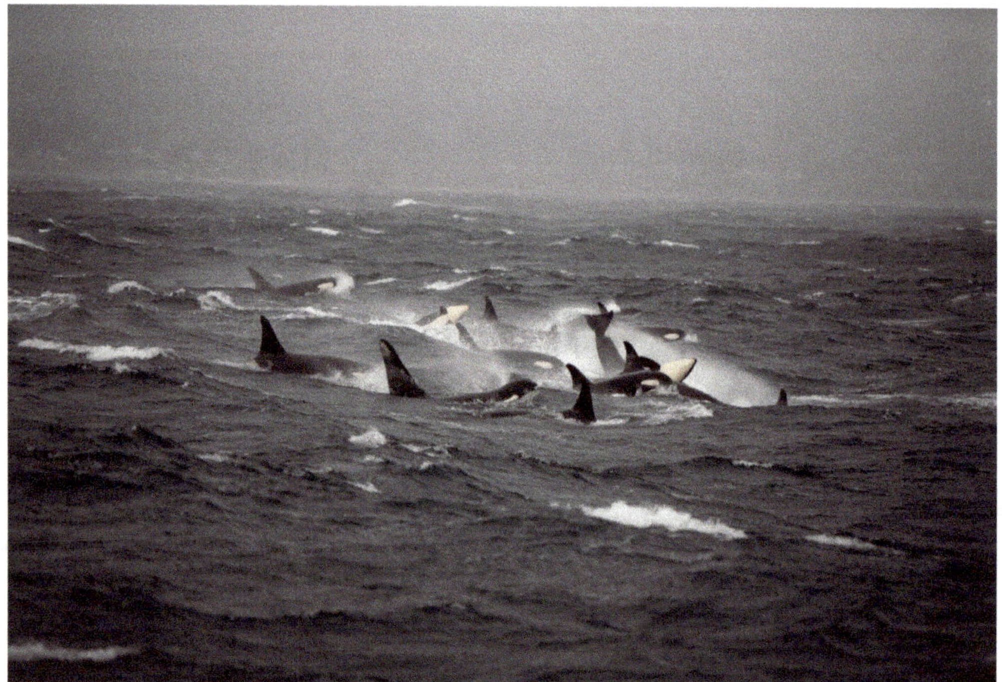

Resident killer whales (part of K & L pods)   © Nancy Black

One of my most interesting wildlife encounters was back during the winter of 2000, when we came across a group of killer whales that were pretty spread out. There were quite a few of them, over twenty at least, when we first got there. And they were spread out, maybe a half-mile to a mile in small subgroups of five here, then two there. So, I first thought they were the offshore type of killer whales, not the transients we usually see. There seemed to be too many to be transients, and just their behavior and how many there were and how they were spread out was different.

I was very excited just because they were offshore, because we don't see them very often—maybe once a winter, maybe once or twice. Some years we don't even see them at all. Anyway, we were getting the cameras ready. I wanted to identify as many as we could, because we want to learn as much as we can about the offshore type. They're the ones we see that range all the way from Southern California up into the Bering Sea. There's just one population. The very same group of animals is seen down in Southern California and all the way up to Alaska.

They aren't in separate groups like transients. There's one type of transient that is down here in Monterey Bay, and a different transient population that's up in British Columbia. Then you get a different set of transients in Alaska. Same with the residents. Anyway, the offshores are really exciting to see, and we really want to identify all of them. There's over 300 of them.

As I started taking pictures, I was looking at them, and some of them had open saddles. Where the white goes into the black there on the back just behind the dorsal fin, there was some black going into the white, and that's called an open saddle.

So, then I'm thinking, "Wow, that's kind of weird, for offshores to have that," because very few killer whales really have that, and in offshores, if they do, it's very minor. So, then I'm thinking, "This is something really different. Like, what is going on? Wait, *they look like residents!*" I had been working in Alaska for the previous five or six years at the time, and we'd see residents up there quite a bit, and these were starting to remind me of resident killer whales. But I thought, "No, no it can't be possible they would be down here," because we've *never* seen any resident types in Monterey Bay.

There are three types of killer whales: the transients, which are the mammal-hunters; residents that feed only on fish, primarily on king salmon or Chinook; and the offshore type, which I mentioned. They feed on sharks and squid and maybe offshore oceanic fish I don't know much about.

So, there's three types, eco-types, of killer whales off the Pacific Coast, and maybe another type that we don't know that much about, but much farther offshore. I was the naturalist on a gray whale trip that day, as we looked at these killer whales. And the people were getting really excited, too, because there were so many killer whales, *and,* besides there being so many, they started to get really active. They were breaching. There was some spy-hopping. We saw a newborn calf with little orange marks on it. When they're first born, they're really orangey, so this killer whale calf couldn't have been more than, you know, maybe a month or two old. It was really excited, popping its little head up. It was really cute.

With all this activity, the breaching and bubbly behavior, it really reminded me more and more of residents. "God, this is crazy. I mean, can these really be residents?" And I had not been familiar with the residents that are seen in Washington State at the time, because I hadn't worked with those. I had only been studying the residents in Alaska, and these didn't look like those. So, I'm thinking, "Oh my God, when I get home, I'm gonna look in the book and see. Maybe they're some weird type of offshore. I still thought residents have never been down here, so these can't be residents. What's going on? Maybe there's some other type of killer whale from offshore or something, who knows?"

So, it was a huge surprise, because by that time, by that year, I had been out for the last maybe thirteen years pretty much constantly. I had been working a lot pretty much year-round for the last thirteen years, and nothing! I'd seen no killer whales that looked like that at all. So, this was really a huge discovery of something.

Anyway, we got a lot of photos. I got home that night, and looked at the pictures right away. And I looked in the book for the southern residents, the ones in Washington State. They're currently endangered. And it was like, "Oh my God! One of them matched!" Then I looked at another one, and another match. I'm like, "This is amazing!" I could not believe it!

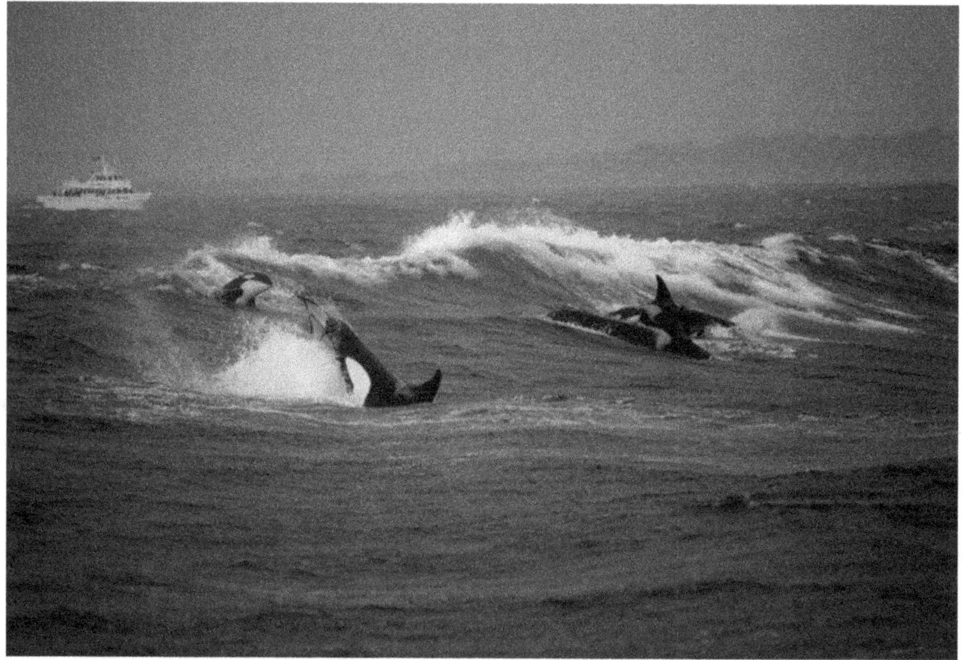

Resident killer whales (part of K & L pods) © Nancy Black

Then I called my friend Dave Ellifret, who works with Ken Balcomb up in Washington State. "I'm sending you these pictures now to confirm it," because he knows all of them by heart. He's got them all identified in his head. And I sent him these pictures, and he said, "Yes, it's part of the K and L pods." I mean, are you *kidding*?

And he was going crazy, too, because they had never been seen this far south before. I don't even think they'd been seen, you know, south of northern Oregon before or Washington in previous years.

As soon as he saw them and the word spread, you know, up in Washington State, it was immediately on all the news media up there and even down here. And everybody up there was worried, "Oh my God, our killer whales have left!"

They thought the whales had left the area, and maybe they were gone for good, because the salmon population was very low, even back then and that was sixteen years ago. Now it's really low, the salmon. Those whales are starving to death right now, sadly. And that was the beginning of it. We think they were traveling farther to look for food, because their salmon was depleted and still is. Since then, we have seen the residents down here almost every winter or every two or three winters. If they haven't made it to Monterey Bay, they've been seen in Northern California.

So that was a huge discovery, and that was like the biggest surprise of my career out on the ocean, seeing the southern residents in Monterey Bay.

[See Nancy's bio after the following story.]

The Pursuit: Killer Whales and Risso's Dolphins

Nancy Black

(Date of Interview: 1/16/17)

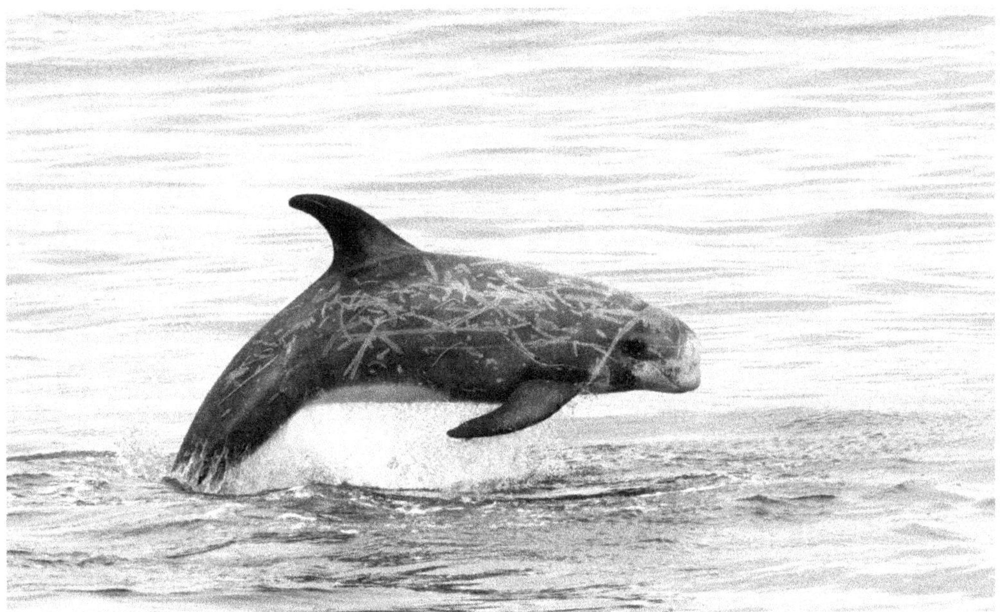

Risso's dolphin porpoising

Back in about 2003 or 2002, early 2000s, we were out on one of our whale watching trips. I think it was in the fall, and we were watching a small group of transient-type killer whales, the ones that eat marine mammals. We'd been following them for maybe twenty minutes or so. They were just slowly traveling, and then we came upon a group of scattered Risso's dolphins. They're a larger dolphin, about twelve feet long, that feeds only on squid.

Killer whales don't really prey on Risso's dolphins very much. There's been just one time during my thirty years on Monterey Bay that we've seen killer whales attack and kill a Risso's dolphin. But beyond that they really don't. Risso's are not one of their main prey.

So in this case, the Risso's were scattered out, and all of a sudden the killer whales took off porpoising. *But* this time, it was the Risso's that were chasing the killer whales! It was *really* unusual. Very strange! The killer whales were being pursued by the Risso's, which are known to be kind of a bullying, aggressive dolphin.

We're like, "What's going on here?" We quickly realized it was the killer whales that were being pursued, not the other way around. The Risso's were kind of flanking them on the side and in the back, behind them. The killer whales were grouped together, tight. And they were going fast, away. We were trying to keep up.

The Risso's chased after them for, I don't know, maybe it was like five, ten plus minutes or so. They caught up to the killer whales, and then some more Risso's ahead of them blocked them to the point where the killer whales stopped. They were surrounded by the Risso's, and it was like they were trapped in a fence almost. The Risso's had them trapped and bunched up.

The killer whales were completely surrounded by the Risso's, and they couldn't get out. Somehow the Risso's were keeping them trapped. It was the strangest thing ever. I've never seen anything like that since, and I hadn't seen the Risso's do that with other dolphins before either. So, they had these killer whales trapped for maybe—it could have been up to five, eight minutes or so. And the killer whales were stopped like they were trapped in a net or something. It was so similar to that.

Then, all of a sudden the killer whales broke free. They broke free and they just fled out of there as fast as they could. The Risso's did pursue them for a little bit, and then just gave up and that was it. But it was the strangest thing. What was going on? It was really a mystery. Very unusual.

NANCY BLACK

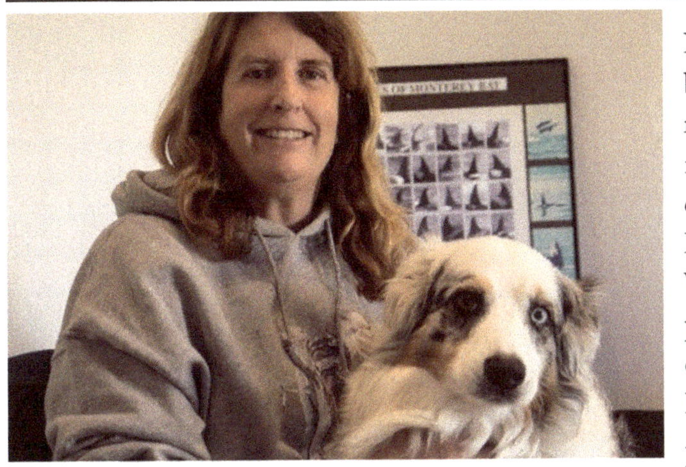

Nancy Black is a marine biologist and killer whale researcher with the California Killer Whale Project. She's also owner of Monterey Bay Whale Watch, which runs multiple whale watching trips daily out of the Monterey harbor.

Nancy was born in San Carlos, California, and grew up there. She attended the University of California at Davis as an undergraduate and came to Monterey Bay to attend graduate school at Moss Landing Marine Laboratories. There she studied Marine Mammalogy in the Marine Sciences program in the Birds and Mammals Lab. She received a master's degree in Marine Science from Moss Landing. While at the lab Nancy had different part-time jobs to help pay the bills. She got her start working as a naturalist during the gray whale season on boats out of San Francisco and Half Moon Bay and at Randy's in Monterey. During that time, Nancy started running her own whale watching trips for school children to earn additional income. She chartered the boats and worked as the guide. The program was so successful that some schools are still bringing students out twenty-five years later.

During her time as a grad student, Nancy also worked in the Bahamas over four seasons (summer and fall), with the Oceanic Society, helping on wild Atlantic spotted dolphin trips. They took groups out to sea on a sailboat for a week at a time to swim with the dolphins and assist with research. Nancy was a biologist/naturalist for that program.

This gave her the idea to do something similar in Monterey Bay. Overlapping with her time working on the Bahamas' project in the early 1990s, Nancy collaborated with Cascadia Research Collective out of Washington State on a program in Monterey Bay. The program was similar to the Oceanic Society and Earthwatch projects. Nancy took ten to fifteen people out on the bay on the *Point Sur Clipper* where the participants helped with data collection and photo IDs. They mostly focused on humpback and blue whales, but they gathered data on killer whales, too, if the whales showed up. Nancy still captains the *Point Sur Clipper*, taking passengers out on all-day trips searching for killer whales.

Killer Whale Classroom

J o d i   F r e d i a n i

(*Date of Interview*: 10/1/19)

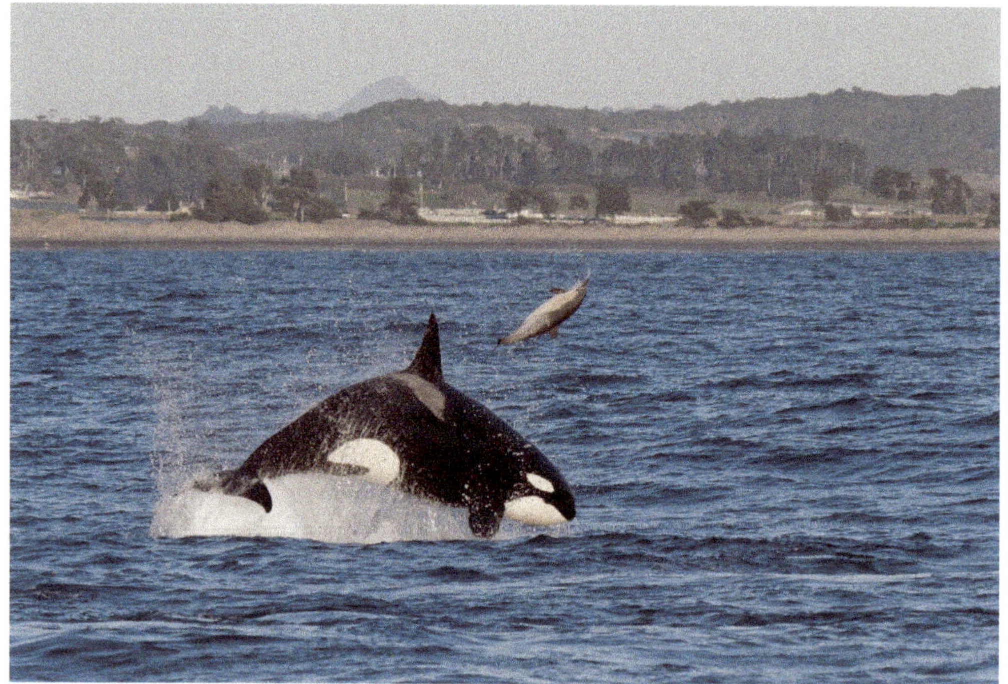

Killer whale tossing common dolphin

The encounter that always rises to the surface for me, even though Monterey Bay is just full of amazing encounters, happened about six years ago. And I think part of why it's so important is that it was one of those things where everything came together, and then amazing stuff happened.

I was at home that morning working on my computer, and at that point in time my cameras were always already packed and ready to go. The clothes I needed to have on a boat were in my truck. And the phone rang. It was Nancy Black, who was the captain of the boat I was going out on at the time, and she said, "We've just been out. We found killer whales and they're hunting. I'm taking the passengers back to the dock, then I'm gonna turn around and take the boat back out again. Can you make it down here?" That was just barely enough time for me to grab my things, get in my truck and drive all the way down to Monterey, but I said, "Yup, I'll be there."

So, I fly down there, I get to Monterey and get on the boat, and it's Nancy, another photographer named Daniel, and me. We head out from Monterey, and we go back over toward Moss Landing. There's another captain out at that point. He has no passengers, just a couple of deckhands on his boat, and he's got the killer whales.

There's a female named CA138 and her two offspring, and maybe one or two adult males. There's at least one male, Fat Fin, who is an orphan that was adopted by this female. So, we're trying to follow them and Fat Fin's off over there, and CA138 is porpoising along over here, and her kids are porpoising along after her, and we can't really tell what's going on. We're trying to follow them, and somebody says over the radio, "Oh, she's got a harbor porpoise!"

Next thing we know, CA138 turns and heads back toward the harbor. She's only three miles offshore. It's a beautiful day, sunny, mellow, and the water's calm. And as we turn around to follow, we see her and she suddenly does this *huge* tail throw. Her tail comes up, and 'whoosh,' big splash like that. Real powerful! I'm standing up at the bow. I'm clicking away with my camera, and I'm not sure exactly what's going on at that point it's happening so fast. But the next thing I see is CA138 porpoise completely out of the water. And as I'm looking through the lens of my camera, I see this bowling pin flying through the air in front of her! I say something like—and I paraphrase here—"Holy crap!" But I continue snapping away holding the shutter down, when she leaps out of the water, and this little porpoise or dolphin flies through the air. It lands on the water and the next thing I see she has come over to her offspring.

At that point, I'm so intent on photographing I don't actually see exactly what's happening. It's not till later when I go through my images that I am astonished for a couple of reasons. One is, I got it all! And I got it all in focus. And the other photographer did not. So, I had a series of photos that nobody else had. And in looking at my images, I could see this turned out to actually be a common dolphin flipping through the air, having been batted by CA138 as she came up. She just like 'boom' hit it through the air, and it did a 180 and then landed on the water. The next thing her two offspring come over. You could see mom come to check them out, and you could see the blood in the water by the mouth of one of her kids.

Basically, what happened was a training exercise, where her kids have helped her, or at least followed her, in the hunt. She managed to catch the dolphin, and if I look closely at the large files of my photo, I can see tooth marks. She had this dolphin—her tooth marks are right on its back—she actually had it in her mouth. She could have just bitten down and that would have been it. But, no, she grabbed the dolphin—well, I'm not sure which came first, the bite or the tail throw, but she took her fluke and she batted the dolphin to stun it, and then she porpoised out of the water, and with her head she tossed the dolphin through the air. That completely stunned it so it couldn't get away, and at that point her kids came in and *they made the kill.* Not only was it photographically really exciting for me, but we got to witness a natural experience of hunting and teaching in the wild. The whole thing was incredibly exciting. I was absolutely ecstatic!

And then the story and my photos got picked up by a top national Brazilian magazine. They ran with the photos. Actually, I think it probably started before that with a journalist I knew who had been writing for our local paper and then began writing for *Wired*, a national publication. She ran with these photos in *Wired*. Then the Brazilians nabbed the story. And then working with both Nancy Black and Alisa Schulman-Janiger, who knew the history of this particular female, I was able to write up the full experience. And with Carl Safina's assistance, I prepared the story, illustrated the story, and he ran it on his *National Geographic* blog.

Overall, it was an absolutely incredible experience for me. I still think about it all the time. CA138 is my favorite killer whale, and I can actually recognize her, which is pretty amazing, since I'm not all that good at recognizing killer whales. But it was very exciting, and it really helped give me a name in the marine photography world.

JODI FREDIANI

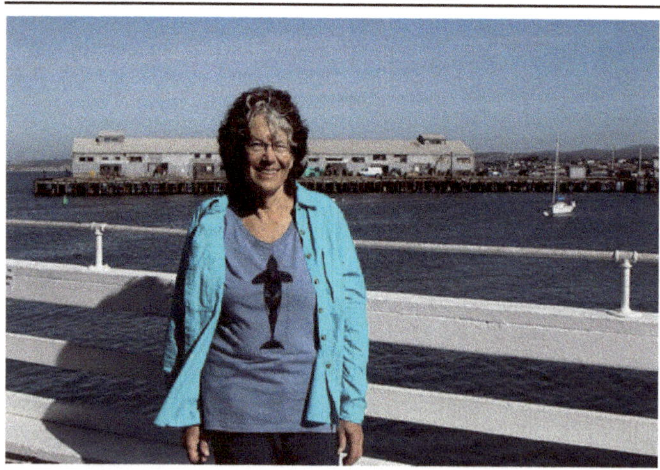

© Katlyn Taylor

Jodi Frediani is an award-winning wildlife photographer focusing on marine species and the marine environment. She is coeditor of this volume, *Wild Monterey Bay*, which also features her photos. Her images have appeared in numerous local, national and international publications as well as on BBC TV and in *National Geographic* blog posts. Her photos have also garnered awards in multiple prestigious international photo contests. She has spearheaded fluke identification efforts in the Silver Bank waters of the Dominican Republic, where she has been swimming with humpback whales for the past twenty-two years. She is currently collaborating with CEBSE, an environmental NGO, and Whale Samaná, on a comprehensive fluke ID catalog for the Dominican Republic. She has coauthored multiple scientific papers on humpback whales and is a member of the Whale-SETI research team focusing on humpback whale communication.

Jodi was born in Los Angeles and grew up in the San Fernando Valley suburbs of Los Angeles. As an only child, her 'siblings' were her family's cats and dogs, parakeets, tortoises and chameleons, leading to a lifelong love of animals.

After a year at the University of California (UC) at Davis preparing to study veterinary medicine, she transferred to UC Santa Cruz, which had opened just the year before. At the time, Environmental and Marine Studies were in their infancy. At UCSC she studied biology and art, but took a long, circuitous route to finally getting a Bachelor of Arts degree, with a focus on photography, many years later.

After taking one quarter off to travel, where she met her husband-to-be, she returned with him to Santa Cruz, got married, had two children and started an organic farm, where they grew fruits, vegetables and dried flowers and raised an award-winning herd of dairy goats. In addition to raising and showing dairy goats, she also became a TTOUCH® instructor, training animals and training people to work with animals. Simultaneously, she worked for thirty-five years as an environmental consultant, protecting forests and forested watersheds.

Jodi had traveled extensively through Europe and the USSR with her parents as a teenager. She took up travel on her own after her marriage had ended and her children had grown, and has not stopped traveling since.

However, it wasn't until the early 1990s, when Jodi went on a couple of Earthwatch projects involving whales and dolphins, that she was smitten by the marine 'bug.' She initially went to the Bahamas on a project led by Ken Balcomb on beaked whales. However, weather conditions led to colder-than-normal seas and no whales were seen. On returning home, Jodi decided to check out the whales in her own backyard and went whale watching on Monterey Bay. She was soon introduced to the world of fluke identification by Adam Pack on Maui after joining his Earthwatch project a couple of years later. Curiously, she had had a vivid, memorable dream as a child about her family and a whale, which in retrospect seemed to have been prophetic.

In 2009, Jodi gave her first photographic presentation to the Monterey Chapter of the American Cetacean Society. She was then invited by Nancy Black to go whale watching with Monterey Bay Whale Watch whenever she wanted. Jodi took up that offer and has been photographing whales, dolphins and other marine creatures in Monterey Bay and around the world ever since.

Harbor Seal Rodeo

Jim Harvey

(*Date of Interview*: 10/29/18)

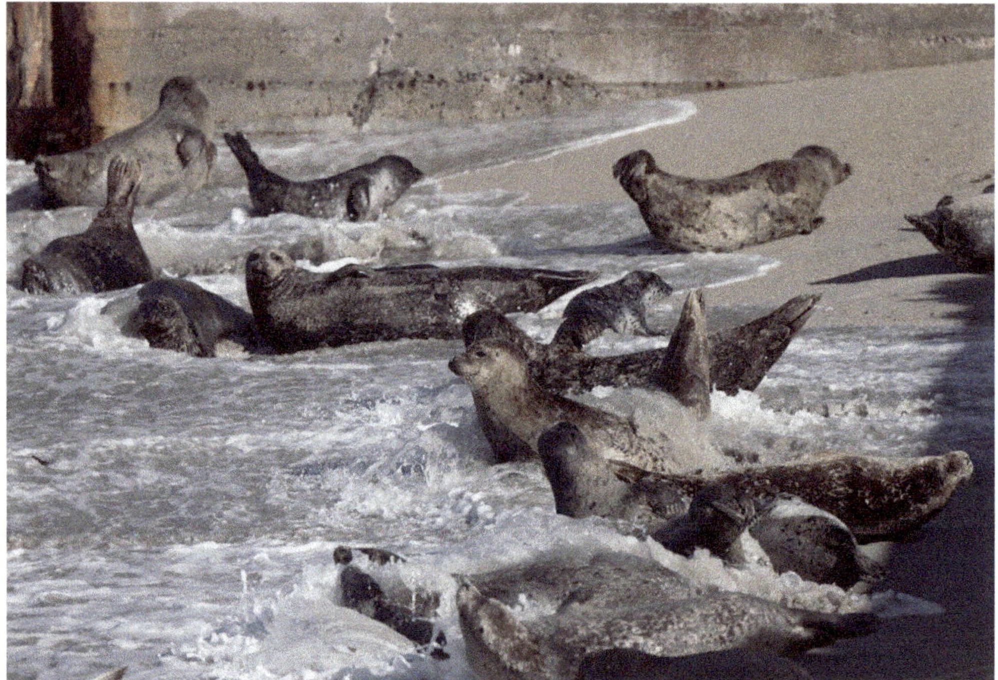

Harbor seals

I'm going to tell a little story about a capture event for harbor seals here in Elkhorn Slough. Harbor seals are very difficult to capture, because they are very wary of humans, first of all. They are sitting right next to the water when they're on land and resting, so they're capable of getting in the water and fleeing very rapidly. And because they are in an estuarine system, they're really used to getting in the water whenever there's a disturbance.

It's taken a long time for us to develop methods to be able to capture these harbor seals for that very reason. You start coming close to them and they immediately get into the water, and it's difficult once they get into the water to catch them. So we devised a method of capturing harbor seals that uses a net on the back of a boat that's set at a very fast pace. Basically, you're doing a big beach seine, with a net around the harbor seals. And if you do it properly and the seals behave properly, the largest number of animals we've caught in one net was eighty-five, which was *way* too many seals! But mostly, with harbor seals in Elkhorn Slough, you don't catch that many. You oftentimes catch none, or you catch what is probably the optimum number of about ten or fifteen.

The way this is done, the seals are on the haul-out site, resting up near the water on the mudflat, and two boats come up to the seals at a pretty fast pace. The first boat is the one that has the net in it, and as you get close to the seals, the seals most likely will start going into the water. Hopefully, some portion of them won't— those that are sort of unsure what they should be doing. They may be standing there looking around like, "Oh, look at these boats coming. What am I gonna do?" If there's a slight hesitation on their part, this happens: the first boat comes up; they drop a buoy, attached to one end of the net, off the back of the boat, and then the boat proceeds to go around, kind of making a curved arch around where the seals had been or maybe still are. And in that whole time the net's playing out off the back of the boat.

That net's about 150 feet. Well, no, it's about 300 feet long, and about 14 feet deep. It's a pretty good-sized net. It's set, like I said, very rapidly. The second boat then comes, picks up the buoy and pulls that first part of the net to shore. Now you presumably have a net that goes from one end of shore around and then back to shore again. And any seals that were on the shore are hopefully gonna get caught, and any seals that got into the water and never swam too far away may potentially get caught.

This happens all in the course of about maybe three minutes. So you're doing it really quickly. The two boats have extra people in them, and as soon as you get to shore both boats' occupants jump out of the boat. The first thing you train yourself to do is put an anchor on the shore, because we've done this before where you didn't put the anchor out, and all of a sudden you look around and the boat's floating off. You learn very quickly that somebody throws the anchor on the shore. Now you have both boats on shore. People jump out of their boat and grab the net, and now you start pulling it to shore. And what's supposed to happen is the seals are in the water now swimming around trying to find their way out, and you need to get them back to shore pretty rapidly. Because, if you don't, the seals may start to figure out that there's no escape. They can go up on shore, but they can't get past this net that's in the water. In that case, the smart seals will start thinking about it and just jump over the net, the surface part of the net and they're free.

That's why you want to get to shore really quickly, so you don't give them a lot of time to think it through. And if you do it properly, the net gets pulled to shore, and now you've got a series of seals, maybe; like I said, optimum would be ten to fifteen seals in this net. They're in the bag of the net. You're pulling both the top of the net that has the floats on it, and the lead line that's the heavy part of the net, and you're pulling these two in together, and now there's this big bag of the net that has the seals in it.

As you pull the net to shore, you now have this bag of seals, basically, that you're pulling to shore. That's why you can't do this with just one or two people. You have to do it with a large group. And we typically have twelve to fourteen people that are helping us pull this bag of seals to shore.

Now the hard part comes. That part's relatively easy, but once you've got this seal in the bag in front of you, especially if it's in mud, it's very difficult to walk in that space, let alone do any kind of work. So, the way we have to do this is you have to open up the top part of the net. Somebody has to go into the net where the seals are all going like this [*gesticulates wildly*] and biting at you, and barking at you—well, screaming at you. And then you have to grab their rear flippers, and pull them partially out of the net. And somebody throws another individual net that we have—we call them 'hoop' nets—that are about eight feet long. They're a cone-shaped net with a rubber around the outside of the ring, so you can have this opening that you flip up in front of the seal. Pull the net over the seal, or, oftentimes we just let go of the flippers and the seal will want to go forward back to the water, and in so doing it gets into this net. Then we twist the hoop net, so the seal is in its own bag, and you pull the next seal out of the big bag net into a hoop net and back up onto shore. Then we grab the next one, and we keep doing that over and over again, until we get all of the seals out of the bag net into their own individual bags.

The hard part, as you might imagine, is going in if there's a whole bunch of seals that are free inside the bag, and you have to be able to grab the net, or grab the flippers and not get bit. And, oftentimes, some of these animals—the big males—are up to 250 pounds, 260 pounds, so you're sort of fighting a linebacker in the bag, which is what it feels like. You oftentimes can't move something when it's stuck, so you now have a seal that's turned and is coming toward you, and you can't move because your feet are in the mud. So, you just fall backwards. You sometimes will throw a bag in front of the charging seal, one of our capture nets in front of it, or somehow try to keep the seal from biting different people, who most of the time do pretty well at not getting bit. But every once in a while somebody gets bit by a seal. It's not a pleasant thing, because seals, the way they catch their food, especially large fish, is they grab their fish and then they shake their head to tear it. They do the same thing with your hand or your arm or anything else. They'll grab you like this [*mimics seal latching on*] and start shaking. Before we go capturing seals, I tell those people who are handling the seals it's sort of not intuitive. If you get bit, *r e l a x*. Because if you hold your arm stiff and they grab it and start shaking, they're just gonna rip through your skin. But if you relax, you'll go with 'em and it'll be less painful with a lot less damage. Which is hard to do. Think about it: "Oh, *relax*! My arm is in the seal's mouth, *relax*, everything will be fine." It's a hard thing to do. But I've trained myself, and a lot of the other people who've done it have also gotten pretty good at, when they do get bit, just r e l a x i n g. At some point the seal will let go of your arm or your hand.

So now you have the seals in their individual bags. Oftentimes, we will transport them to someplace that's got a little more stable ground and go about tagging them there. That involves weighing them and putting a little tag in their flippers that identifies them individually. Often, we will put a radio tag on them, and the way we do that is basically glue it to their hair.

My good friend and colleague, Robin Brown at the Oregon Department of Fish and Wildlife, and I are the ones that pioneered that technique in the world, of gluing tags to seals and sea lions, which is now done everywhere. We were the first ones to do that with seals in Oregon. And it works out really well, because you can glue the tag to the hair. If you do it well and the seal is in good shape, it'll carry that tag for about eight to nine months, maybe a little longer, and then it molts and the hair falls off, and the tag falls off with it. So basically, the seal gets rid of the tag after about a year, and most of our radio tags last about a year. So, it works out really well. The seals don't have to carry this thing around after the tag stops working. Nowadays, the traditional way of doing this, the standard way of tagging elephant seals, sea lions, or whatever, is to glue things onto their hair. We did that early on, learned how to do it, then told the rest of the world how to do it, and everybody else has been doing it since then.

So, yeah, the harbor seal captures are always like a rodeo. There's just lots of things going on. There's lots of yelling, because it's so dynamic. Seals are going after different people, or different things have to be done, and it's rarely a calm event where you're able to sort of just slowly do it. It's like, "oh, get this, grab that line, put your net down!" So, it is fun, in the sense that it's a rodeo. But at the end of the day, hopefully, if it's been successful, you have a bunch of harbor seals that are now tagged and running around. They get over the event probably—in my estimation based on watching them—probably in about an hour and have gone back to totally forgetting what just happened to them.

We've been tagging seals in one location, where we had the seals in one spot and continued to process or tag them there, and the animals we just disturbed are hauled out about 200 yards down the beach from us. It's very common and pretty obvious, I think, that the seals don't quite understand that the disturbance we just created is gonna happen again. They sort of independently think, "Oh, it happened. Some of those guys, those crazy people, you know, disturbed us, and now I'm just gonna go about my way and continue to be a harbor seal." That happens right next door to where we were working. I think the seals get over it really rapidly after we've disturbed them.

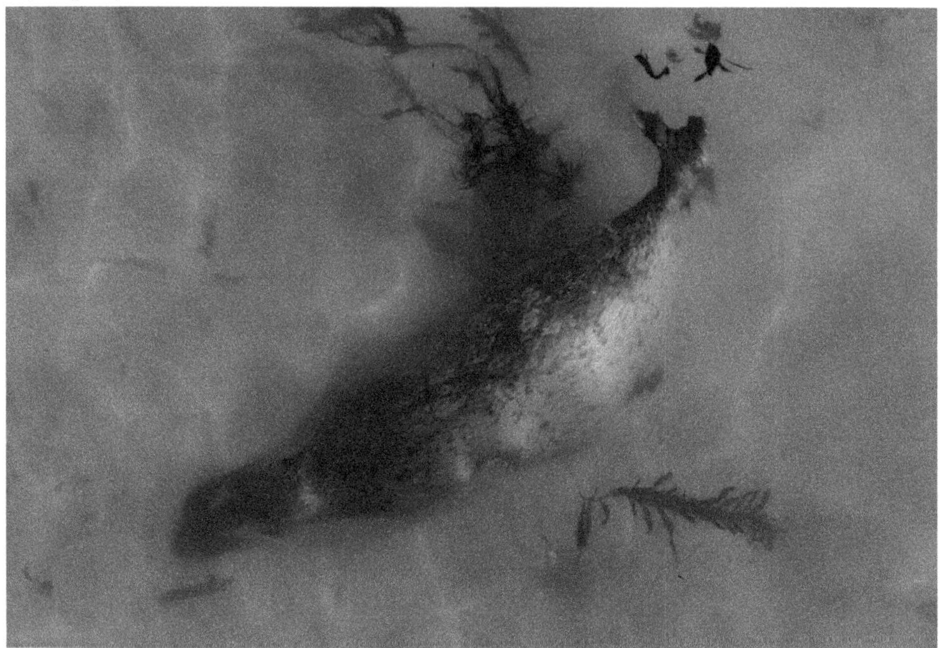

Harbor seal

I think that's pretty much the story. Now, there's lots of little caveats about that, though. Each time we do this, something else bizarre happens. Or we have to improvise how we go about capturing seals. It all depends on the location and what's going on with the seals. We've had one place in Elkhorn Slough where the seals went up this little tributary. So now we had a couple of seals way up this little, narrow tributary—it might have been six feet wide, so we came up with a brilliant idea. Let's just put the net right across the little tributary and then we'll go walk up along the mudflat and scare them down into the net. And that worked.

It ends up being a little bit scary because the seals, once you're moving them down into the net, swim very rapidly so all you see is this wake, where the seal is under water swimming and you can see the wake of this seal coming. And the net's sitting there, and we're all standing there holding the side of the net going, "OK, what's gonna happen?" Then all of a sudden, the seal *hits* the net, and you grab the net and hold on. You've got to do the same thing I mentioned before, where you've got to pull the animal out of the net and make sure you're not getting hurt, and the seal doesn't get hurt at the same time.

It's a technique we've developed over a long period of time, and we've been very successful at catching seals that way. And now we've tried out a variety of other ways of catching seals, some of which use tangle nets, where it's like having a gill net for salmon, but it's for seals, so it's got a bigger mesh and you put it in the water. It has really thin lines so the seals don't quite see the net in the water, and they'll swim into the net, get caught, and then you've gotta pull them up into the boat, take them out of the net and put them into these little hoop nets, as I mentioned before. And then go ahead and process them, weigh them, and put tags on them, that sort of thing. But it all depends. It depends on the seals and what location it is, and how the seals are behaving.

Jim Harvey

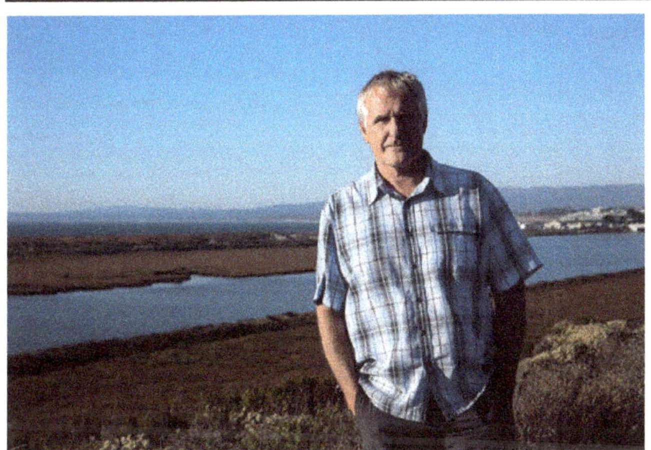

Jim Harvey is a Professor Emeritus and former Director of Moss Landing Marine Laboratories (MLML), which administers the Master of Science degree in Marine Science program for the California state universities in Northern and Central California. Jim joined the faculty in 1989 and taught there for twenty-three years. He then became Chair of the Department for four years, with responsibility for the academic program, before being appointed Director in 2013.

Jim was born in San Diego and lived there for just one year, before his father, who had been getting his master's degree at San Diego State, moved to Berkeley, California to do his PhD in botany. Jim was raised in the Santa Clara Valley, now more well known as Silicon Valley, where he went to San José State for his undergraduate work.

Jim always had an interest in marine biology, but the path to his current career wasn't foreordained. His father taught at San José State University (SJSU) as a botanist, with a strong geology background and extensive knowledge of birds. Jim knew he could never compete with his dad. While out surfing one day Jim had an epiphany: 'marine science'! His dad didn't know anything about marine science.

After getting his bachelor's degree at SJSU, Jim attended MLML, where he completed a master's degree, studying the feeding, reproduction and aging of blue sharks. He got his PhD from Oregon State University, completing his doctoral thesis on harbor seals. Jim continued his studies, spending two years at the NOAA facility in Seattle, Washington as a postdoc student.

During those two years, he was considered a jack-of-all-trades, as he already had tagging experience, aerial survey experience and animal handling experience. When gray whales got caught in ice and NOAA wanted to tag them, they sent Jim. When the *Exxon Valdez* spill occurred in Prince William Sound, Alaska, they sent Jim to do aerial surveys for oil and its impact on wildlife. He recollects that they sent him to every natural and man-made disaster in Alaska for those two years.

Just as Jim finished his postdoc, a position opened up at MLML, then a small, dynamic marine lab. This was exactly the kind of job he had hoped for, and he'd geared his work experience toward the skills he'd need, purposely taking jobs and training that would enable him to get the kind of position he wanted. Little did he know that even his 'natural disaster' experiences would come in handy.

Jim became a professor at San José State in 1989, stationed at MLML. He arrived two months before the 1989 6.9-magnitude Loma Prieta earthquake destroyed the lab. He was in the lab at the time, as the foundation moved three feet toward the ocean. The whole lab didn't fall down, but ended up severely tilted. He recalls it was pretty exciting. A geological oceanographer was helping teach the class, and the two of them had just finished and walked out the classroom door as the quake started. Jim yelled back into the room to get the students out, and they were already running as he yelled '*Earth.......!*'

Jim and his colleague ran into the atrium as students tried to run out the main door. A two-story seawater tank outside was swaying from side to side with about five feet of water sloshing out the top. Students were going to run right beneath it, and Jim yelled, "NO, NO, come back!" So they all stood there trying to keep their feet under them. Cracks were forming in the ground at least a foot wide and three feet deep. According to Jim, you were just kind of dancing around trying to stay upright. The shaking only lasted fourteen seconds, but it seemed like two minutes. Built on sand, the whole area liquefied, causing great damage to the structures. The building was red-tagged and about to be knocked down with everything in it, including master's theses.

Jim and others convinced the county to put in structural supports, and for two days, staff and students passed stuff out the door through a human chain. Everything was stored in Salinas. And for the next ten years, classes were held in trailers in Salinas, some twenty miles from Monterey Bay.

Spooky Dives at Año Nuevo

John Pearse

(*Date of Interview*: 1/16/17)

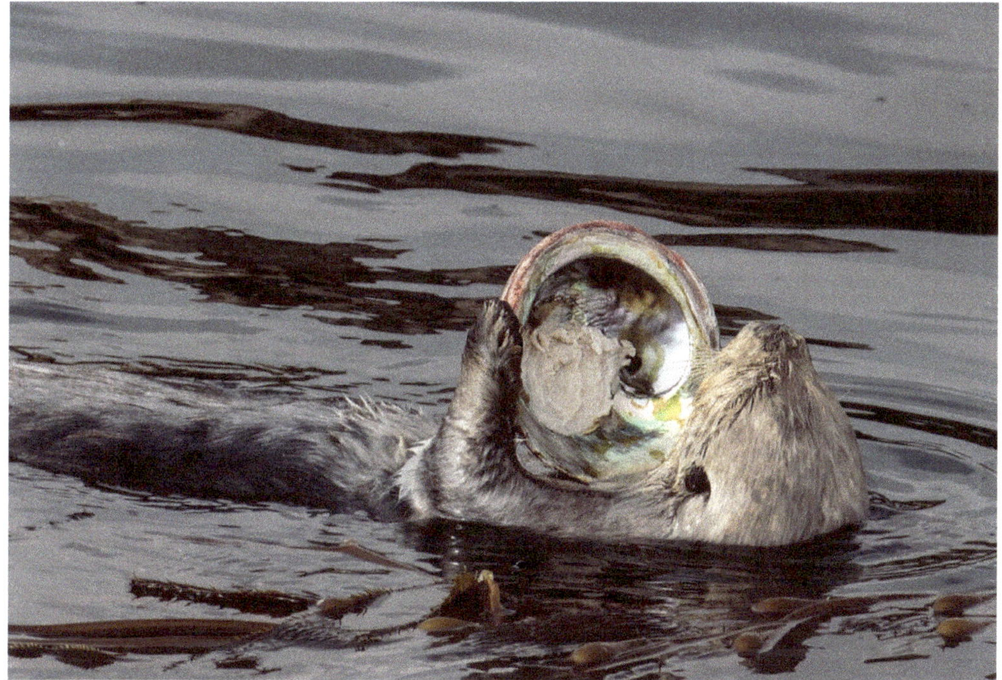

Otter feeding on abalone

I'll start talking about a really hairy diving story I have, stupid actually for me. This was in the 1970s, and we were working on sea otters. Sea otters had just come back to establish themselves, and they were just moving their way up to the Santa Cruz coast. We were trying to establish what they really do to sea urchins and abalones, and we wanted to find a place where otters and abalones had not been collected very much. We started working in Santa Cruz, and right up the coast from Santa Cruz there's Lighthouse Point. At that time, the kelp forest was very narrow right along the coast, and on the outside it was covered with sea urchins. We anticipated otters coming up and taking out the urchins, so we did a transect there. But we were talking to people, and they said, "Oh, you should have been here ten years ago. There were abalones all over. That was mainly abalones there. People were collecting them, and they collected them all out. That's why you don't see abalones anymore."

We wanted to find a place where there were abalones, and they were at Año Nuevo[32]. I got two of my graduate students—three of us—and we went up to Año Nuevo, all ready to go diving. By that time, there were also quite a few elephant seals there, plus harbor seals and Steller

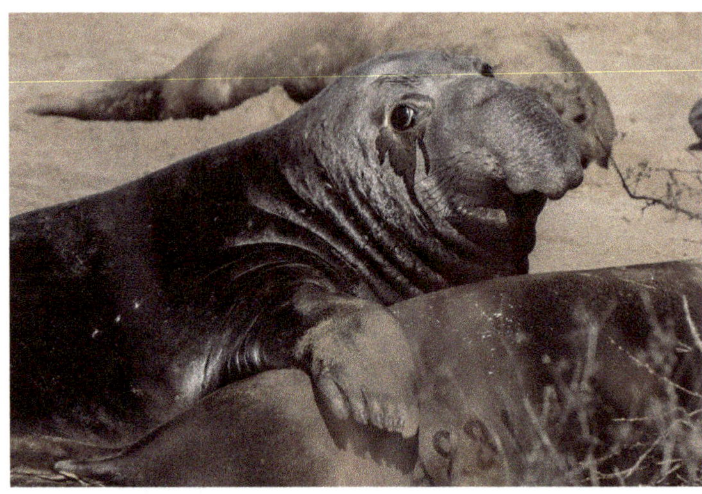

Northern elephant seals

sea lions. They were all on the island. It was also known that there were a lot of sharks there, but we were going diving. We didn't have to worry about sharks. So, we went in. We went in to some underwater channels. It was really interesting diving. It was very 'surgey.' The visibility was maybe three feet at the most, two or three feet, so you couldn't see very much. And we kind of slid down, almost held hands as we went down.

Then we ran into a seal without a head. That made us just a little bit nervous. But we were able to actually go down, and we dove down repeatedly. We found that the bottom was just coated with abalones. Everywhere. And the urchins were all along the sides of the channel. It was really just quite spectacular. So we collected a bunch of abalones. We measured them. We put them all back. And by the third dive, one of my students, Val Gerard, who was a very strong-minded woman, said, *"I'M THROUGH WITH THIS PLACE!! I'M NEVER COMING BACK HERE!!"* She was really off with that. But it *was* one of the scariest places, when we started to think about it, and it was just nuts to do what we did there.

But I didn't learn, and I had another student who really wanted to go and see this system, so I took her out; just the two of us went out. We went down one of the channels and got down about twenty feet. There was a lot of kelp slopping back and forth, and as we're wending through the kelp, I put a hand down there and there was a dead sea lion—buried and all, and it didn't have a head. We were out quite a ways by that time. And we were staying really close to the bottom. I didn't want to get up on the surface, where we were more likely to run into a shark. But that dead sea lion set us off. And we didn't realize how much it had set us off

---

[32] Año Nuevo is a well-known haul-out breeding and pupping site for Northern elephant seals about 25 miles north of Santa Cruz.

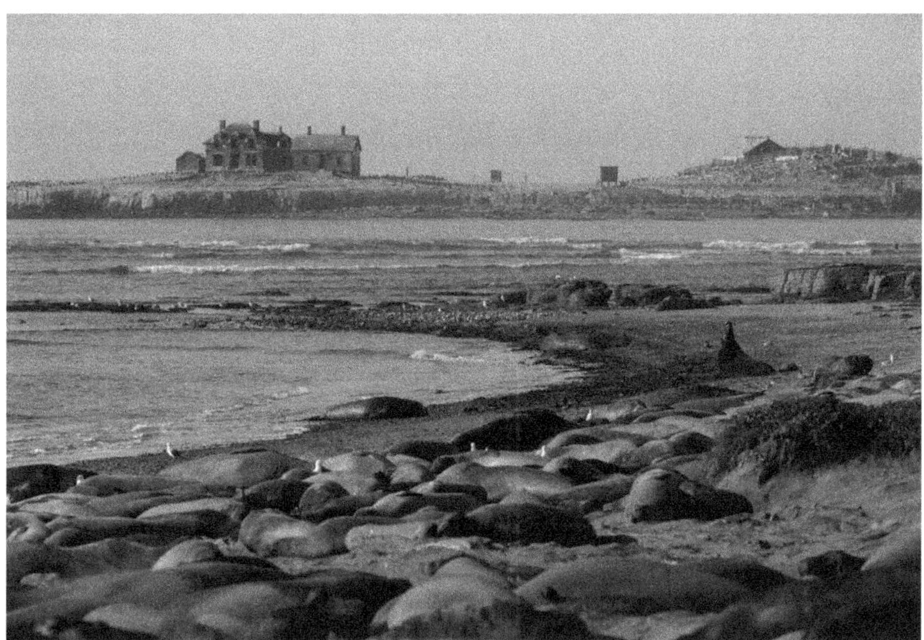

Año Nuevo Island in the distance

until we got quite a ways out and were breathing pretty heavily, and suddenly we were out of air! We had no choice but to come to the surface. That was really a spooky thing. We hit the surface, and the island was *way* off. You know, we didn't realize how far out we were, and we had to swim back on the surface where the sharks were.

We came in, and we could either go all the way around the island to a beach where we could get out, or there were some rocks right there with some Steller sea lions on them. The surge was pretty high, so we came up to the edge of that rock and waited for the surge. The sea was going back and forth, back and forth. And my student was right behind me. "I'll go first and you can come right behind me." And the surge came up high, and I just jumped and got up on the rock. I didn't think that as soon as I hit that rock, all those Steller sea lions were off that rock, diving right down on top of her. [*laughter*]

Anyway, she finally got out. But it was a memorable dive, which we never did again even though I would have liked to. We used the data for a paper we did. That was one place that had lots of big abalones we could compare with Hopkins[33], where the abalones were all small, hiding in cracks and crevices. I've often thought we should go back and see what it's like now, but I don't think it's responsible. That was when I was skilled, young and stupid, not that I've gotten that much smarter. I really shouldn't have taken students out there at all. [See John's bio after the following story.]

---

[33] Stanford's Hopkins Marine Station in Pacific Grove, California.

The Sponge That Might Have Been Us

John Pearse

(Date of Interview: 1/16/17)

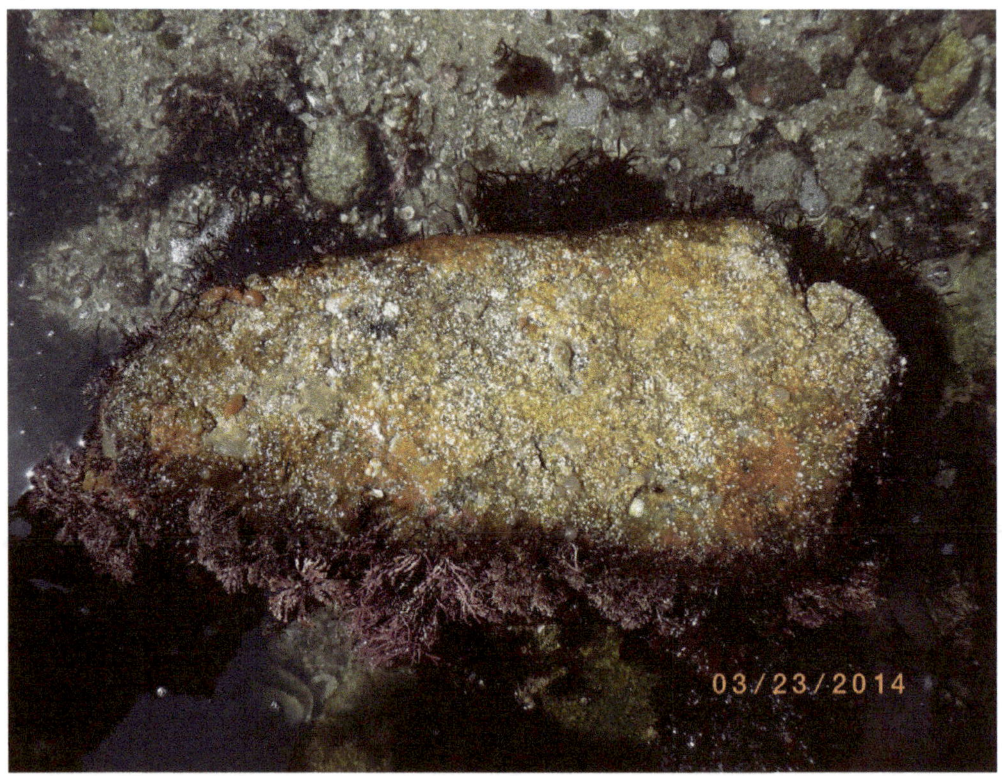

Sponge named Oscarella   © John Pearse

The other story that I really wanted to talk about a bit as a scientist, that maybe people would appreciate, is that I had a lab in Santa Cruz where I did a lot of experiments. We had running seawater in the lab, and we started to get a brown scuz growing on the glass. I scraped some of it off and looked at it under a microscope, and I realized it was a sponge. But it was a sponge that had no spicules. Most sponges have lots of either calcareous or glass spicules that hold them up. This one had no spicules at all. It didn't even have the fibers that make up a spongy sponge. It was just tissue. It's called a slime sponge. It's just a slime that's on the rocks. I'd never seen anything like it.

I thought I knew that there was supposed to be a sponge here that didn't have a skeleton, and I'd never seen it, and I thought it must be that. I was spending a little bit of time looking at it. It was fascinating! I could look with the microscope right through it and see the feeding chambers inside and the embryos it had. So, I thought this would be a fantastic animal to look at in a Petri culture. But nobody's ever been able to culture it. However, we had a graduate student who was really good with sponges, and she was from Venezuela. She came in the lab, and I said, "Christina, what do you think this is?" And she said, "Oh, I don't know, I'll take it back with me. I can't tell. I'll have to look at it with a scanning electron microscope." And she came back and said, "John, that's *Oscarella*, a genus that is known only in the Mediterranean and in Europe. It's not found here." Oh, my goodness. How did it get here? It's a slime.

Then I was up at the aquarium[34], and I saw it there, in the aquarium. Maybe the aquarium brought it here, for some kind of thing. They have animals from the Mediterranean, and it GOT OUT! Got somehow into my lab. I couldn't figure out how it could get into my lab. I talked to people at the aquarium, and they said, "Oh yeah, it's terrible! It grows up sometimes in the spring, and you have to scrape it off quickly. What is that?"

Well, I was worried a little bit about it. After I retired, I used to take my students to Carmel Point, all along here actually, but Carmel Point was one of my favorite places. At Carmel Point there's a little red flatworm that is described as endemic to the Monterey Peninsula. It used to be everywhere. You'd go out and there'd be a green sea lettuce, alga, there, and there'd be red spots on it. And that's another one of those things you remember from the past, and it's not here now.

I used to take my students out, and I'd stop and say, "Look at these little flatworms. These are the simplest flatworms, simplest animals," and I'd go on about them, and the students would look at me and go, "What's he talking about?" To me they're really fascinating, really interesting bilateral animals. They don't have a gut. They just have a kind of incision, and they're predatory. They jump on lower crustaceans and enclose them. It's a terrible way to go. You can see the thing inside trying to get out, and it's engulfed. But the flatworms almost disappeared. After I retired, I thought, I'm gonna have time to really look for them, see what happened to them. They were so abundant here, but they've all but disappeared now, and I can hardly find them.

As I was out looking for the flatworms, I found this sponge. And that's when I thought, "Oh my goodness, the damn thing's out." It's gonna take over the coast. We need to find out what this is! I wrote to Christina who had gone back to Venezuela by then, and said, "Can you help me? We need to find out what this is!"

---

[34] Monterey Bay Aquarium.

And she said there's one person in the world who knows anything about this and he's Brazilian, and he did his PhD in France.

So, I contacted him, and he said, "Yes, if you'll fix them for a transmission electron microscope, that's the only way we can tell them apart. They have no characters." Well, I did, and he found some characters that he said he'd never seen before. It's a different species. So, we described it. It was the first species of that whole group of animals found in the Pacific. About the same time another species was discovered, which is found in Vladivostok, in Siberia. At any rate, there it was. It turns out this sponge is really fascinating, I think, because it's a sponge that doesn't have any characters like typical sponges. But it does have some characters that other sponges don't have, that we humans have, in its cells, the tissue most animals have as kind of a basement membrane underneath the epithelium. Sponges don't have those—*but this one does!* So, its sperm is more like the sperm of other animals than that of most sponges. This one looks like it could almost be a sponge that was us five hundred million years ago, although it turns out it's probably not.

Since we described it, here's another interesting thing we've learned. There's a student at UC Berkeley who was very interested in sponges. I met him at a conference, and he gave an organizer's symposium on sponges. I went up to him and said, "Scott (his name was Scott Nichols), have you looked at *Oscarella?*" He says, "NO, NO, *I can't get any!* Those French! You know those French, they have all that *Oscarella*, but they won't send me any. They are so secretive and oh...." "Well, come to my lab!"

So, he came down to my lab. Did some nice studies. We published all of them about the characteristics, because he looked at them as somewhat of a transition between spongelike organization, and the rest of us. He did molecular stuff on them, too, and found that they are certainly a different species. In fact, there are two species now on a molecular basis. He hasn't named the second one yet, but they now have their own genome. If you're in biology and you have these relationships with genomes—with different groups of sponges—now there is this species, which was only described in 2004. So that to me was very exciting. It's a very different kind of story than diving for abalones at Año Nuevo, but it's my story.

JOHN PEARSE

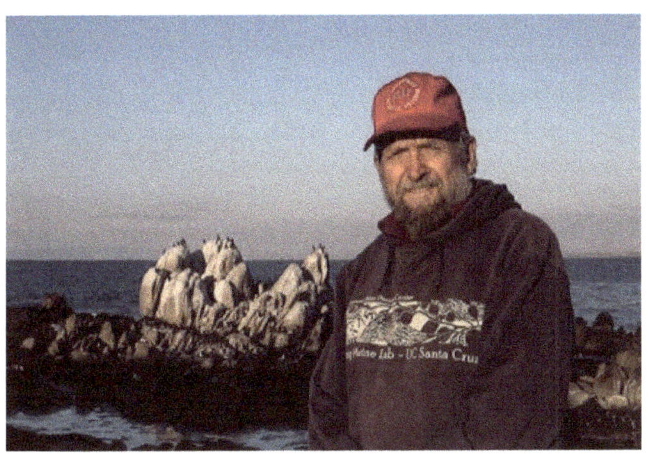

The late John Pearse was Professor Emeritus in Biology at the University of California at Santa Cruz (UCSC). He was also Research Professor in the Physical and Biological Sciences—Ecology and Evolutionary Biology Department of the Institute of Marine Sciences. John passed away in July 2020.

John taught at UCSC for twenty-two years before retiring. Though retired, he continued to stay active in the field of marine biology.

He was born in Boise, Idaho, where his father was stationed as an experimental agronomist with the United States Forest Service. John's family moved from there to Utah, where they stayed for five years. Their next move was to Washington, DC, where his father was stationed for another five years. During that period, John spent a lot of time at the Washington Museum, the Botanical Gardens, and out and about in the field. He would note with a smile that he was a naturalist from the very beginning.

The family's next move was to Tucson, Arizona, where John spent his formative years. During that period, he worked at the Arizona-Sonora Desert Museum. As a high school kid, John was hired to build the trails and take care of the animals before the museum opened. He always thought he was going to be a desert biologist.

But after their time in Tucson, his father worked for the U.S. State Department with his first assignment in Egypt. John attended the American University in Cairo for a year in 1954–55. During this period, John spent time at sea, and his father had a station on the coast of the Mediterranean, where John spent a good part of the summer snorkeling and discovering marine biology.

However, the American University did not offer courses in biology. John's father came from Chicago and had gotten his master's degree from the University of Chicago, but left Chicago as soon as he could. He hoped that because he was an alumnus of the University of Chicago, John might be able to get a fellowship, and he could stay with his uncle, who lived there. John followed in his father's footsteps, attending the University of Chicago for his last three years of undergraduate work, where he got his bachelor's degree.

Even though most of the students at the school were in premed—only three graduated in zoology—the university wanted John to stay for graduate work. But he wanted to go into marine biology.

John applied to several schools and ended up at Stanford University, where he was able to take classes at Stanford's Hopkins Marine Station in Pacific Grove, California. He took a seminar in reproduction of marine invertebrates. Fascinated by the questions surrounding invertebrate reproduction, where temperature rules the timing of reproduction, John took the opportunity to study in Antarctica, where Stanford had a contract. John did his thesis there on the reproductive cycles of sea stars and he's worked with echinoderms ever since.

His academic career took many turns following the travels of his early years. He taught at the American University in Cairo for two years, working on reproductive cycles of animals in the Red Sea. The Six-Day War sent him packing. He considers that to have been one of the luckiest things to ever have happened to him.

John's first wife was from Southern California, so they went to live there, but the American University paid him for a year as they wanted him back as soon as it was safe. John had a friend at the California Institute of Technology lab, and was invited to work there for the year. Things still weren't settled in the Middle East at the end of that year, and John was offered a position by another friend to work on sea urchins.

The next turn came when he got an offer from Todd Newberry (they were grad students together), who was teaching invertebrate biology at UCSC. Newberry wanted a break and asked John to teach his class. Richard Peterson, one of the other founding faculty members in biology at UCSC, had started to work out at Año Nuevo, as a behavioral pinniped biologist. Following Peterson's death, John got his position. He taught at UCSC for twenty-two years.

Seals on (and off) the Beach

Joy Reidenberg

(Date of Interview: 10/27/17)

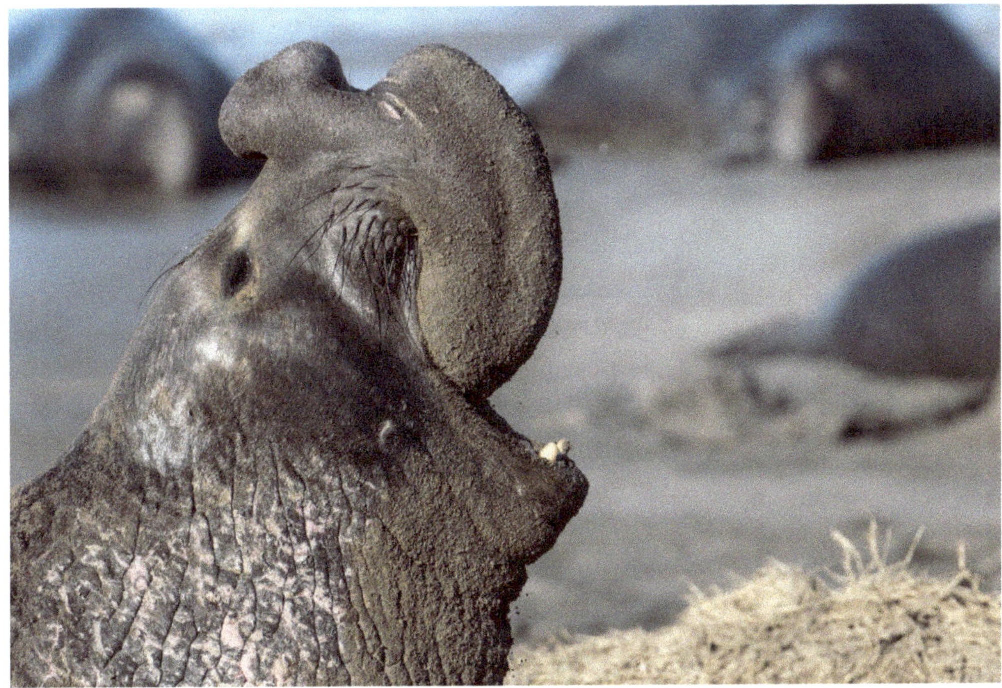

Roaring bull elephant seal

My first trip to Monterey Bay was in 1989, I'm pretty sure, because I was there for the very first time I attended a Marine Mammal Conference. The conference was in Pacific Grove, but I made time to see Monterey Bay at some point. I remember that pretty well because I was also pregnant at the time. And I was in the beginning of my eighth month so it was the last time I could fly. I had to get special permission to fly to the conference. I was very excited about it.

I was not a student. I didn't know about the Society (Society for Marine Mammalogy) when I was a student, so I came to my first marine mammal conference as a faculty member. Being pregnant did not stop me from investigating all the marine life I could. I was so stunned… First of all, I looked west and the sunsets were beautiful! I'm looking out over the Pacific Ocean and I can see the sun setting into the Pacific Ocean! In New York when I look west at a sunset, you know what

I see? I see New Jersey. [*laughter*] I see oil refineries and ships that are docked there. It's not a very pretty sight to look west and see New Jersey for your sunset.

I was living in New Jersey then, so when I got out to California, I said "WOW! You have beautiful sunsets here. I just can't tear myself away from the coast and looking at the sunset." And then I looked down and what I saw were seals—on the rocks, like really close! I had never seen a seal. I knew they existed. But in New York, you know, we don't have any shoreline that isn't hardened at this point all around Manhattan and New York. Seals don't come up and beach themselves, because there's no beach. And if you go to the beach, it's like Jones Beach. It's like, you know, 3 million people on the beach, so no seal's gonna come up there.

So I'd never seen a seal—alive. I've seen dead ones. I do a lot of work in anatomy, so I see a lot of dead animals. Well, I saw these seals, and pregnant me, I didn't care, I climbed over the fence, I went down on the rocks.[35] I got really close—this was before the age of digital cameras. I only had my little, you know, regular camera, and I didn't have a zoom lens because all of my research work was on dead animals. They didn't move. I could get really close to them, so I didn't need a long lens.

I'm not knowing if I can get a picture of these seals because I don't have a telephoto lens. I got closer and closer and they didn't move! They just stayed there; they didn't seem to care! I stayed far enough away that they couldn't bite me or anything, but I was just stunned that I could see them so well. And then the sea lions came in, and, "Oh, my God, *there's sea lions now, too!*" I didn't realize how different males and females were. That was the first time it really struck me that males are called sea lions because they have this giant mane around their head! You know, it's not really long fur like lions have, but there is this giant *thing*—then one opened its mouth and *belched*. Ok, that was their roar! It's *like* a lion's roar, but it's this BIG *belch*. Ok, now I get why they call them sea l i o n s. So that was my introduction.

Then I drove from Pacific Grove a short distance to Monterey, and saw the Monterey Bay Aquarium. Now, the animals there are cute—they have the sea otters, which are adorable—everybody falls in love with the sea otters. But the thing that grabbed me the most at the aquarium was having this display of jellyfish, of all things. They were the most *beautiful* things I'd ever seen. Before that, I hated jellyfish. They were nasty things that sting you. You never want to see one when

---

[35] A word of caution: it's very important NOT to climb over the fence in Pacific Grove when seals are on the beach. These are pupping areas, and people disturbing the pregnant seals or moms with pups can lead to separation and death of the pups.

you go in the ocean. But they had them in this really cool display with beautiful blue backgrounds and soft music was playing. They put a little bit of a current in the tank, and it made them swirl around. And they had this great lighting on them—ultraviolet light—and they were glowing. They were the most beautiful things. They looked like flowers floating around in circles. I was mesmerized and they couldn't get me out of the aquarium. It was closing, and I was still there looking at these tanks.

So that was my introduction to that area. Of course, I had to come back. So I made liaisons with friends who were working in Santa Cruz, which is directly across Monterey Bay from Pacific Grove and Monterey, and said, "I want to do some anatomy out here." I was invited back, and we got to work on elephant seals.

Now elephant seals are pretty cool animals. Most people think they are mad ugly, but I think they are really, really interesting. Especially the males, when they open their mouth and they start to, you know, make these giant bellowing noises that are sort of *bbbbbbbb* [*hand over mouth, patting lips while blubbering, imitating a male elephant seal's vocalization*]. What's going on with these things? And I thought it was coming out of their nose! They have this giant, elephant-like nose. But I came to realize that the nose was simply blocking the mouth like this [*Joy places her hand over her mouth again, patting it while vocalizing like an elephant seal*], and it was blocking the mouth that was making these punctuated sounds. I thought that was really, really cool.

I wanted to get a good, really close-up view of them, so I went out with some of the people who work in the area. Guy Oliver took me out on an expedition along the beach. I did not realize that with the right blue jacket and the right permissions, you could actually walk right up next to these things. I was terrified at first, because, you know, each one is like the size of a truck. They're HUGE, really, really, really big! An adult male can weigh as much as 4500 pounds! But mostly they're very lazy, so unless you piss them off [for instance, if they feel their harem is threatened], they're not going to, like, hurt you. [They can move exceptionally fast, though, so it's best to keep quite a distance.] But I really had to avoid the business end. I'd walk around the tail and that was fine, and we'd look at the tags, and if the tags weren't facing the right way, Guy would reach down and yank on the flipper so we could get the tag visible, and then they would turn around and say, "OK, I'm outta here!" and I would back *way* off. But I would watch this whole scene as he was doing, like a bullfighter, this dance with these elephant seals, just so he could see the tag, so he could get a picture of the tag so he could see what number it was. I was stunned that I could be so close to them.

Then we went over to see some of the females. They were adorable. They'd just lie there relaxing like they're in a spa. And Guy said, "You can get really close to them if you lie down." And I said, "Really?" So I lay down like I was a seal. I was able to snug up pretty close to them. "This can't be legal, what I'm doing." "Well, you're under a research permit, so it's ok. You're here to get pictures of them and you need to get close," so that's what I did. And I got a lot of really great pictures of them. But somehow in the snuggling down in the sand, I lost my big, giant, purple hat. So someday you're going to see an elephant seal out there wearing my big, purple hat, because it was cold that day. I never found it. I'm sure it's sitting on top of some elephant seal's head out there.

Then we got into some elephant seal research. And that meant recovering a specimen. Now these are *big, big* animals. It's really hard to recover a specimen from them. What I remember is that I got a call from Sara Kienle; she had gone out to recover this elephant seal that had died. But it's really big. She says, "I can't bring the whole thing back, so where should I cut it?" So I'm giving her directions over the phone, and she's trying to cut the head off so we can get the specimen we need. And she ended up putting it on, like, a kid's snowboard/sleigh thing. You know, like those sled things you go down the hill with, and you hold onto the sides. Looks like a little plastic toboggan. She put it on something like that, and they were dragging the specimen across the beach. Which at this point was primarily a fifth of the whole animal, but it was still humongous.

And then she said, "I've got it in the freezer. Now you have to fly over and see it." So, of course I did, and I wrangled a few other people to come and help me. Jodi, for example, was there taking pictures. We had a wonderful experience. We got to dissect all of the muscles of this area [the head], really understand how these animals are put together and how they are able to move their mouth and bite things and make sounds. We were looking at the larynx, which is the voice box, and how they make sounds.

My other experience in Monterey Bay happened when I was there for some filming. We were doing work for PBS on a series called *Big Blue Live*. Just before the series started filming, I had an opportunity to go out to sea. I went out on Fast Raft's boat *Ranger*[36]. Kate Spencer is a friend of mine. She took me out. And I got to see a whole bunch of firsts—for me they were firsts. It was the first time I'd ever seen a blue whale. It was the first time I'd ever seen Dall's porpoises. It was the first time I'd ever seen killer whales! It wasn't the first time I'd seen a great white shark, but we did see a great white shark. It was the first time I'd seen an ocean sunfish, *Mola mola*. And I don't remember what else we saw at this point, because my head is boggled up with it all. But we did get some pretty good views of humpback whales, which are really, really cool animals. [See Joy's bio on p. 100.]

---

[36] Fast Raft Ocean Safaris, owned and operated by Kate Spencer.

Welcomed by a Frisky Harbor Seal

Brandy Gale

(Date of Interview: 12/11/16)

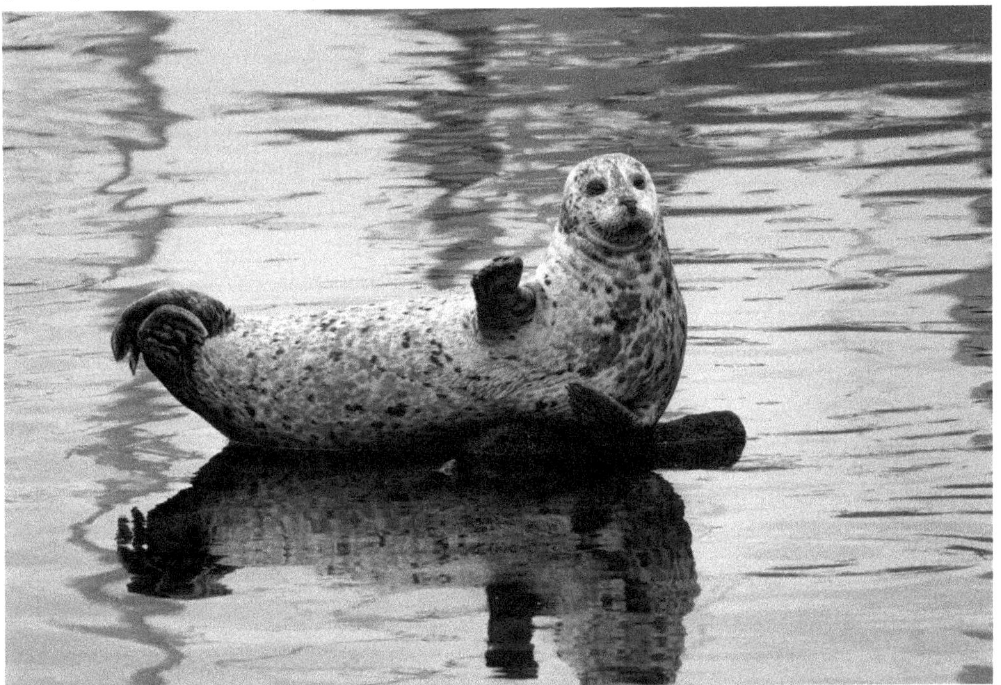

Harbor seal

I was always terrified of water. I had a *really* bad childhood experience in the water, so I just never went in again and never went swimming. I'd go to a pool party, and I'd not go in the pool. I went to Barbados several times and didn't go in the water. You know, I made paintings from the shore, did photography, and enjoyed all of it, but water, no, that didn't happen.

But then, many, many years later, I moved here to the Monterey Bay area. I'm looking at the ocean thinking I've got to get over this! And so I went back to Canada, and found an instructor who teaches adults who are terrified of swimming, to swim! And she had me take baby steps. You know, put your feet in, and I'm *bbbllllahh*, gonna be sick, but anyway, eventually she got me in the water, and I learned to swim. And in 2013 I put my head in the water for the first time since I was a kid, and it was like—I came up, and thought, "I can do this!"

When I came back to Monterey Bay, I went snorkeling. And it was really great! I wasn't afraid, in fact, I was really comfortable. My partner even said, "Wow, you're doing really well." I also had a good snorkeling experience in Hawaii that involved dolphins, but that's another story. Next thing I know, my partner said, "Why don't we teach you—get you lessons at least—to try scuba diving?" I'm like, "Well, ok." And we're talking about someone who would throw up if she went into the kiddie pool. I'd have an actual panic attack. But I went ahead, and I took an introductory course in scuba diving. I sat on the bottom of the ocean, and just loved it. I was so calm and it was terrific! Then I went and got certified. And during my certification in Monterey Bay, I'm trying to do the little lifesaving test they make you do, down at the bottom and, you know, switch your regulator and do buddy breathing and all that. And there's this *wonderful* harbor seal who wants to play with my flippers, my bright yellow fins. I got to do all of these exercises with this *wonderful, frisky* harbor seal. And I passed the test, thank goodness. I had a wonderful teacher, Dave Babineau, over at Pro Scuba Dive Center. That harbor seal just made me feel so welcome. It was like I was being welcomed to the ocean after all these years. And the harbor seal encouraged me to go back out with my camera and start exploring the Monterey Bay area. [See Brandy's bio after the following story.]

Tasting Tide Pools

Brandy Gale

(*Date of Interview*: 12/11/16)

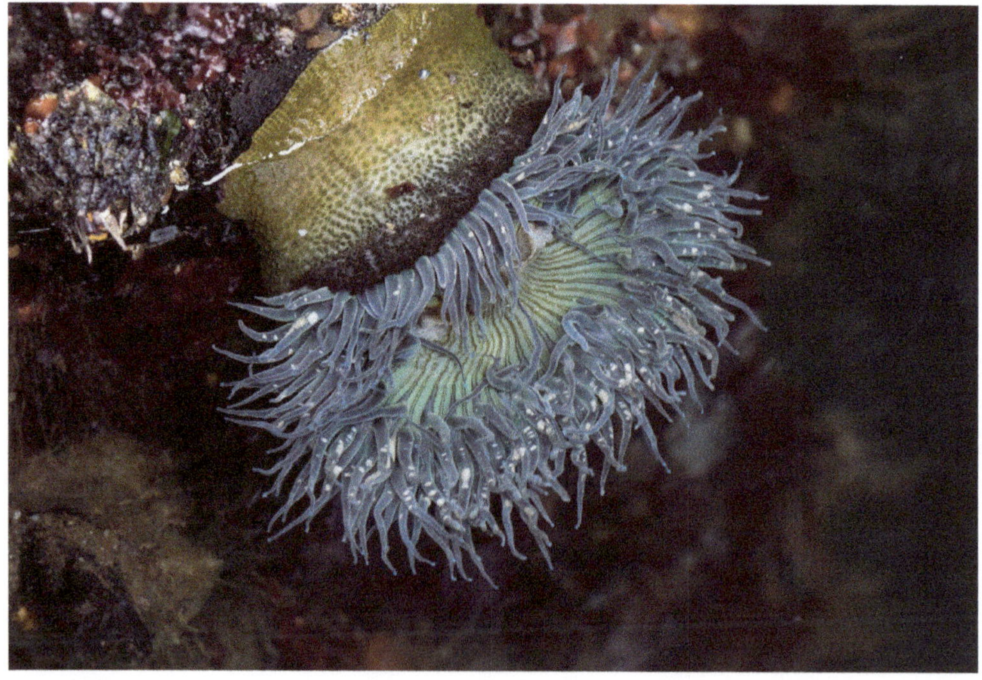

Sea anemone

I started exploring along the shore and the tide pools and found that my real passion was shooting these little invertebrates, tiny little nudibranchs, or sea slugs. They have the wildest colors and some of them swim like this way and that, very fluidly. They move in the water so beautifully and are all different colors.

And sea anemones! All these wild sea anemones! I'd never seen a sea anemone before. They're so exotic and almost erotic! I love shooting them. They have *amazing* colors! I don't really know for sure why, but maybe their colors come from what they eat, like different kelp or various fish or other critters.

As a synesthete, I experience the critters through all my senses. I find they do have personalities. They do have tastes. They have textures. To me, each anemone has a different taste! Some have no taste at all! (I don't actually eat them!) I do find that watching them when they're eating is really fascinating, particularly

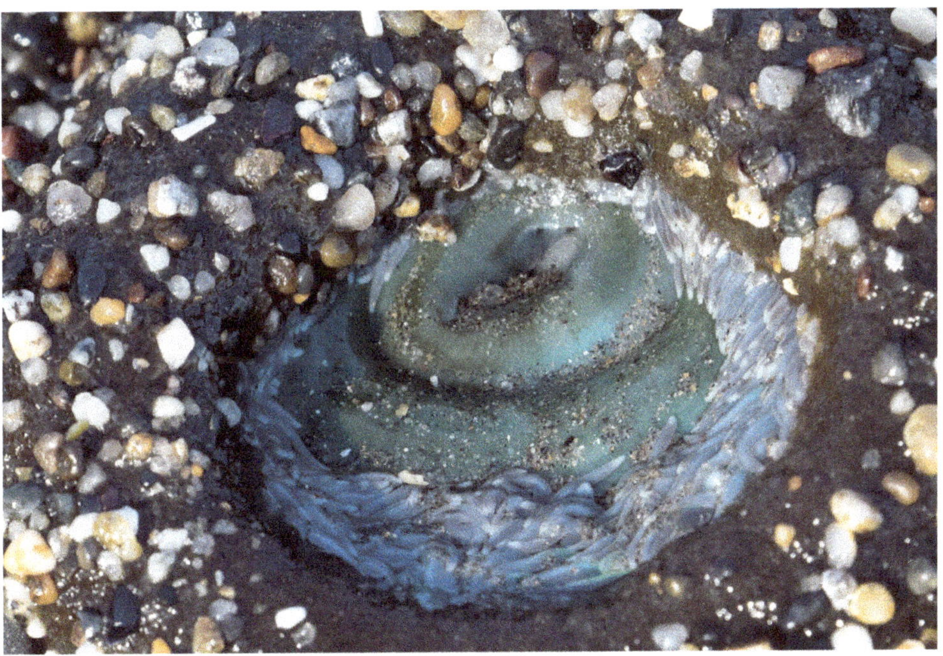

Sea anemone encrusted with pebbles

the things they spit out. They have the detritus from their meals all around them and on their bodies, like beautiful décor. They are almost jewel encrusted, because of the bits of shell and so on left over from their meals. I find this fascinating.

I do have my favorite sea anemones, and I like to go back and photograph them over and over. Some of them, I've been told, are really old and have been there forever and ever. That's so cool! So, I'm very interested in sharing time with them, exploring them some more and getting to know them as individuals.

BRANDY GALE

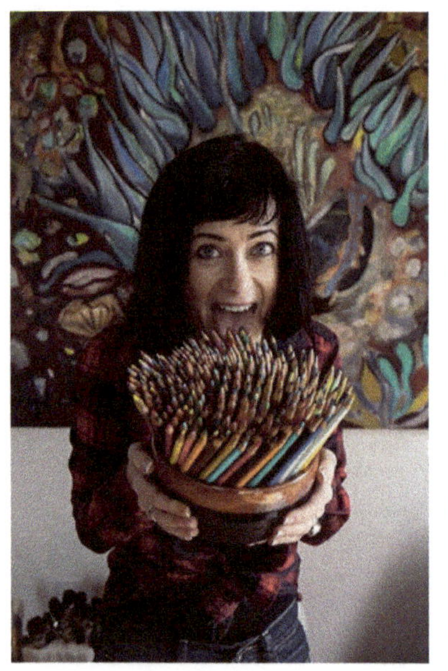

Brandy Gale is a *plein air* landscape painter and photographer. After having painted in a studio for years, in 2001 she was encouraged to get outside by her mentor, J. Bardini. Brandy fell in love with painting in nature with all its challenging distractions. She also enjoys working outdoors because of her full-spectrum synesthesia, which means that all five of her senses are crossed.

Because of her synesthesia, Brandy tastes colors when she hears sound, or she might feel a texture from a visual experience. So when she's outside painting from life instead of a photo, she may smell what she sees, then another sense is triggered, then another, and she puts all of that into the painting. If the mountain seems really red, she paints it red. The synesthesia informs her painting a great deal, and informs her photography as well. As she says, if she has a synesthetic response to the subject, she takes the photo and it makes all the difference! Most of her paintings are done along the intertidal areas of Fiji, Hawaii and California, and she is currently focusing her underwater photographic images on tide pool critters of Monterey Bay.

Brandy grew up "all over the planet, all over the place." As a military brat, she was born in Marville, France, but grew up in Belgium, Germany, the United States and Canada, as well as France. She attended five high schools, including one in Livermore, Kansas.

Brandy was born with synesthesia. It's the only world she's ever known, but the first week of school, the teachers called her parents and said there's something really weird about your kid.

Brandy laughs and says she has zero marine background! It's a new playground for her. The website OKCupid.com brought her to California. While she had been here previously on a couple of art-related visits, it wasn't until getting picked up at the airport (just after OKCupid.com) and driving down along the coast, that she found herself weeping with the beauty and couldn't believe how gorgeous it all was.

Brandy had lived in Canada off and on most of her life and had been settled on a charming island in Lake Ontario, Canada, called Quinte Island, in Prince Edward County. She was very happy there, but lonesome, hence OKCupid.com. She now lives happily in Bonny Doon, California with her partner, and a spectacular view of Monterey Bay and the Pacific Ocean.

Magical Lights

John Mayer

(*Date of Interview*: 8/4/16)

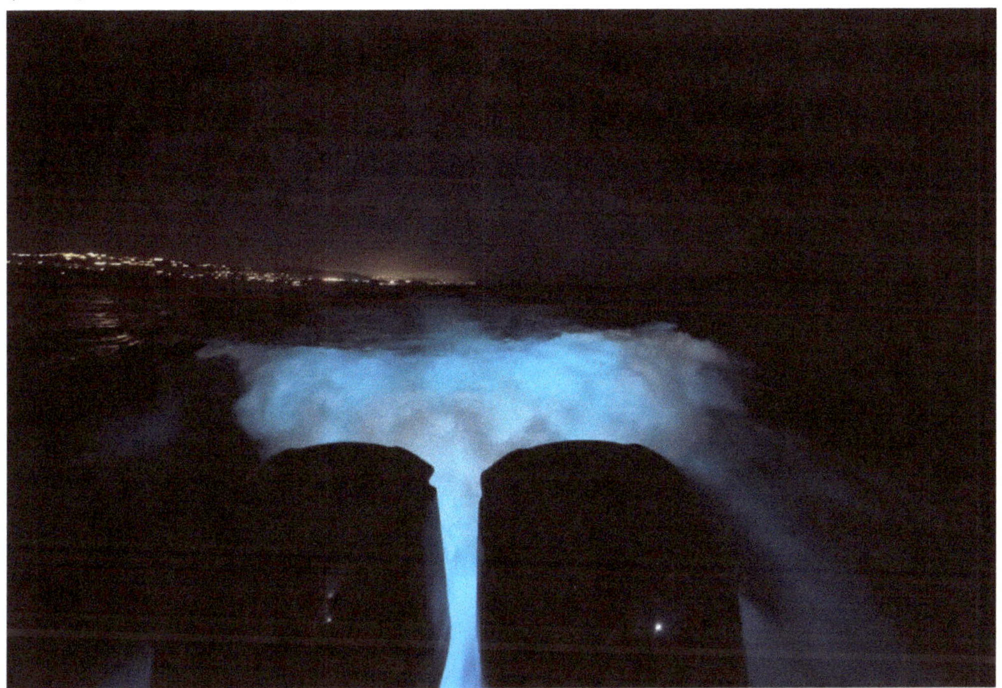

Bioluminescence   © Mark Girardeau

There've been so many memorable wildlife encounters, but I'd say out of all of them one stands out as truly magical. I haven't seen it again like that, so I'm gonna have to say that it was probably the most incredible and interesting experience I've ever had. Forgive me, but I don't think I have the facts down very well, because I can't remember for sure what year it was. But I do believe it was during the 1997–98 El Niño. We were fishing albacore. They were close enough that we were fishing on the *Randy I*, which is an old wood plank boat that we used to operate out of Randy's Fishing Trips. We were leaving that morning, very early, and heading offshore for albacore. The skipper, I believe, was Raul. Anyway, we were heading offshore by Cannery Row. It was just a beautiful, dark night. I don't remember if there was much of a moon. It was superdark, but the lights from Cannery Row were reflecting really beautifully off the water. It was very placid.

We were heading out and I went to use the restroom. This little boat had no lights in the bathroom. So, when I went in there, well, you just had to shoot by Braille, you know? So I'm in there doing my thing. As I'm looking in the toilet, I see little specs of light going through the water. I'd never seen this before. Now I know what I was looking at, but then I had no idea what I was looking at. I'm seeing lights in the toilet, and I'm thinking, "I have to have hit my head." In my head something's going on, and I'm thinking this isn't right. I'm in there trying to finish up doing what I'm doing, and I'm looking at the lights in the toilet. The reason why—I'm gonna back up a little bit—is we used to circulate seawater through the toilets, and I never really put that together at the time. But anyway, I'm seeing lights going through the toilet and I'm starting to get kind of wigged out, and I open the door and say, "Hey Skip, we've got a problem here. Either I'm losing it or there's something seriously wrong with this boat. We got light going through the toilet water and it's really freaky."

He doesn't even look down at me. He just says, "You need to come upstairs." And I'm like, "No, no, you don't understand. There's an issue down here. There's a problem with the toilet." Hah! Anyway, we kinda go back and forth, and finally he says, "Get your butt up here and take a look at this." And so I'm, "Fine. Ok." I walk up top and it's an open-top drive. So where you're driving the boat from, suddenly you've got a beautiful view. I walk up in front and what do I see? The entire surface of the ocean lit up. Unbelievable! What it was was cence. And it was happening that night. The sea was flat, beautiful, and practically no moon. The illumination was so bright and so vivid it was stunning. And what made it even more stunning was the fact that there was baitfish everywhere for miles.

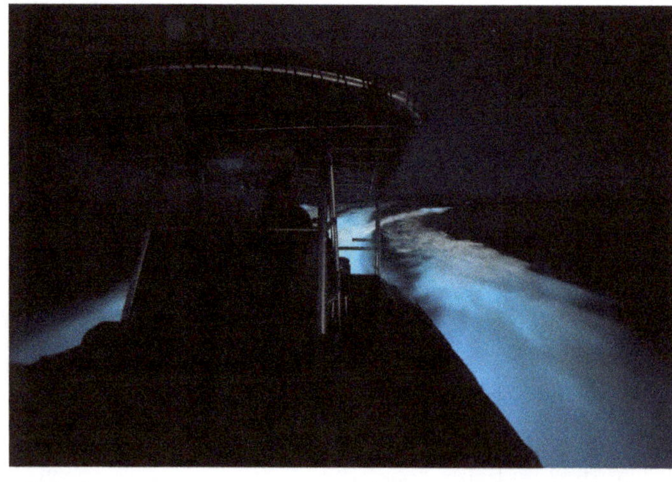

Bioluminescence   © Mark Girardeau

As the boat was pushing through the baitfish, they were exploding in every direction. Just exploding fish! And as the fish would speed up they would leave a little bioluminescent trail, and you can imagine this, extrapolating, thousands and thousands of these little fish. It was just mind-boggling! After staring at it—I'd never seen anything like it, never even heard of it—it was unbelievable! Just set me back!! We're watching this as we're going along, and we're just going through acres of this stuff. Heh, heh—then out of nowhere, these great green bursts of light would just shoot through the bait: one after another, three at a time, four at a time. It was dolphins! I assume it was dolphins. It might have been porpoises, thinking back on it. But still, it was amazing. These dolphins started shooting through this bait. As they were shooting, you'd see beams—big, bold, long streamer beams of light—going off in these masses of fish. And when the dolphins hit the surface of the water, it was like fireworks, and you'd see the streamers and they'd explode, and *pow*, the fish would just blow up in sparkles! And we watched this go on and it was like a dream. Looking back on it, in my head, it was just as fantastic as I'm describing it. It was just amazing. I've seen bioluminescence plenty of times since then, but *that* particular night was a once in a lifetime shot.

JOHN MAYER

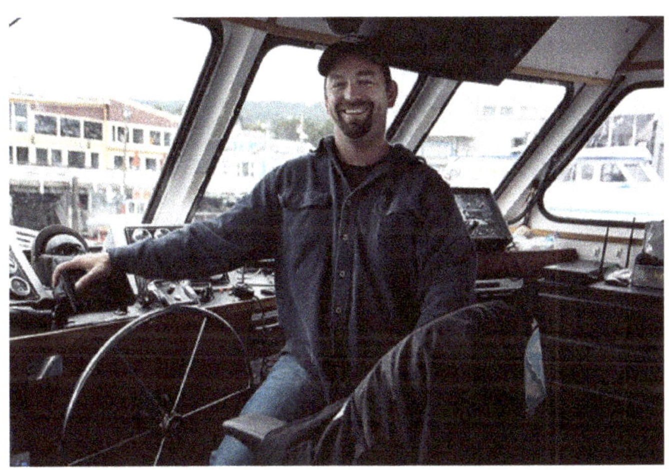

Captain John Mayer was the captain/operator of the *Blackfin*, a vessel owned by Monterey Bay Whale Watch at the time of his interview. He later went on to open and co-own Discovery Charters Inc. on Fisherman's Wharf in Monterey. He was born in Santa Cruz and grew up in Pacific Grove, Carmel Valley, Monterey and Seaside. He got his feet wet, so to speak, in the marine world at the age of fourteen. John says he stumbled down the wharf when a gentleman asked him if he'd like to wash his fishing boat. John said yes, had fun and did a good job, so he was asked to come again, and he kept on doing the job. Then a skipper noticed him and asked if he wanted to go fishing. John accepted and he's been on the water ever since.

When the Sea Sparkles

Meg Kikkeri

(*Date of Interview:* 1/20/17)

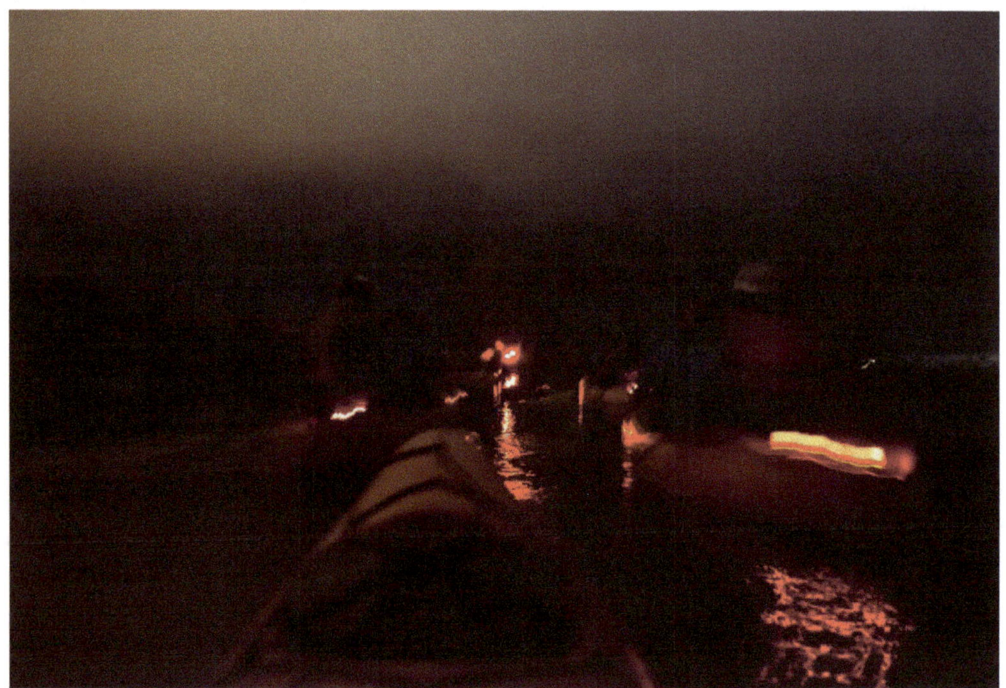

Nighttime kayaking

One of my most memorable wildlife encounters in Monterey Bay happened this past summer. I was working at the Monterey Bay Aquarium with the Education Program, and I got to live in Monterey for free at like some people's houses. I had my godmother's kayak with me, which I'd just strap on top of my car—which made me feel *so cool!* Just driving around with a kayak!

And I knew, like around August, that there's like bioluminescence typically that happens in the water. So, one day I called up a bunch of my friends, and was like "Yo! Wanna go like kayaking in the middle of the night and see what happens?" I knew there was bioluminescent kayaking, but like I didn't tell them about it, and they were like, "No that's weird scary." And I was like, "No, totally! Like come do it, it's gonna be totally cool!!" So, I got a group—I had two kayaks, two single kayaks—and my friends brought like surfboards and paddleboards, and we all came out like 11 pm at Lovers Point. It was *incredibly* foggy, and you couldn't see anything in front of you. And they were like, "Meg. Like what? We're not... Are you *kidding* me? Like it's so… This is, no… You're silly." And I was like, "No, trust me, trust me! It'll be *so* good!"

We go out, and like, because it was *sooo* foggy and so dense and was so dark you could like see the bioluminescence like immediately as we went out. And it was like everyone was just quiet for ten minutes, because they were like, "Oh my…." It was *sooo* magical. It was like, it was like sitting there in a kayak like waving your hands through the water thinking about like how amazing like nature is. And thinking about, "Wow, I'm here right now experiencing this beauty that not very many people even *know* about, and it's like, it's unbelievable.

We kept kayaking out, like passing the aquarium, and all of a sudden, if you just stayed really still, if you just hung out, you could hear the harbor seals pop up right next to you with their little nostrils, and then just like check you out, then go back down, and you could see their stream of bioluminescence pass you, which was *UNbelievable*. We were out like till 2 in the morning. It was *incredible*. It was one of the best experiences I've ever had in Monterey Bay.

It all tied together recently. I had brought my friends from college to Monterey, and I was just like explaining *why* this place was so important to me. And like realizing the difference of people who've never experienced Monterey Bay. And trying to *get* them to understand why I love it so much made me realize how important it was to me.

MEG KIKKERI

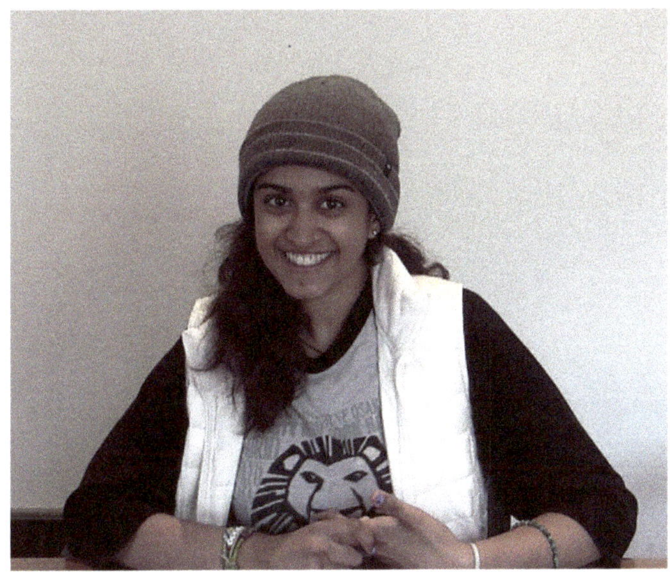

© Katlyn Taylor

Meg Kikkeri is a second-generation South Indian–American who was born and raised in the South Bay area. They have been interested in the connections of the natural world and people for a long time, starting with getting lost looking at tide pools and smelling flowers in the neighborhood. Meg graduated from Smith College with a Bachelor of Arts in Biological Sciences and Environmental Geoscience.

After hearing photographer Jodi Frediani give a PowerPoint presentation on Monterey Bay marine life at a Rural Bonny Doon Association (Santa Cruz County) monthly meeting, Meg enthusiastically asked how to get involved in the marine world. Frediani advised them to apply to be an intern with Monterey Bay Whale Watch, which they did. Meg was accepted, and learned to photograph whale flukes for identification purposes and how to keep data logs during the whale watch trips.

Meg has also volunteered and been a paid employee at the Monterey Bay Aquarium starting as a freshman in high school when they became a Teen Conservation Leader at the aquarium and a mentor to girls in the aquarium's Young Women in Science program. In 2016, Meg was recognized by the Monterey Bay Aquarium and the Paul Walker Foundation for their contributions to studies of ocean and conservation issues and awarded the Paul Walker Youth Award. The Paul Walker Foundation provides a scholarship to each award winner to pursue marine science/environmental studies in college. Meg has also volunteered with the Marine Mammal Center in the San Francisco Bay Area and at Woods Hole Science Aquarium in Massachusetts.

Meg currently (in 2024) works for Save the Bay as a Native Plant Nursery Assistant growing California native plants for marshland restoration all around the San Francisco Bay. They are passionate about engaging with the public, creating accessible and inclusive spaces for folks historically left out of environmental movements and conversations, and facilitating connections of the natural world in hopes of fostering more environmental stewardship.

Just Basking with Sharks

Randy Randazzo

(*Date of Interview*: 10/16/18)

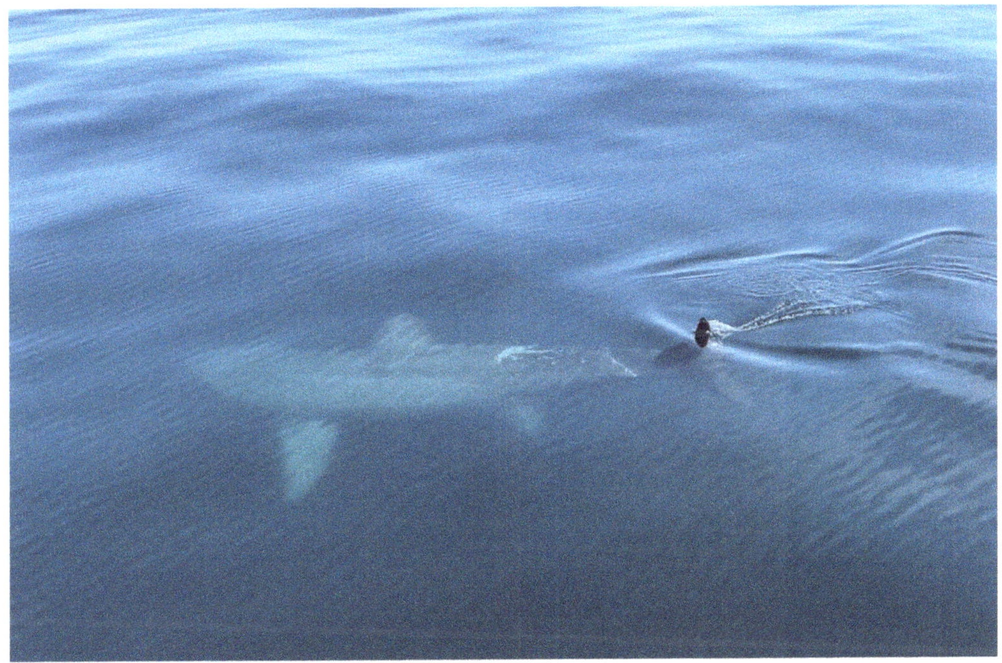

Basking shark © Katlyn Taylor

The basking shark? My brother and I, we were fishing gill net. We had a gill net and we used to lay them out here, and we used to get halibut and sole and crab. There used to be a lot of crab down in here. I mean loads of crab. Every morning we'd go and we'd pull the net and take whatever was in there. Take it in and sell it. This was a fish market—a Japanese guy—and we would sell him all the stuff.

Anyway, we go out there one day, and there's a basking shark that's just as big as a whale. And there used to be a lot of them. You don't see them no more. But we used to see them *all the time*, basking on the water. That's why they call them basking sharks, they were just sleeping. He was all tangled in the net, so with our little thirty-footer, what were we gonna do? We untangled whatever we could. We cut out whatever we could. And he's just floating. Big. You could almost walk on him.

So, we tied his head on the front of the boat, and on the back we tied his tail, and we headed for Moss Landing, because we knew Moss Landing in those days was processing whales. Basking sharks—anything you brought, they'd process it. They cut it up and they made oil.

"What year was that?" Gee… "After the war?" No, no. No, that was before the war, that was in the thirties. That was in maybe—how old was I? If I was born in '23, say in '38, I was what, twelve, fourteen? At fifteen I was fishing sardines.

So, we towed it. It took us seven hours. I'll never forget. Took it to Moss Landing, and they took it; they had a big ramp at the cannery there, where they went into the water. They hooked it up. They pulled it up the ramp. Oooooh. About three or four guys came out with knives, and they start cutting it up. And then they gotta boil it. In those days they used to boil it to get the oil. And they gave us $70 for it. $70. Wow, that was big money then.

Katlyn: Was the shark bigger than the boat?

Randy: Oh yeah. The skiff was like a thirty-footer, and the shark was bigger than that. Oh yeah. The boat was thirty feet. The shark was just, *psshaw* [*gestures with hands*]. Good thing I remember, it was nice weather. We were just cruising along slow. You don't see 'em [basking sharks] anymore. We used to see 'em all the time. Years ago. Lotsa whales now, but no basking sharks. I don't think you've seen 'em, have you?

Katlyn: I've never seen one. But there've been two sightings since I've been here.

Randy: Wow. They were huge and I guess they call 'em basking sharks because they bask on the surface. You'd usually see them—half of it, out of the water—like they'd just be kind of floating. He was just basking.

RANDY RANDAZZO

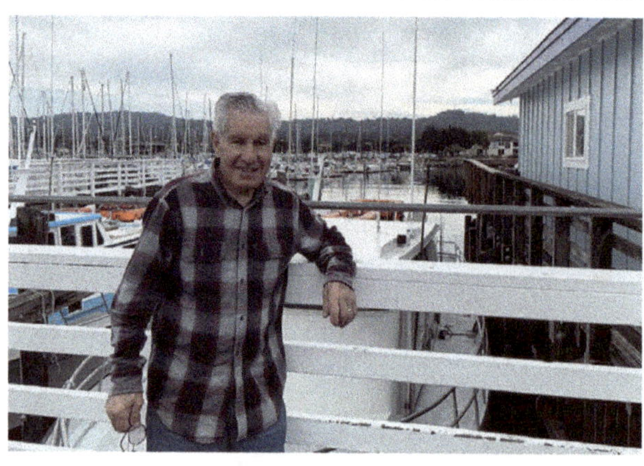

© Katlyn Taylor

The late Salvatore "Randy" Randazzo was born in 1923 and raised right here in Monterey by Italian immigrants who met in Monterey and started a family here. He started helping his dad on fishing boats when he was a young boy. He also worked as a commercial fisherman, a party boat captain and even fought in the U.S. Navy in World War II. He only attended one day of high school before he enlisted and headed out to sea to fight for the United States. Randy spent his whole life on the ocean.

When he got home from the war, he worked as a commercial fisherman during the sardine heyday. He paid $500 for a share of the boat and went to work on a purse seiner. In two years, he had made his money back. In 1948 he bought part of the Monterey Fisherman's Wharf, and piece by piece built it into Randy's Fishing Trips. The original pier he constructed was made of refurbished materials out of the scrap piles of the canneries being dismantled on Cannery Row. He also owned a small mooring field, skiffs for rent, and a little bait and tackle shop.

In 1957 he built his first boat, *The Randy I*, for his charter business. By 1961 he had enough income and enough demand to build a second vessel, *The Randy II*. At the peak of his operation Randy had five party boats leaving from his shop on Fisherman's Wharf.

In 1981 Randy decided to retire from his business on the wharf and sold it to Peter Bruno and John Lupo. They continued Randy's legacy until 2017 when Peter Bruno sold the business to John Mayer and Mat Arcoleo, who rebranded the business into J&M Sport Fishing and Discovery Whale Watch.

After his retirement, Randy still filled in for many years as a party boat captain for the other fishing companies on the wharf and commercially fished in his own small fishing vessel. Randy passed away in 2024, but even into his late nineties you could find him down on the wharf every day looking at the day's catches and chatting with all the owners and workers on the piers. Randy really was a piece of living history and had many amazing stories.

A Shark Named Elvis

Sal Jorgensen

(Date of Interview: 10/22/18)

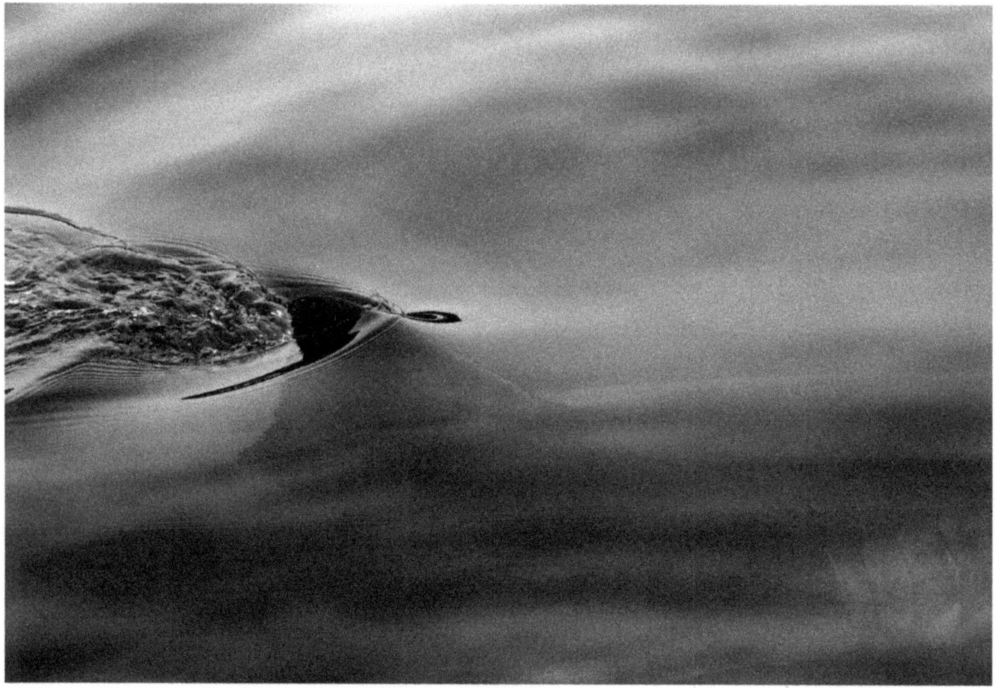

White shark

I think this is a good story choice, because it kind of tells the whole story of California white sharks that are central to the Monterey Bay area.

Last Friday we went out to the Farallon Islands for tagging and doing our photo ID work. The Farallon Islands, Año Nuevo Island, Point Reyes—this whole region of Northern/Central California is a place where white sharks come and aggregate. They're looking for their prey and October to November is a peak time. We're in the middle of October right now, in the thick of white shark season. Sharks are coming here essentially to eat juvenile elephant seals that are hauling out at this time of year. We were out at the Farallon Islands, photographing the sharks, and looking to get a profile shot of the dorsal fin, which is basically their fingerprint.

We use a decoy; it's a silhouette that looks like a seal. We float that out underwater behind us. And we're anchored at this point at the Farallones. So fifteen minutes in, and we have a shark up. And we got some video and it was great. We didn't recognize that shark, and then about midmorning, we were just about to pull the anchor and go try a different spot. The decoy was already reeled in and in the boat, and we looked down and suddenly see there's quite a large shark, around sixteen and a half feet long, swimming around the boat. It had lots of scars, you know, and it looked like a real old-timer. We started looking closely and finally the shark surfaces and we can see the fin, and it's a shark we call Elvis. We recognize at the tip of the fin it's got a little flip, sort of a rounded part, like the hairstyle of the legendary singer. Elvis is a real special shark, because he was first photographed at the Farallon Islands in 1989. So this Friday, we have a new record—the longest span between when a shark was first ID'd and when we've most recently seen him. It's twenty-nine years! The previous record was twenty-seven years, which still is impressive, and there's one at twenty-six years. So, it's incredible!

My colleague, Scott Anderson, photographed this shark in 1989 when he was in the Farallones, actually studying birds. That was before he shifted his lens from the birds over to the ocean and started studying the sharks, where he really started this photo ID program. A lot of the ID photos we're looking at today, we'll go back to match to some of the historical photos. It's been twenty-nine years, and in that time, I've seen Elvis… the last time I saw him was two years ago in 2016. And also, I think in 2015, 2014, and then 2013 and 2011. In 2006 I remember seeing him. Not every year, but we see him out there frequently and it's really exciting.

What it tells us really illustrates the story of white sharks in this area. These sharks come back here every single year. The males every year, the females every other year, or sometimes they take a break, but basically throughout the whole of their life. Where they go between seal hunting seasons is offshore to the White Shark Café—to Hawaii. It takes about a month for them to swim out there. But just like clockwork, they come back here every year. It's just amazing to see the same individuals come to the exact same spot. We could have been anchored there ten or fifteen years ago in the exact same spot and seen Elvis. And if we didn't have our satellite tagging program, you would think that these sharks never left that exact same tiny little area. But when we started attaching electronic tags, we saw the tracks head off into the ocean. In fact, they spend more time offshore in the open ocean than they do at the coast, but they come back every time.

The reason this is so significant is that these sharks are able to cross, traverse, the ocean. They swim to Hawaii regularly; they could clearly just keep on going to the other side. There are white sharks on the other side. But they come back. They're kind of like salmon. Salmon return and give birth where they were born. And that's why we have these genetically distinct stocks of salmon. Some of them are distinct within a particular fork of the same river. Well, we have our white sharks here in California and northern Baja California. In this area, which we call the northeastern Pacific, they are genetically distinct from all other white sharks in the world. And we think this is due to this site fidelity, philopatric[37] level of place, so there's a tendency to go give birth where you were born.

Elvis is a male, obviously, but the females are doing the same thing, and the females will come and give birth in Southern California and northern Baja California. So, that's pretty cool.

[See Sal's bio after the following story.]

Aptos Warm Nursery

Sal Jorgensen

(Date of Interview: 10/22/18)

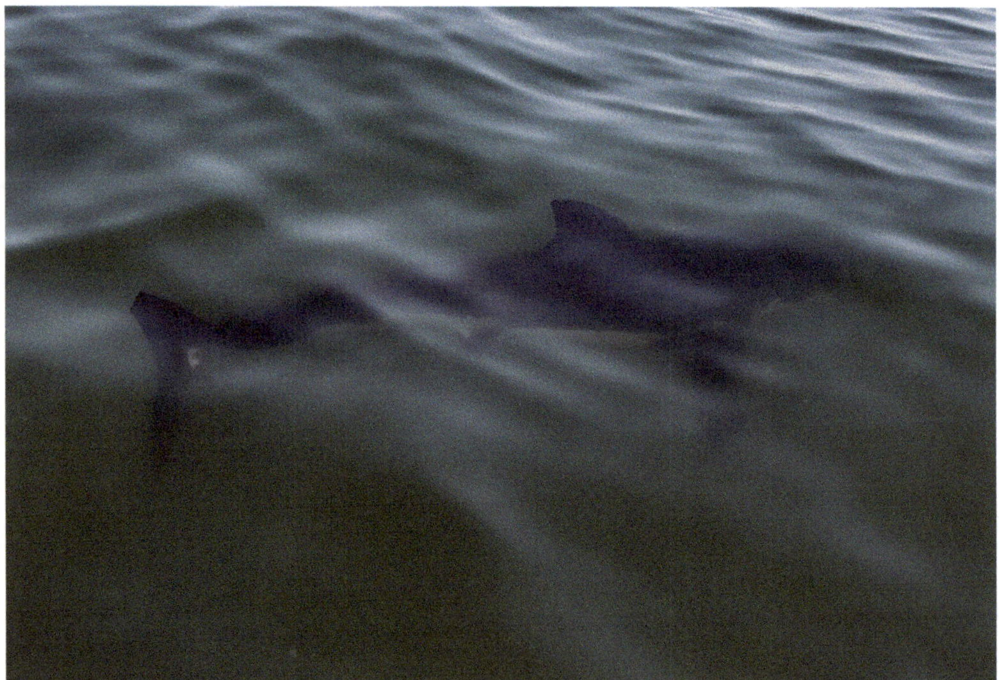

White shark

Ohe of the really cool, interesting new things in Monterey Bay, with regards to our white sharks, is that since 2014 we've started to see a lot of small sharks off the northern Central California coast that we've never really

---

[37] Tending to return to a particular site or area.

seen before—in particular, in the northern part of Monterey Bay off of Aptos and New Brighton Beach. We first started seeing this around 2014, and we've done some work looking at the types of temperatures these smaller sharks prefer, because white sharks are endotherms, and they have to maintain a warm body core temperature. Usually, when they're born, they're confined to warmer waters. In California, that means south of Point Conception, so the Southern California Bight.

However, in 2014 we had this warm 'Blob,' a body of warm water that really warmed up the coastal waters of Central California. In 2015 we had El Niño, which extended to 2016, so there were three or four years in a row of exceptionally warm waters along the northern Central California coast. When we plotted where we would expect to see juvenile white sharks and newborn white sharks, according to the water temperature, suddenly the area that should be accessible to them was above Point Conception, into the Central California coast and even up to Monterey Bay, which is thought of as Northern California. And so theoretically, looking at the temperatures, we could predict that they should be in Monterey Bay, and that coincided with the observations that indeed we started to see up here.

Even this year, they're back again. So, we're trying to figure out what exactly is going on. We think that it's clearly a temperature-related phenomenon to see them up here. We think that this might become the new normal; certainly twenty to fifty years from now as the ocean temperatures warm, this will happen more frequently. This was what we predicted, and it may, in fact, eventually be just warm enough for these juvenile white sharks to be up here regularly. The interesting thing is, it's only warm here part of the time, part of the year. In the spring we get the winds and they stir up the water. We get the upwelling. We get the cold deep water coming up to the surface, so our entire coast starts to get a lot chillier.

But there's this really interesting pattern that happens, because the northern part of the bay is hooked over and it's south facing, and it gets a lot of sunlight, and the current that's running alongshore, along the California coast, kind of has a little eddy into the northern part of the bay. As the water temperature cools off along Central California in the spring, there's always this warm pocket of water inside the bay right off of Aptos. And we've worked out a way to see when this warm pocket is prominent and what the temperature differences are. I've seen this spring that the temperature difference between that warm pocket and the outer waters of say Año Nuevo, can be five to ten degrees. And that's a huge amount for a small-bodied animal that has to stay warm.

You know, people have been seeing a lot of sharks off of Aptos and wondering why there are so many in that one particular area. We think that what happens is we have these abnormal warm years. Water generally in Southern

California is fairly warm, so the sharks can come up here, or maybe they're even born here, because the mother recognizes it's a warm-enough area. Then the wind blows, the area cools off, and everything starts cooling except for that one warm spot. We think this has the effect of corralling all those sharks into that area. That's the hypothesis that we're working with right now. We've been out there this spring putting on tags that measure temperature, that have video cameras that record their behavior and record the types of things they're seeing.

White shark sunning at surface

The interesting thing is that these little white sharks, when we see them in Aptos, are swimming at the surface. They're kind of basking in the sun. It's the warmest spot. We can tell from our tags that this is the warmest time of the day and this is the warmest place to be that they've found. And that's when they linger around. Typically, when we see white sharks in a hunting mode or a foraging mode, they're swimming deep, and they're not looking to be detected, so they're trying to be stealthy and use the element of surprise to come up on a seal or sea lion or something. We don't think that the surface milling is a predation behavior. We think it's a thermoregulatory behavior. Indeed, it supports the idea that they're trying to stay warm. The way to do that is to be in the warm spot—not only that, but to be right at the surface and getting some solar radiation in that little warm layer of water. That spot's not getting much wind either. It's really windy outside, but you duck into that little cove, it's just so calm and warm. If you've gone there from Monterey, you can really feel the difference.

So that's a pretty interesting new development. You know, it's a changing place, and we've seen since 2014 a lot of new species up in this area—different birds, snails, pelagic crabs, all this new stuff associated with warmer water. I think the smaller juvenile white sharks are just one more piece of that puzzle.

SAL JORGENSEN

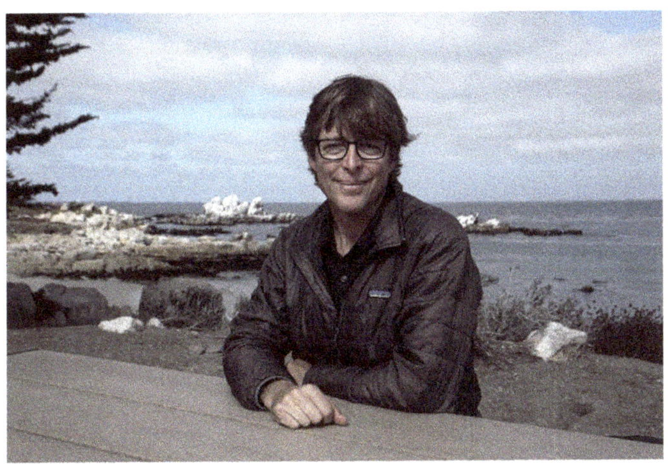

Salvador (Sal) Jorgensen was a Senior Research Scientist at the Monterey Bay Aquarium in Monterey, California at the time of his interview. He was conducting research on white sharks in the wild hoping to learn more about their place in the local ecology and how their numbers are changing. Currently, he is a marine ecologist and faculty member at California State University, Monterey Bay (CSUMB) researching the movement, population dynamics, and ecological interactions of ocean predators.

Sal was born in Seattle, Washington, but grew up a little bit all over the place—Seattle, California, Africa, Canada, and then back to California. At age nine he moved with his family from Canada to Mozambique off the southeastern coast of Africa and lived there for five years. His parents were university teachers participating in Canadian University Overseas, like a Peace Corps for university teachers in developing countries. His family settled in Montreal, Québec, Canada after returning from Mozambique. Sal notes that while Montreal is a beautiful inland city, it is an island on a river and very cold in the winter. As a teenager he was counting the days to finish high school and community college and go explore warmer areas that were coastal.

After meandering through Central America and Mexico, Sal ended up in California again. He'd always considered himself a West Coast person by birth, and he and his parents lived on the West Coast of North America from Southern California to Canada. After living in Africa, he became very much drawn to the ocean.

Sal got his undergraduate degree at Sonoma State University, then attended graduate school at the University of California at Davis. He had been working at the UC Davis Bodega Marine Laboratory in Bodega Bay, so had already started to put his roots down in coastal California.

After graduating with a PhD in Marine Ecology from UC Davis, where he studied the movements and population dynamics of fish, Sal heard there was a job offering at the Monterey Bay Aquarium to study white sharks. That was around 2005 when the aquarium had been the first to successfully display a white shark. A lot of people would come to visit, and the aquarium saw this as an opportunity to invest extra funds into studying this enigmatic species. Sal was intrigued by the idea of studying white sharks, applied for the position and was hired.

Like every diligent nine-year-old, Sal had done a lot of research on white sharks and scared his mother a lot. When he first had the opportunity to study sharks as a biologist, he called his mother and said, "Hey, I've got this great opportunity to study schooling hammerhead sharks at a seamount in Mexico, and I'm going down with a world-famous shark scientist, Dr. Peter Klimley, to dive in the water and count the sharks." There was a long silence on the other end… "Mom, are you there?" "Maybe I could get you some shark repellant," she replied. He explained that Jane Goodall didn't wear chimpanzee repellant when she was out in the field.

As a marine ecologist Sal has always been interested in how movement affects population dynamics, and why animals move. He has studied rockfish movement and movements of fish around seamounts in the Sea of Cortez in Mexico. Those studies included hammerhead sharks and communities of species such as tunas and jacks. Studying sharks through the aquarium was a way to continue along this path. Sal realized during college that he was studying species declines. As a kid, he didn't know and doesn't think anyone knew that much about whether we could deplete the oceans. However, in college he realized it's a real problem for sharks, because they take so long to reproduce and have so few young that they'll have a hard time recovering.

Sal notes that the problem with sharks is that they have a bad reputation. Getting people behind shark conservation is not as easy as asking people to save the whales. At the Monterey Bay Aquarium, Sal worked to change people's perception of sharks as part of his job dealing with the white shark, which is the poster child of the perceived threat sharks pose to people.

A Sweetheart of a Turtle

Scott Benson

(Date of Interview: 11/10/16)

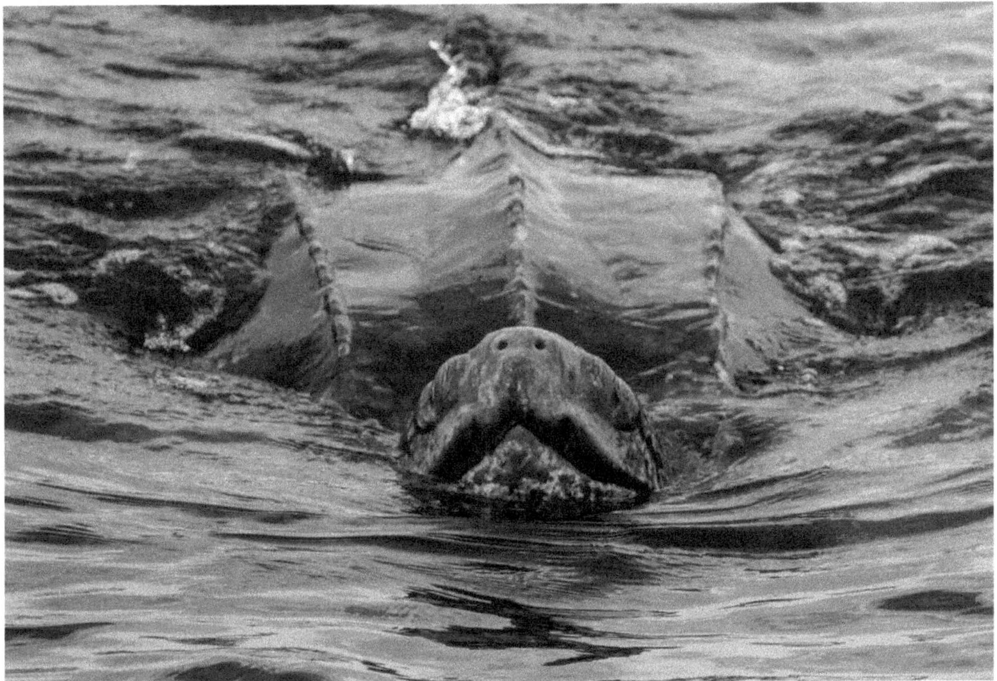

Leatherback turtle

Memorable wildlife encounters. Well, I've had a few of them. I'm on the whale disentanglement team here. And I've done lots of work out here with marine birds and mammals. I did that for my thesis work at Moss Landing.

You know, with the leatherbacks, which is what I primarily do now, I've sampled lots of different turtles, and it turns out that, believe it or not, a reptile like that can have a personality. Yes, it turns out that they do. Some of them are pretty easy to work with, and others put up quite a fight. They all have different kinds of attitudes. I wouldn't have believed it at first if you told me that, but now that I've seen enough of them and interacted with enough of them, I totally believe that.

One time we had this very large turtle (607 kilograms, or over 1300 pounds) that we were trying to capture for sampling. I looked over the side, and I saw how big it was—and I'm using a hoop to catch these turtles. So we're not tranquilizing anything, but we've got to put a hoop net on them and then bring them onboard.

I can say some of them can put up a bit of resistance. And I saw this animal and thought, "Oh goodness," and I looked behind me and saw the crew I had. I didn't have my regular crew. I had a bunch of substitute folks. And gosh, I'm thinking, maybe this is not the right group for this one. But even though the turtle looked really huge, I really wanted to try to sample this one. So we went for it. We captured and sampled this animal, and she was just a sweetheart. I mean, she was so calm and patient, and beautiful! A large animal without any scrapes on her—she was just a magnificent animal.

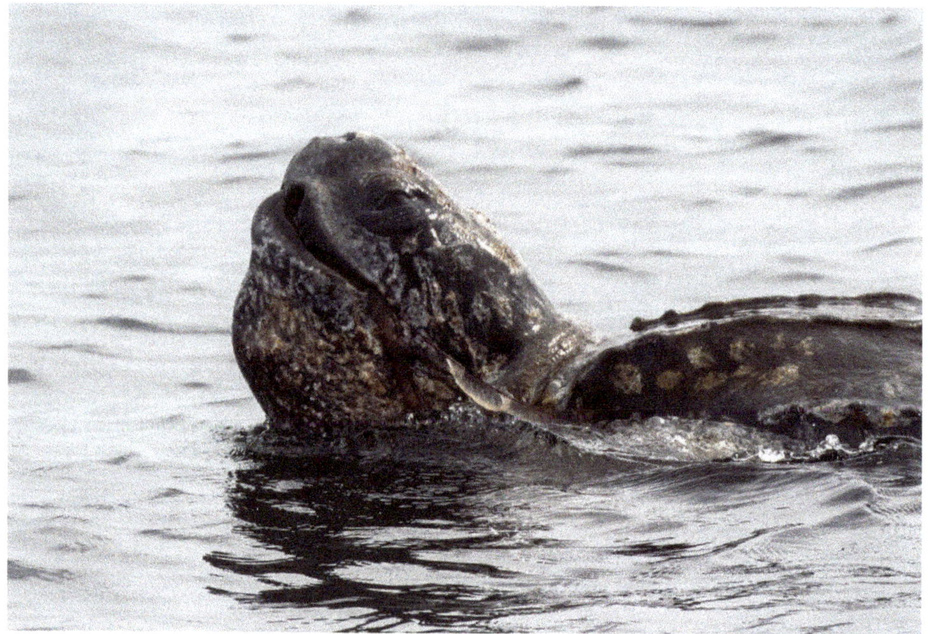

Leatherback turtle

Then we put her back in the water and she went to swim away. It's the only time this has ever happened to us. She got in the water, and she did two big, powerful strokes. And these are animals that have these long flippers and are very powerful. True swimming machines are what these animals are. They can lift you off the boat with their flipper, and, you know, understandably so; they're swimming all the way across the Pacific Ocean to get here. Anyway, she did two big flaps with her flippers then put 'em out straight, and then turned, and did a power glide. She essentially moved off, exited the boat going that direction then got in this power glide and turned around and did a swim by our boat. I could see the whole thing underwater. It was the most impressive thing I've ever seen. The power and magnificence of this animal swimming past us like that. Without, you know, really doing anything startling. It was just two strokes and then this power glide turn going past the boat. It was unbelievable!

SCOTT BENSON

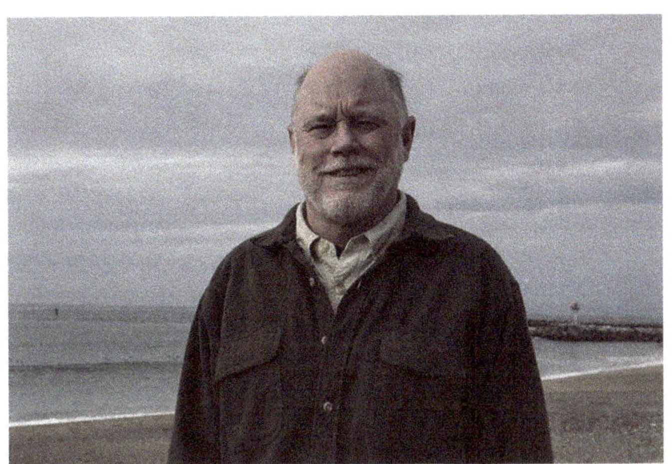

Scott Benson works in the Marine Turtle Ecology and Assessment Program at the Southwest Fisheries Science Center, which is part of NOAA. He is the lead researcher or Principal Investigator for leatherback turtle research. Scott is based in the Monterey Bay region because the leatherback turtles are here. He notes that this area is a well-documented foraging ground for leatherback turtles. They migrate across the entire Pacific Ocean from Indonesia and come here to consume jellyfish. The turtles are seasonal constituents of the local ecosystem, though Scott is based here year-round.

Scott was born in St. Louis, Missouri and moved to Southern California with his family when he was five. He grew up in southern Orange County (Laguna Niguel/Dana Point), back in the days when Interstate 5 was under construction and the coast road was the only route to San Diego. Dana Point was a truly small town then, smaller than today's Moss Landing, where Scott's office is located.

Scott came to Monterey Bay in 1994 to do graduate work in marine science at Moss Landing Marine Laboratories. Prior to that he worked for NOAA for ten years or so. He spent four to six months every year at sea counting whales, dolphins, seabirds and sea turtles as an Identification Specialist. In that capacity, he was sent around the world identifying marine species from on board ships, most of the time in the eastern tropical Pacific between Hawaii and mainland United States, and Latin America. But Scott was also sent to the Atlantic Ocean, southern Indian Ocean, and other locales. During that period, he spent a lot of time at sea. Some field surveys went on for four and a half months before the ship returned home again.

Scott would usually work for six months of the year doing survey work. He was also a state beach lifeguard for California. Scott reminisced that each time he came back from his adventures at sea, he had time on his hands and a pocketful of money, a rarity to have both at the same time! As a result, he spent his time off traveling the world—Asia, the Himalayas, South America. Scott explained to people he was front-loading his retirement.

Serendipity and Rare Birds

D e b i   S h e a r w a t e r

(Date of Interview: 5/12/19)

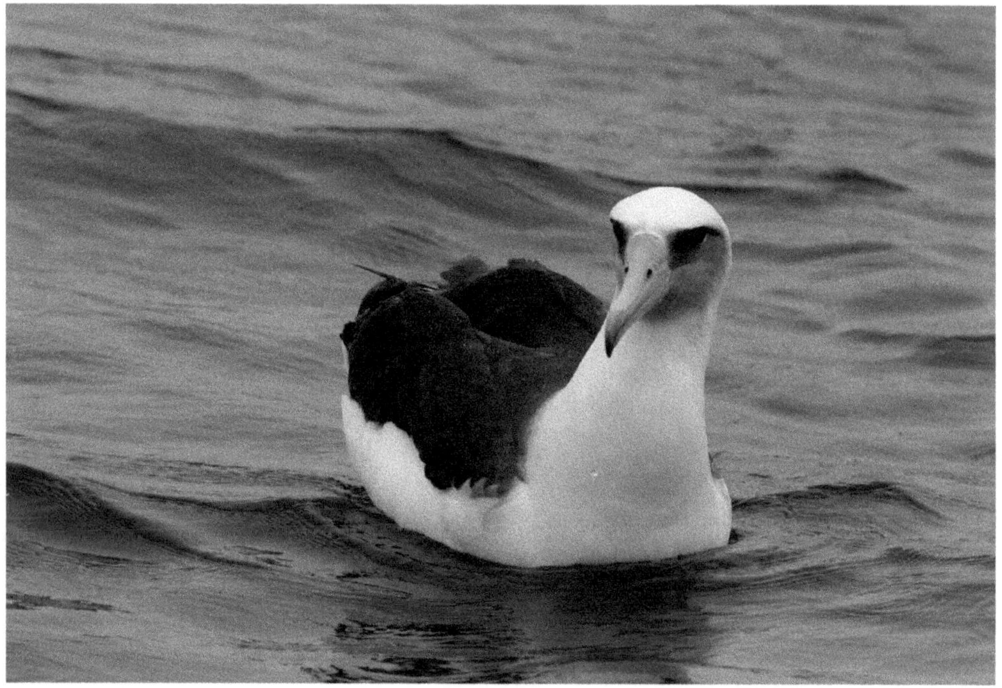

Laysan albatross

So, I got to Monterey. I did these boat trips, a couple of boat trips. I thought it was a lot of fun. I started talking to local people, and I'm like, "How do you get to see a Laysan albatross? I've seen the black-footed albatross." And they said do a winter trip. But nobody does winter trips. There's nothing out there in the winter. Well, I'm gonna do a winter trip. So, I set up a winter trip—a February trip. I believe it was 1978, on the *Star of Monterey*, which was a little boat in Monterey at that time. With David Lemmon—Big D. So, we're gonna go out there in February. I've got all these bird-watchers in 1978 that come up from Los Angeles to go on this boat with me. I'm advertising and we're gonna go way out there and try to get a Laysan albatross.

Now, in those days, you have to understand, it was not easy to see a Laysan albatross. Why? Because the Laysans breed on the leeward chain of the Hawaiian Islands, Midway and stuff, and basically they shoot toward the Aleutian Islands for feeding, whereas the black-foots come to us in Monterey. Now we see Laysans more often, but that's because around 1985 Laysan albatrosses began nesting on islands off of Mexico. But in 1978 we didn't even have those Mexican Laysan albatrosses.

Well, we go offshore, and we're looking, you know. I don't remember the beginning of the day. There wasn't much to it. Hard core birders! *Hard core birders!* And David and I, we spot these blows. And they're going like this—angling forward. Wow, well! I don't know anything about whales still, but I brought this NOAA publication, 444, that has black and white photos of all these dead whales, and that's how I learned whales! And according to that thing, if the blow is going like this, forward, that's gonna be a sperm whale. And I've never seen a sperm whale!! Gotta see a sperm whale!! You gotta have that! David was into it as much as I was. So, we spot these things, and we think they've got to be sperm whales. He says, "Do you wanna go for 'em?" "Yeah, go for 'em!" So, we do, and of course, they dive. Well, you know, if they're sperm whales, it's gonna be a long wait. So, I'm thinking, "This is gonna be dicey. The bird-watchers are *not* gonna like this," so I stop the boat and I tell them, "We're gonna wait for these sperm whales to come up."

It's quiet on the boat. Very quiet. Then everyone starts breaking out their lunches. The gulls that have been following us all day chumming behind the boat, they sit down on the water. And there's this young lady on board. She is not a bird-watcher; she's the girlfriend of a bird watcher. So, this young lady says, "You know there's a funny looking gull back there." A Laysan albatross was sitting on the water behind the boat! Everyone absolutely went berserk! And I said, you know, I know you guys are probably all cursing me under your breath, because I stopped to wait for these whales. Let's see in a show of hands, how many people is this a life bird for? Virtually everyone on the whole boat. That was a Laysan albatross. Just like that, while we were watching for sperm whales. Then it began to sink into me, that, man, you better be looking *at* everything. You better be looking *for* everything, because one thing leads to another. And it just always seems to work that way.

Then there's one other story. I thought, you know, well I asked, "How do you see a Laysan albatross?" Go on a winter trip. Do a winter trip. But then I thought every winter trip was gonna be like that. Not, *naha.* [*laughter*] It doesn't work that way. But I did have another idea. You know, like my most-wanted bird for a long, long time was the tropicbird. How do you get to see a tropicbird? You gotta go out in the summertime, July. Nobody goes out in the summertime. Nobody does that. It's not a good time of year. Well, I'm gonna go out. You gotta go *way* offshore. Well, I'm gonna do it. I'm gonna go out, and I'm gonna go to the Guide Seamount in this little boat called the *Silver Prince*, a little *tiny* thing owned by some guy in the Navy school.

So, we get on the boat. Ron Ransom's with me, and we go out. I mean, we left in the dark because it's a *long* drive out to the Guide Seamount. Very long drive from Monterey. And we get way out there in the middle of nowhere. We're chumming. And the captain has to take a leak, so he's going down to the head, and as the boat was stopped, hovering over the boat is a red-billed tropicbird. Just like that! I thought, ok, you're on my trip and you get to see a red-billed tropicbird. It's gonna happen every summer! Nope.

In the beginning, you know, I'd have this idea. The way it was going, I thought it was magic. I thought it was *magic*!! You just do it, and the birds will be there! It'll happen then! We had an albacore trip one time. We started doing these albacore trips. You'd catch an albacore. That's a heck of a lot of fun. Oh my gosh, *FISH ON*!! There's nothing like yelling *FISH ON*! I love it! And so, we're catching these albacore and having lots of fun. Saury are jumping right here! All the terns are trying to feed on the little baitfish that the saury are chasing. The Jaegers are coming down on top of the terns. You have a whole ecosystem laid out right there in front of you. Underneath you've got all the animals that are trying to eat the saury, in addition to the albacore. You've got the fish, you've got the birds, you've got, you know, probably sea lions, all kinds of other things.

Well, it's one of those typical foggy, overcast days and we're out there, and now my "I-want-to-see list" is really ratcheting up. Now I want to see a red-*tailed* tropicbird, not a red-*billed* tropicbird, a red-*tailed* tropicbird. All the red-tailed tropicbird sightings in California are two hundred or more miles offshore. Well, we're not gonna make it two hundred miles in one day. No, not even close. And there's only two or three records of those birds, on top of that.

So, we're out there on this albacore trip, and it's an overcast day, real foggy, and you know, when you're bird-watching out there on the ocean you're either looking like this [*away*] or you're looking over the top of the water. And in the fog we get a fallout in the fall season of a lot of warblers that get lost, and stuff like that. So, we have this warbler coming behind the boat, and we're all looking up at it, and into our field of view flies the red-tailed tropicbird. If we hadn't looked up, we would never have seen it. [*laughter*] There's a lot of serendipity out there, that's all I can say.

DEBI SHEARWATER

Debi Shearwater was the founder, owner and operator of Shearwater Journeys until she retired in 2021. She took people from all over the world on trips out on Monterey Bay to see birds and other marine life. Debi taught bird-watchers that if

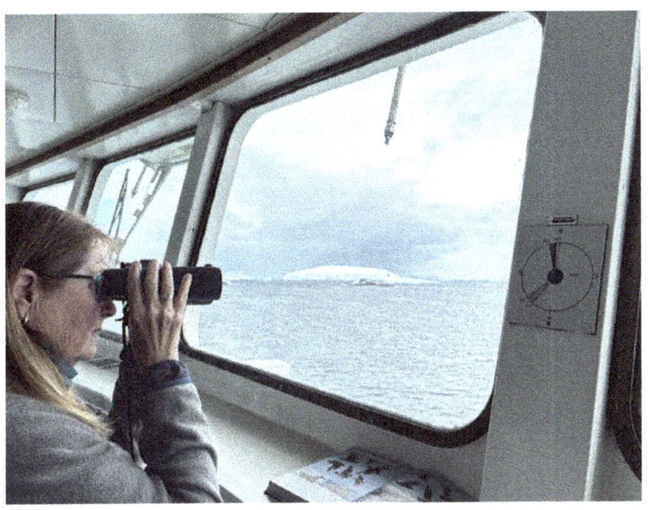
© Robin Welch

whales are feeding, birds are probably nearby, and it's worth looking at everything that is out there. Her trips included Half Moon Bay and the Farallon Islands off of San Francisco Bay, but over the years she led trips up and down the California coast. She also led expedition voyages at sea, including the Galápagos, Antarctica, South Georgia Island, the Falklands, Svalbard and the Russian Far East.

Debi was born and grew up in Brookhaven, Pennsylvania. She married an Army officer at eighteen, and together they lived in a number of places, mostly in the U.S. South. When he was transferred to the Naval Postgraduate School in Monterey, Debi came kicking and screaming all the way—too many people and cars!

Debi's path into bird-watching was fortuitous. While her husband was in Vietnam, her little brother found a baby bird. Not only did it not die, but Debi raised it and the female house sparrow became her pet bird. Debi's husband sent her a pair of binoculars from Vietnam, and she began to look at the birds in her backyard. That piqued her interest and Debi then bought books on birding and decided to join the National Audubon Society. By then she and her husband were living in Texas, where she joined Audubon field trips and met her birding mentor, Connie Hagar. Connie walked the same route every day and found all kinds of birds that people knew nothing about. That planted a seed in Debi's mind and she thought someday she'd find her own place and walk the same route over and over again.

The next move took her to Virginia, where she went on her first pelagic trip to see shearwaters. There she met a birder who lived in Monterey, who told her if she liked seabirds she'd love Monterey.

By then Debi had become a serious bird-watcher. After her move to Monterey, she went out on a National Audubon Society bird trip on Monterey Bay and was hooked. She then organized her own trip with the Santa Cruz Bird Club, and on her first outing they saw a special Japanese shearwater, the streaked shearwater, and that bird triggered her to start leading regular bird trips. However, she says the birds wouldn't have sustained her; it was the marine mammals. After her divorce in 1977, Debi began seriously putting trips together. She ran eight the first year, and in her top year she ran eighty.

The Universe Below the Surface: Orcas, Polychaetes and Wolf Eels

Skylar Campbell

(Date of Interview: 1/20/19)

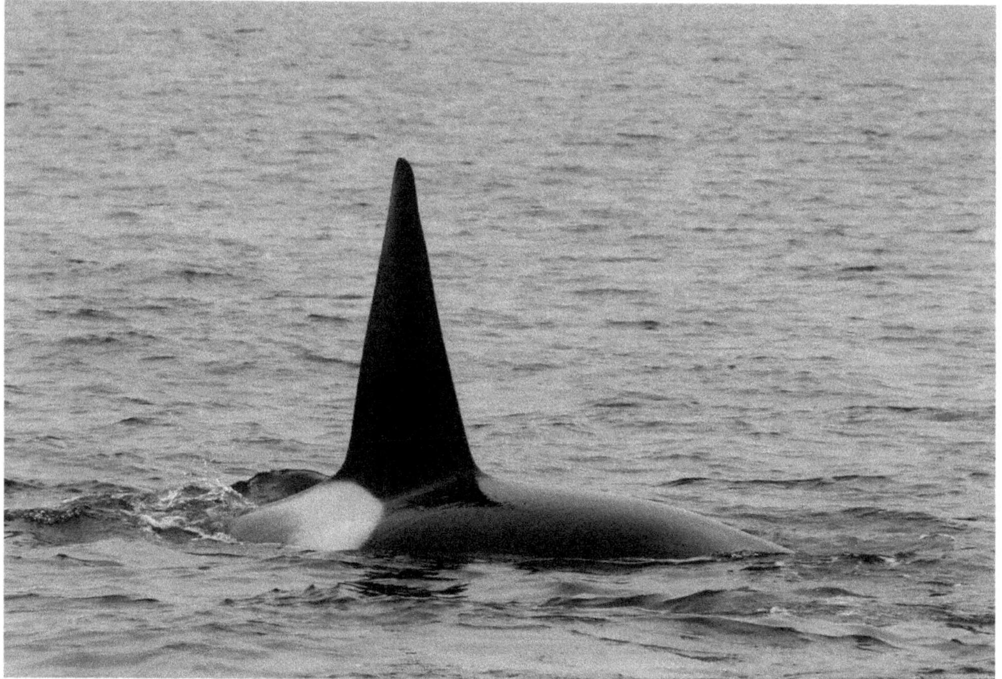

Male killer whale

To me that question about my most memorable wildlife encounter kind of seems like there's an event, you know, that's made an indelible mark on me. But being in the line of work I'm in, it feels like that all the time I'm on the water: all the hours and the days where you see the seasons change, and you see what comes into the bay, what leaves the bay, what starts showing up—you know, jellyfish, or anchovies, or squid, this and that. It's like a bombardment of just the coolest stuff all the time.

Every day, even on the worst day, it's like a really cool *National Geographic* magazine. Our area is not the Caribbean. It's not a coral reef. It's not, you know, the most pleasant place to be as far as temperature, but the diversity of life in the ocean in this area is incredible. It's just the nature of the Monterey Bay that it's so dynamic. There're not a lot of places where you can go and see such incredible stuff. Out of Moss Landing, you go a mile out of the harbor and you're already in over a hundred fathoms, and it keeps getting deeper and deeper and deeper.

It's all happening for me on a daily basis, because I'm in the business of taking fish, as in a 'take' means killing. I deliver a lot of product, but I know where it's going. I see a lot of stuff out on the water. I see everything from the whales that come by my boat and spook me, you know, to little tiny sand fleas that come up, or little octopuses—I see hundreds of these. Just with the volume of what you see every day with the wildlife, you're able to notice little changes. Oh, the anchovies are a little bit bigger, or there's a different kind of mud coming up in the traps. Oh, there's a polychaete[38] that came out of the mud in the traps. What does that mean, you know? There are all these little indelible marks.

One incident that just comes to mind, and I thought about it, is a whale thing. We were heading out to go crabbing. We were going up to Half Moon Bay, so we left from Monterey with a load of gear on the boat, and it was getting dark, and I'd never seen a killer whale before, an orca before. I was having a cup of coffee on the back deck, as we were probably making it past the whistle buoy near Point Pinos, and I saw this huge killer whale. And the white parts that I thought in my mind were gonna be white were actually like a dark gray. And I don't know, it was only just a glimpse of it, and it was following us. And it spooked me! It was really unsettling, but it just kind of reminded me of the universe below the surface, how it's incredibly dynamic and diverse. That's a whale story, but it was one of those things where you just kind of look over, and there's like the most amazing thing you've never seen before.

I've also seen great white sharks cruising between our boats when we're hook-and-line sea bass and halibut fishing. You know, blue whales, whales running right up to our boats and everything like that, but that one— the orca—that just pops up in my mind every time. But here's another short story about something

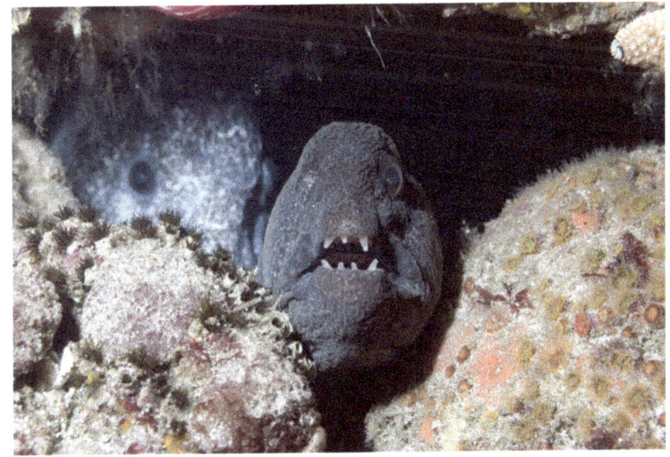

Wolf eel   © Chad King (OET/NOAA)

---

[38] A type of bristly marine worm.

kinda different. Sometimes we get wolf eels in our shrimp traps; I think that's what they are, the purple ones, yeah, and we're having to fight. *Gotta get the thing out of the trap*! It's in there! I've got to put it back in the water! Just had a battle with a wolf eel off of Cyprus Point!! He was big, too! I don't know how it got in the shrimp trap, which has an opening like this. [*makes a 4" hole with hands*] Somehow this, you know, four-foot-long eel got in. Have you seen their teeth? They're like fangs… and the jaw on the thing, it like bit through my boot! It was just altogether a really hectic thing, but it was pretty cool.

SKYLAR CAMPBELL

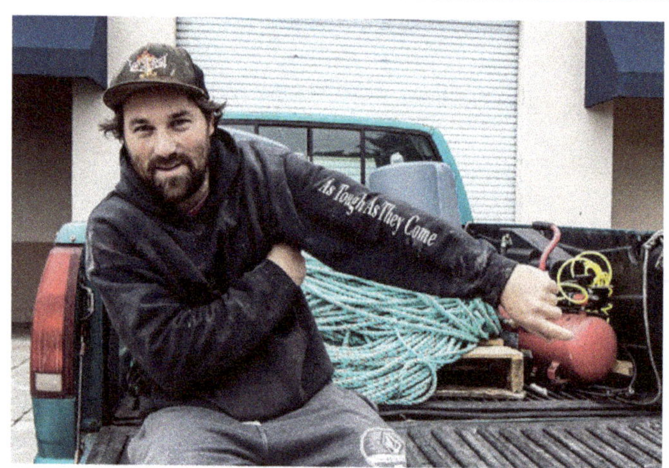

Skylar Campbell is a commercial fisherman in Monterey Bay by day and a professional musician by night. As he says, he has two part-time jobs that amount to two full-time jobs. Skylar's day job is operating his own commercial vessel for open access (unrestricted) fishing. He currently fishes for hagfish, also known as slime eel, which is not an eel, but a jawless, boneless fish without vertebrae. Skylar says they are more like a prehistoric type of sea worm. He also fishes for rock crab, open access, and has a limited-entry salmon license. At night he plays music in local bars and clubs. As a musician he plays drum set and saxophone. He came up through the Monterey Jazz Festival, taught music and now plays gigs locally.

Before owning and operating his own commercial fishing vessel, he worked on a spot prawn boat for four years. It was a nine-month season, but he worked during the extended California drought ('three years of summer'). Ocean conditions were insane all the time. No wind, no swell. Fuel prices were down and the price of prawns was up. They made hay while the sun was shining. He averaged being out on the water every other day. Now he figures he's on the water six months out of the year. The other six months he's on the boat doing other things like unloading his catch, boat maintenance and various odds and ends in the harbor.

Skylar sells his catch to wholesalers that sell to restaurants. The hagfish are shipped straight to South Korea, as there is no local market for these odd, eellike, slime-producing creatures. The crabs and salmon go to Robbie's or Monterey Fish or Fisherman's Choice. Skylar notes that a fisherman's work is constrained by a series of permits from the city, county and state. In frustration, he voices his opinion that fishermen are considered criminals before they commit a crime.

Skylar was born at home in Pacific Grove, California in 1987. He grew up in Pacific Grove and lives in the house where he was born. His mother is also a Pacific Grove native, but his dad came to the United States from Bavaria when he was fourteen. He joined the U.S. military, moved around a lot, and ultimately came to Monterey where he met Skylar's mom.

Skylar has no formal marine education, but has spent most of his life in, on or around the water. His parents' attitude was basically do whatever you want, check in after school, then be home for dinner. So, Skylar and his brother would go down to Lovers Point where they spent time figuring out how to poke pole[39] in the rocks at the end of the pier. They'd also practice jumping off the rock over on the west part of the beach, or what they call Beach II. As kids they used to call it The Cliff, because it was the biggest thing you could jump off of and not kill yourself. That's how Skylar spent his weekends and after school. The boys were always in the water, always free diving, fishing with a Hawaiian sling[40], shooting perch, stuff like that, and surfing. Skylar's brother followed the surfing gig, while Skylar preferred skateboarding, but they were always going out on the pier and fishing for stuff.

When he was seventeen, Skylar got his first boat—a little boat with a little outboard on it, which enabled him to continue to spend time in, on and around the water. And the rest is history.

---

[39] Poke pole fishing, aka 'poke poling,' is a method of procuring rockfish and eels from the intertidal zone that is as effective as it is peculiar—a method of fishing that uses a tool, referred to as a 'poke pole,' continually thrust into cracks and crevices, this fishing style is actually one of great antiquity.

[40] Hawaiian slings and pole spears are somewhat similar in that they both make use of a sling or band to fire the spear shaft, but there are some key differences in their appearance and how they are operated. The Hawaiian sling makes use of a shooter, traditionally made of wood, that uses a high-powered rubber strap to fling a spear shaft forward—similar to a bow and arrow.

Magic Mola on Metridium Mountain

Brian Phan

(*Date of Interview*: 1/20/19)

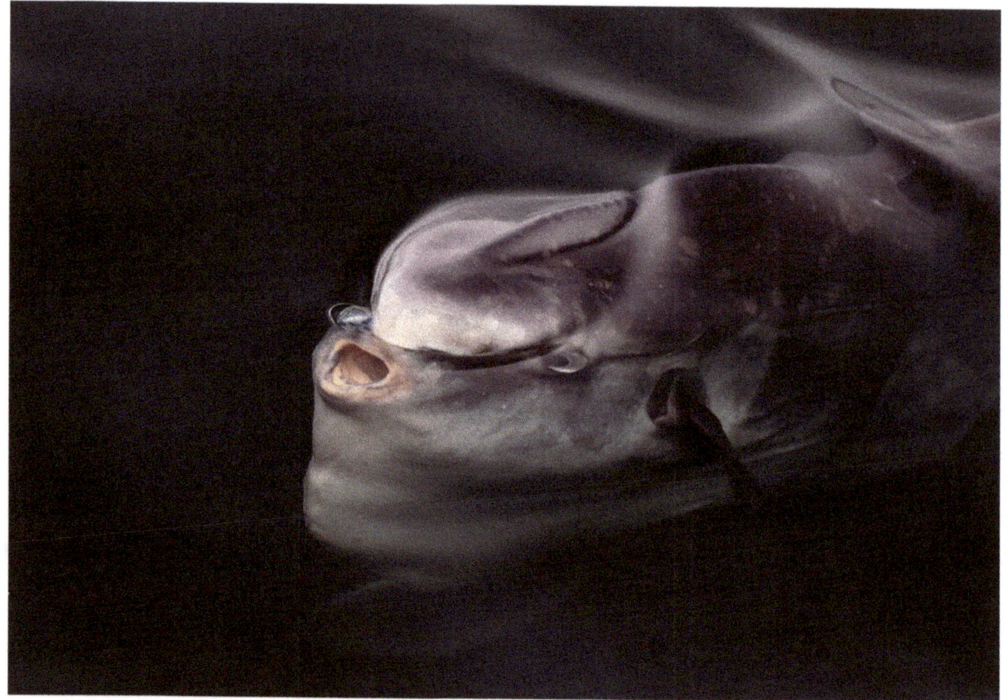

Mola mola *(ocean sunfish) with* Velella velella

It's hard to choose a single special moment as I've seen many amazing things, from walls and walls of jellyfish all over themselves, to thousands of sardines and anchovies swimming around trying to escape from you, because they think you're something that might eat them. The bay is one of the most amazing places, when you get in the water and sit there and just watch God's light coming through the kelp and fish. I spent a whole dive in one spot, peeing in my wetsuit over and over again to warm up, just watching that one moment. And I'm so glad my friends are photographers, because they sit in the same area over and over again, so I can just take it all in. People who dive in Monterey Bay know what I'm talking about. They see the magic and they get it. It's amazing. Even the breakwater has so much life. You can look at crabs, tiny fish, different types of barnacles, anemones, and you can literally hang out in one area for the whole dive.

One of my most memorable encounters, though, was off Cannery Row, off of a boat. We were doing an advanced dive class at a place they call Metridium

Mountain. You slide off the boat into the water, and you go down the anchor line. The anchor goes straight onto this pinnacle that is filled with Metridium—three-foot high, ghostly white anemones. So, that whole mountain's filled with them. And as a cold-water diver, you also check out the tiny little things. You're just sticking your head in cracks, looking at all this cool stuff. Soon I was following a bunch of little fish. "They're so cool. They're so cute." [*pretending to scratch a little fish*]

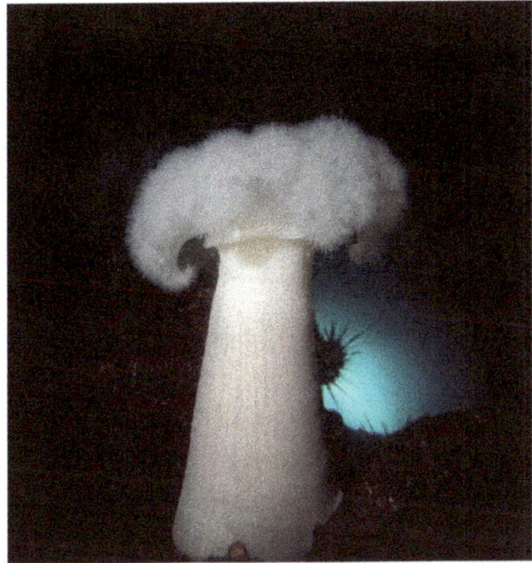

Metridium anemone © Brian Phan

But all of a sudden, I hear my buddy just screaming. [*holds hands over mouth and makes sound like a trumpeting elephant*] And I went, "Oh my goodness, what's happening?" I look over, and he grabs me and starts shaking me. And he turns around and points. And over there was a five-foot-long *Mola mola*, an ocean sunfish, about fifty feet away—five feet long and probably about five feet tall. It's just swimming fifty feet away, and the visibility was about eighty feet that day. It was totally gorgeous conditions. And you see all the other groups of divers just staring at this thing. It's a giant fish, but looks more like a blundering object coming toward us, and I'm like, "Oh yeah, got it!" I wanted to go close. I swam up so close to it, about ten feet away, and then I got scared. Because when you see that *huge* animal with an *enormous* eyeball just staring at you, you're like, "I know you're not going to do anything to me, but you're huge." Still, I just started backing up.

My buddy and I, we stayed there just watching. Everyone's just hanging out and looking at it. And it moved fast, surprisingly. It just kept on circling us. All the divers were watching it, and we spent the next thirty minutes staring at a giant *Mola mola*, and then it just swam off into the distance. So that would be my most memorable event with wildlife here in Monterey Bay—that *Mola mola* staring at us with that big eye. Totally creepy, but *yeah*!

BRIAN PHAN

Brian is a science writer and photojournalist based in Monterey. At the time of his interview, he was employed at Monterey Bay Diving in Sand City, California as a scuba diver and technician for scuba divers. He worked on a lot of different gear, including regulators, tanks, buoyancy compensators, and dry suits. Brian has also been a commercial construction diver, where he worked underwater on the wharf using such tools as pneumatic drills, chain saws and torches. During the week you can usually find him working as a naturalist on whale watching boats departing from

Moss Landing harbor. He has also served as Vice President of the Monterey Bay

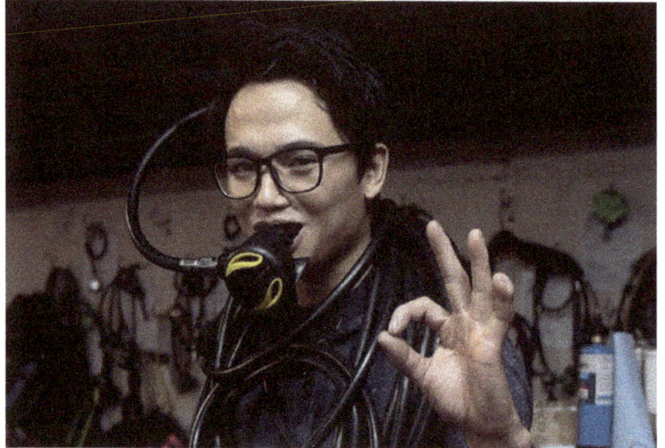

Chapter of the American Cetacean Society. Prior to that, Brian worked at the Monterey Bay Aquarium as an ambassador. He's also been a naturalist on whale watch boats and taught diving to students at California State University, Monterey Bay (CSUMB). A few years ago, Brian went to the Caribbean to do research on social foraging in coral reefs.

Brian was born in San Rafael, California and grew up in Novato, the next town over. His father loved the ocean and was a fisherman in Vietnam. When he emigrated to the United States, he took up recreational abalone diving. There were no catch limits at the time, so he went diving often and took all of Brian's seven siblings diving, but not Brian because he was the youngest. Well, being the youngest was only part of it. Brian's siblings thought he could learn how to swim if they pushed him into the deep end of the pool. But because of his low body fat, he sank. He says he pretty much drowned, and his sister had to jump into the pool, pull him out, and resuscitate him. After that experience he was afraid of the water, but respected it. So Brian hung out on the beach while his dad and siblings went diving.

He always knew he wanted to scuba dive, but didn't learn how to swim until his sophomore year in college, with the help of a bunch of friends. And it wasn't until he was in college that he asked his dad to go abalone diving with him, and his dad said "Yeah, sure." Brian grew up next to the ocean as a kid, went diving as a young adult with his dad, and then came to Monterey to go to CSUMB, where he got a degree in biology (evolution and organismal ecology). Most of his studies were marine biology–related, and while in school he did a lot of research with rockfish. In 2022, Brian got his Master of Science degree in Science Communication from the University of California at Santa Cruz.

But why Brian became a marine biologist has a little different twist. He decided when he was in second grade to study marine biology, because he had a crush on a girl whose parents were marine biologists, and he thought he could impress her and she'd like him. Of course, he hasn't seen her since, but his fate was sealed, at least figuratively, 'with a kiss.' Brian came to Monterey because he knew that CSUMB had a good marine science program. He showed up for orientation, went to the aquarium, hung out at Asilomar Beach, and fell in love with the area.

The Hypnotic Power of a Sunfish Eyeball

Tierney Thys

(*Date of Interview*: 5/11/19)

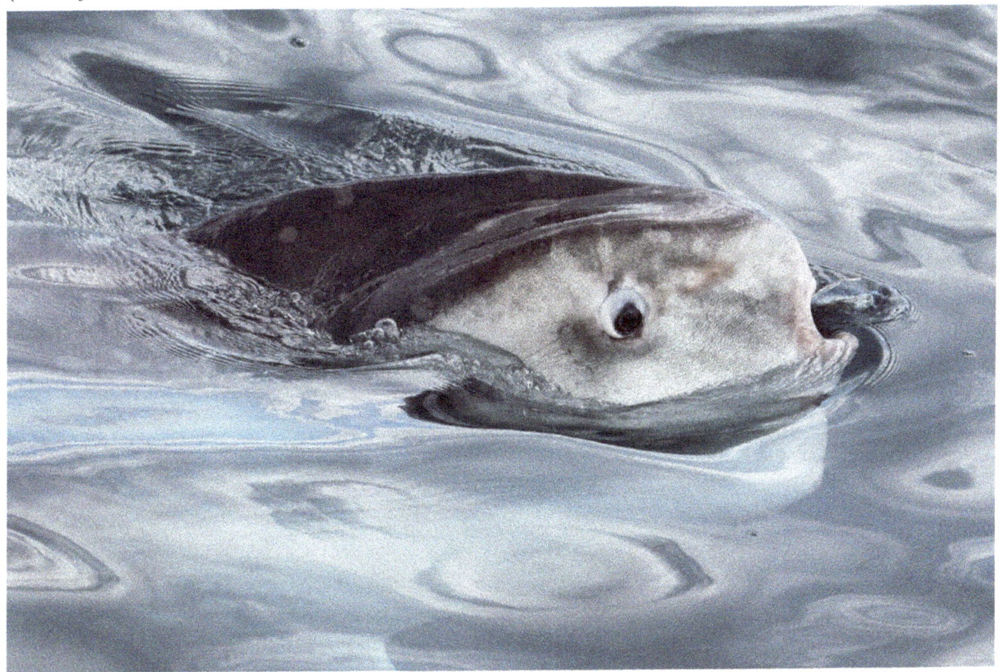

Mola mola *(ocean sunfish) feeding on* Velella velella

This was something that happened a couple of years ago. I was out doing a shoot for *Animal Jam*, which is an online video game—a world where you become an animal to play. I am a Daily Explorer inside the game. When I started, we had a million registered players. Now the game is up to 180 million registered players, so it's really popular. It's like *Club Penguin* but aimed at six- to eleven-year-olds. In the game, I have an aquarium where I can show videos and answer questions—kids' questions—about the ocean and animals.

I was out there doing the shoot on Monterey Bay, but I also work on ocean sunfish; it's my primary study animal. I'm always keeping my eyes open for the sunfish. I'm there with my cameraman, Phillip Powell. I have my expensive lavalier mic and my whole mic system hooked up to me, and this subadult California sea lion—I mean, he's *huge*—he comes up to the zodiac and he looks up. He pulls his head up, and he has this *huge* sunfish in his mouth! And I'm like, *ah*!!

But this is what happens to the sunfish that come into Monterey Bay. It's usually the young of the year and the sea lions rip the fins off, and fashion the sunfish into these perfect, little gray Frisbees. Then they toss them between themselves. This is ultimate Frisbee, sea lion style. Superfun for the sea lions, not so fun for the sunfish, because they end up (ultimately) dying. The seagulls peck their eyes out, and then they sink to the seafloor, and they get eaten by the sea stars, which is a really unceremonious way to die. I saw one do a face plant in an *Urticina*, a fish-eating anemone. I mean if that's not adding insult to injury, I don't know what is. A self-respecting fish, a huge fish, being eaten by an anemone… anyway.

The sea lion shows me this big sunfish. It's like he's showing off right in front of the camera! And then, he drops

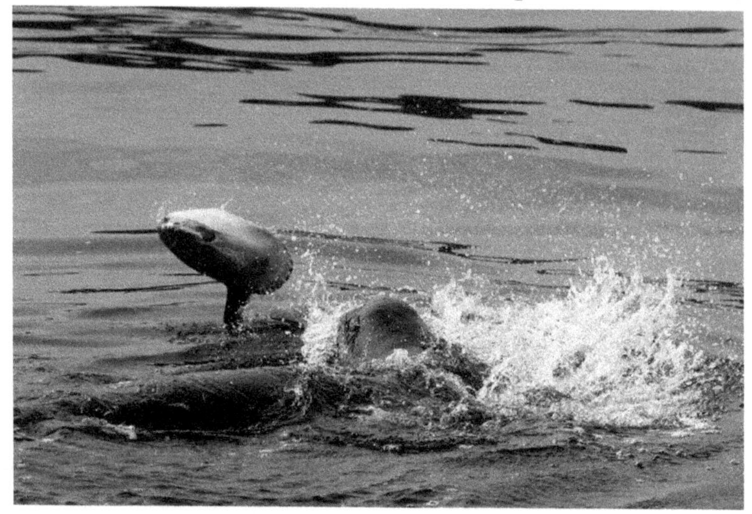

Sea lion tosses a Mola mola *missing a fin*

it. At the time, I was collecting. I needed a sample, because I was looking at the opsin genes[41] in sunfish eyes and I needed fresh eyes, and the sea lions were my perfect henchmen. I didn't want to have to kill a sunfish to get its eyes. Let the sea lions do that. And I'd get all sorts of samples from them. You know, the sea lions rip the fins off, then the helpless fish wash up, and then I get to sample them without having to kill them. So, this sea lion, he drops the fish. Momentarily. And it's huge! And I'm like, "Oh, look," and the fish turns over and it's got this one eye. Like the fish's gonna die, and I couldn't help myself, I just jumped in! I had all the expensive camera gear, all this stuff on me, lavalier, everything. And I jump in, and I get the fish, and I get the eyeball, and I'm so happy!! And meanwhile my camera guy is looking at me because it's his gear. And he's horrified!! And I said, "oh no!!" That was how I ended up paying about $600 for one fresh sunfish eyeball. [*laughter*] But it was worth it. I guess. [*more laughter*]

Science for the sake of the show. But I just had to get that eyeball. It's really hard to get the eyeballs, you know, because when the sunfish wash up, it's usually

---

[41] Opsins are the universal photoreceptor molecules of all visual systems in the animal kingdom.

in the pelagic period, October, which is when a lot of the offshore species come in. The sunfish will wash up after the sea lions rip their fins off, and then if they're fresh I can get all sorts of great tissues. But usually, the seagulls will come in and eat the eyes first, so you have to be there right when the fish wash up. This time I'd gotten a really fresh, big eyeball. But I paid the price.

TIERNEY THYS

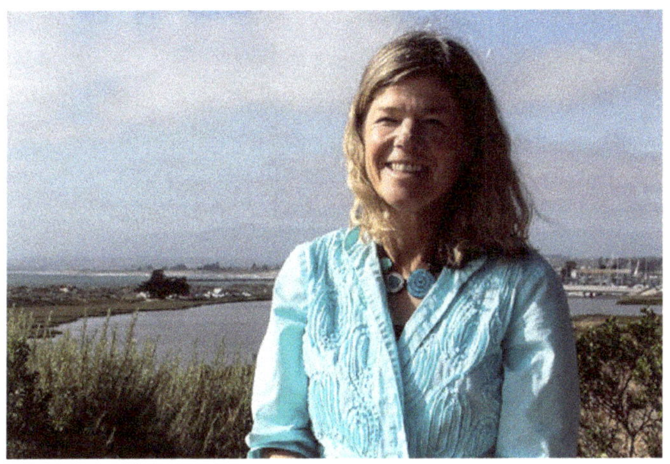

Tierney Thys wears many hats. She is a science media producer and communicator who is also engaged in multiple scientific research projects. The curiously shaped ocean sunfish is one of her signature marine projects. As Senior Editor, Tierney is currently putting together the first big academic book on the sunfish, featuring contributing authors from all over the world. Students will be able to read up on various study themes including reproduction, anatomy, locomotion, fisheries and toxins, and each chapter will end with a list of scientific questions still needing to be answered. This will help focus students so they will be able to hit the ground running when they start their own research efforts.

Tierney was born in San Leandro, California, but at the age of ten moved with her family to the tiny, land-locked town of Norwich, Vermont, where she grew up. She did her undergraduate work at Brown University in Rhode Island where she received a degree in biology. Following graduation, Tierney returned to California for several years where she worked for Sylvia Earle. Tierney then attended graduate school at Duke University in North Carolina and earned her doctorate in zoology investigating the mechanics of swimming muscles in fish, before returning to California.

Tierney first visited Monterey when her sister was attending boarding school in the area, well before the Monterey Bay Aquarium was built. She remembers Cannery

Row, which was ultimately transformed into the aquarium and neighboring shops, as a stinky place back then.

During her first year in graduate school, Tierney came and did research at the aquarium, which was just getting ready to display ocean sunfish. She had already developed an interest in them, and the aquarium had some in captivity that she could study. That was in the early 1990s. Tierney worked with the sunfish for a semester, but couldn't quite develop those efforts into a PhD project.

Following graduate school Tierney returned to Monterey. There she was involved in filmmaking at Sea Studios, located next door to the aquarium, and was able to continue her unwavering interest in sunfish again. Tierney fell for them, as they are such an unusual fish. In graduate school she was studying biomechanics and looking at form and function, and looked at this odd-shaped fish and wondered why they had left their tails behind! Tierney describes them as an abridged oddity, a mistake. Yet, she says that when you see them swimming in the wild, they are just beautiful and graceful, a thing of majesty. They have this major contradiction—they look so cumbersome and yet they are so graceful. For a biomechanist, they were the perfect animal to study.

Concurrent with her ongoing research on sunfish, Tierney has spent ten years in filmmaking. Frustrated with the loss of whole biology courses at the university level, where studies in mammalogy, entomology and the like have been replaced by genetics, she was happy to join the team at Sea Studios in making a documentary series aimed at reinvigorating interest in whole-organism systems. The series, entitled *Shape of Life*, had eight episodes—each one focused on a different phylum. The second series she worked on was about environmental issues from climate change to waterborne pollutants. As Tierney notes, when you work in marine sciences you can't ignore the impacts we're having on the planet. She has consequently become more and more interested in conservation and conservation messaging.

Tierney currently has several grants from National Geographic looking at how our brain responds to nature imagery and also the effects of offering nature imagery to nature-deprived populations, such as the incarcerated. She is exploring the question of how do we take the natural world that we've captured in our cameras and use it as a messaging tool to lessen our impacts.

The Abalone Diver's Dilemma

Tim Thomas

(*Date of Interview*: 12/13/17)

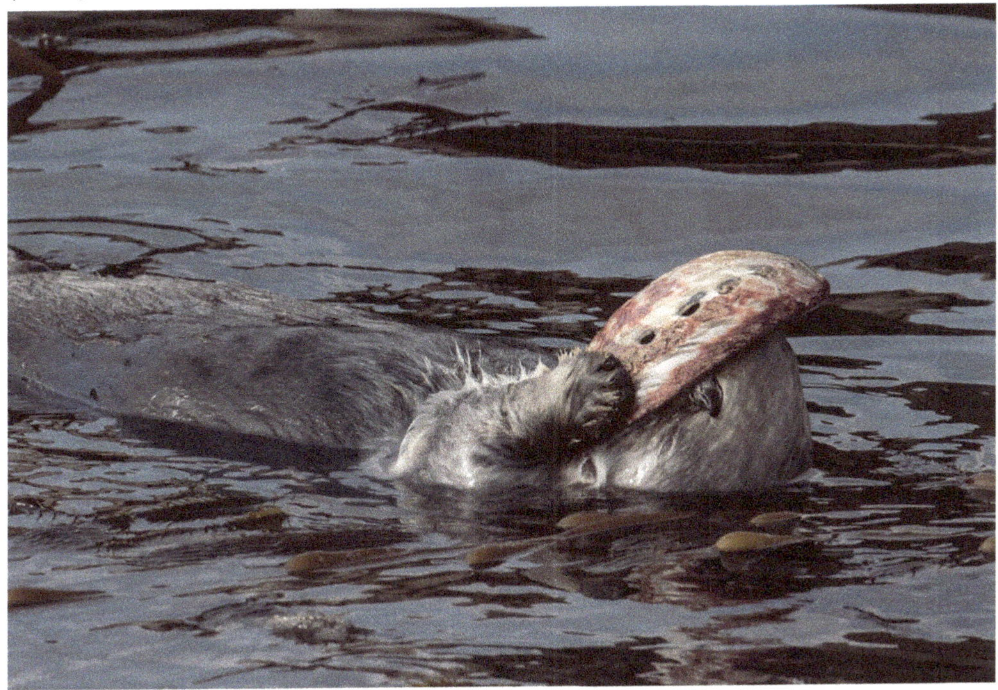

Southern sea otter feeding on an abalone

My old friend Roy Hattori was the last Japanese abalone diver in Monterey. In fact, he was the only diver that was born here. All the other divers came from Japan and with only a couple of exceptions returned to Japan. Roy was born here, just a couple of blocks from the Monterey Bay Aquarium. I asked him how to do this—how to become a diver. He told me that when he was a young man that had just graduated from Monterey High School, his father wanted to get into the abalone business. There was a depression, he had a lot of debts to pay, and he thought, "This would be a good way to make some money." He had no experience in the business whatsoever, but he had friends who were in it. So Roy borrows some equipment and gets on a boat right here in the middle of Monterey Harbor. He's dressing up in this long wool underwear, puts on this heavy canvas diving suit, tacks about sixty-five pounds of lead weight to his front and back, and ties lead to his shoes. Then he bolts on the helmet, and they just toss him off the side of the boat.

If you start running down there, that's how you learn to be an abalone diver. They asked him if he ever had any problems down there. He said, "You know, sometimes the currents were really strong and kicked up rocks." One time a rock kicked up, hit him in the helmet, and cracked the glass on his helmet. You're thirty feet below in Monterey Bay, and you just cracked the glass in your helmet. What are you gonna do? You want to get to the surface, right? It takes a long time! First, he has to release the side valve on his helmet, fill up his suit with air, and bring himself back up. What he did—and I think this was the most remarkable thing— he just reaches into his abalone basket, pulls out that abalone, which is just a big marine snail, takes the abalone, sticks it on the glass, abalone seals up the crack, stops the water from coming in. Goes to the surface, changes the glass and starts all over again.

This is a fond memory for Tim; he knew Roy for over twenty-five years. Roy actually passed away—it was Christmas 2011.

TIM THOMAS

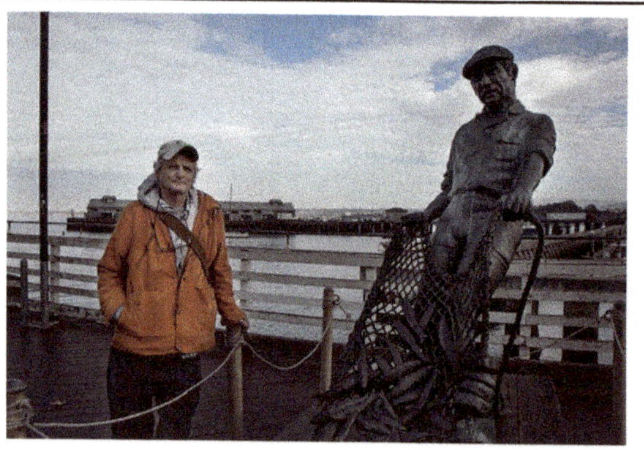

Tim Thomas is a Monterey area fisheries historian. He is a popular speaker and lively tour guide. Tim decided early on in his life to focus on fisheries because Monterey Bay is so important, and everybody who lives here, everyone who has come here, has been greatly impacted by the bay. Tim is also an author of several books, including *The Abalone King of Monterey: "Pop" Ernest Doelter, Pioneering Japanese Fishermen & the Culinary Classic that Saved an Industry*; and—for *Images of America—Monterey's Waterfront* and *The Japanese on the Monterey Peninsula*. A fourth-generation native of Monterey Bay, he was born in Carmel and grew up in Pacific Grove. His interest in local history started when he was quite young. Tim says they did not teach local history when he was a kid, but he spent a lot of time on Cannery Row in the late 1960s among the abandoned canneries. His interest in fishing history was sparked there. It was just something he says he wanted to know more about. When the Monterey Bay Aquarium first opened in 1984, Tim got heavily involved in local historical 'stuff.' He was brought in to help write some living history about whaling on Monterey Bay for the aquarium's initial temporary exhibit entitled *Whale Fest*. That job led to his working as historian and curator at the nearby Monterey History & Maritime Museum for sixteen years. Tim has also worked for California State Parks and the Monterey Bay National Marine Sanctuary.

Whales and Dolphins and Marine Protected Areas, Oh My!

Don Kelly

(Date of Interview: 12/11/16)

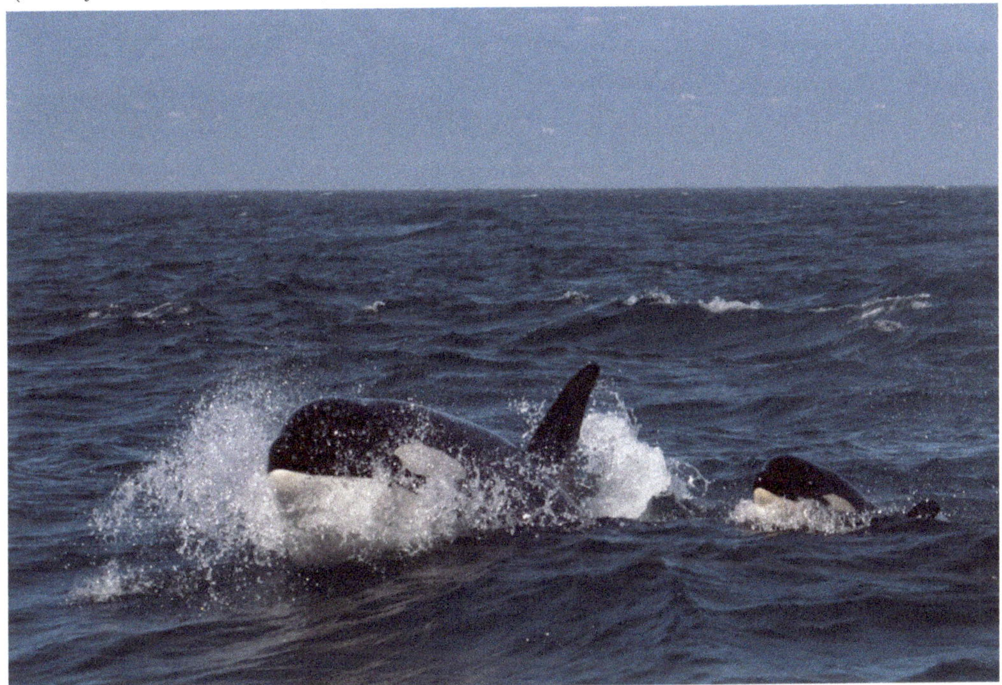

Killer whale mother and calf

I can share a combination of all the things I have done. A lot of people have done very positive things here in Monterey Bay from a research or purely biological standpoint. My story is a little different, in that enforcement usually deals with the negative side of things. As wardens, we are out there to ensure people are complying with the regulations, wherever they have been established, so we are looking for violations. But in looking for these violations, we find some phenomenal things. So few people ever get the opportunity to see a pod of orcas. I've only seen orcas on the water twice in my career!

The nine that we saw the one time was the first time I took one of my brand-new wardens out with me to teach him how to use the boat; there were nine of them and we watched them for a while. I told him, "You know, this is not normal, this is a special occurrence."

The first time I saw orcas, all I saw was this [*hand motion*]. I'm driving the boat, and, "What the heck was that?" I'm watching, and I see it again. I'm going, "What the heck *was* that?" And then I thought, "Oh, I'm seeing dorsal fins coming right at me, so I took a hard left out of their path and stopped the boat and just waited for them to go by. Then I was able to confirm that they were orcas. I wasn't able to confirm it until I actually saw them go by me. This was six weeks ago where we saw that pod of orcas. Phenomenal experience! I told Rich, I said, "Be very careful how you explain how you had such a hard day on the water today to your wife, ok?" [*big smile*] "She may not want to hear how much fun you had." And it is. You cannot script that, you can't do it. It happens when you're least expecting it. No two days in forty years have ever been the same. That's one of the reasons I hate to give it up. I hate to give it up. [Don has just been forced to retire by state regulations.]

I've flown the Monterey Bay area so many times and also seen things, like when a pod of Risso's dolphins comes in following the giant squid. And you see three hundred or so dolphins from the air that are in a feeding frenzy. It is a phenomenal sight. These are the things that people don't get to see from land, because you have to get out there in a boat or a plane.

Then we've gone out to check the albacore fleet at Pioneer Seamount, and on the way out there we had dolphins surfing our bow wake for hours! Those are the kinds of things that are intrinsically valuable that you don't forget about, even though you're focusing on making sure that the people that are engaged in activities involving consumptive use on the ocean and in the bay are complying with the regulations.

We had two minke whales one time coming out there. We were working off a 110-foot patrol boat out of Eureka one day and these two minke whales were coming right at the boat like torpedoes and then at the very last minute they turned right—I mean, you don't, you can't repeat that kind of stuff. It just doesn't happen. And so to be out there and to be out there when things like that happen, it's amazing.

Yes, we're the enforcement division of the California Department of Fish and Wildlife. Our job is to ensure people are complying with the rules and regulations that are set up to protect fish and wildlife and to control consumptive use on the oceans and in the environment. It's negative from the standpoint that we're stopping people from doing something they want to do. A lot of people don't have self-control when it comes to catching fish, or crabs, or abalone or something like that. We're there to ensure that they do.

We also get the positive spin on that when we do find people in compliance, and we get more and more people to buy in on the regulations that are there to protect something that they really enjoy. This is a passion for *a lot* of people as well as a recreation. They are basically coming into a situation where they are part of the solution. And you gain compliance by making sure that they understand what the rules and regulations are and they want to comply with them. Ninety percent of the people will do the right thing if you give them the right information. And so that's another aspect of the job, to get the word out there, "Hey these are what the regulations are, and this is why." Explain to them why. Once you explain the 'why' to most people, they do, in fact, want to comply and make sure that they can continue with their passion, their recreation, and pass it on to their kids and grandkids. It's a very positive thing.

Then there's the Marine Protected Area process. I've been involved with that since 2002. It was the most sweeping change of regulations and regulatory issues involved in ocean fishing in my lifetime. It's been a very difficult road. But what we have seen is that people understand that the Marine Protected Areas can help protect and perpetuate these populations of fish that they enjoy from a consumptive standpoint. They enjoy going after salmon and rockfish and so on and so forth, and to set aside areas that either protect their habitat totally or allow for moderate take in reasonably good habitat was a hard sell right at the beginning. But afterwards we were able to get the word out with the help of the Monterey Bay National Marine Sanctuary, and with the help of a lot of nongovernmental organizations. We were getting the word out to people as to why we need these protected areas, and how we are making a difference. Then there's also been research that's going on to show that this is a positive thing; this will, in fact, help to perpetuate those species well into the future. And that's the plan.

We don't want to see anything get diminished or go extinct, and that's why I've done what I've done for forty years. I want to make sure that continues on, because that's the right thing to do, for everybody. And for the resources themselves—the resources are what our focus is. So, from that standpoint, that's what we're going to do.

DON KELLY

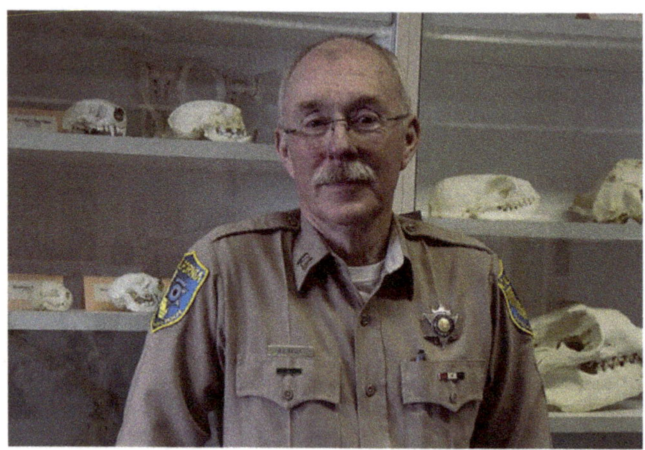

California Department of Fish and Wildlife Warden Don Kelly is currently retired. At the time of our interview, Don was a Patrol Captain for the North Coast District. Don headed the southernmost Captain's District in the North Coast District, which includes Santa Clara, Santa Cruz, San Benito, Monterey and San Luis Obispo counties. He had been with the department for forty years.

Don was born in Los Angeles and grew up on a small farm in the San Fernando Valley, where he had a lot of experience learning animal behavior. He was actively engaged in 4-H, and a lot of his background is associated with the animal husbandry he did in 4-H. Those activities gave him really good insight into domestic animal behavior, as well as wildlife behavior.

His interest in law enforcement arose from a positive experience he had as a child with his grandparents, who took him fishing three times every summer. One time they got checked by a game warden, while fishing at a reservoir in the eastern Sierra. For Don it was an incredibly positive experience, and he told his grandmother, "This is a great job, wow!" That moment stuck with him. That early encounter with a warden, plus Don's passion for the field of biology, being with animals, invertebrates, and everything in the biological realm led him to pursue a career in wildlife law enforcement.

In college, Don got a general degree in biology, but then did graduate work at California State University, Hayward in marine ecology. Cal State Hayward was associated with Moss Landing Marine Laboratories back then when it was just a single-wide trailer. His education gave him a really good sense of the ecological issues involved in the marine environment.

Sea to the Skyline

C h r i s   B e r r y

(*Date of Interview*: 10/26/16)

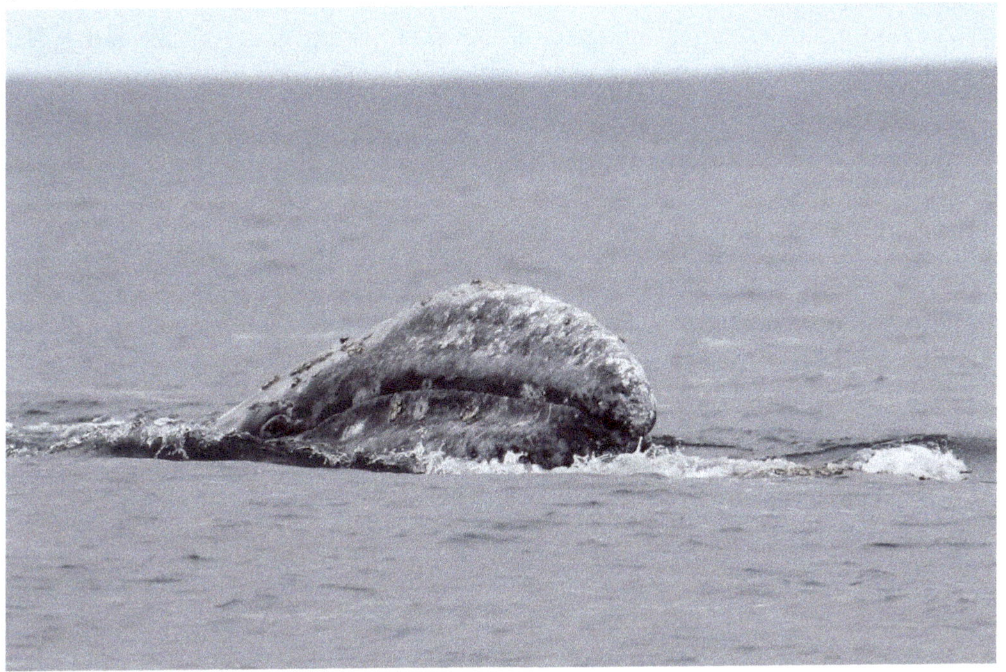

Gray whale

Welcome to Laguna Creek [*shown in video interview and in Chris's bio below*]. I chose this spot, because both as a private person and as a professional, I've had a lot of experiences here over the last twenty-five years or so that have drawn me to all that Monterey Bay has to offer. My story is "Sea to the Skyline," and I say "Sea to the Skyline" as opposed to "Skyline to the Sea," which is what most people say, because my story started in the surf.

I was surfing here long before I had to work here for the City of Santa Cruz, or I should say, 'got to work here,' because when I found out I got to work here, it was like [*arm pump*], "Sweet!!" This is why I don't really worry about how much I earn, because I get to go to a place like this and work.

My first story with wildlife in the bay happened when I was surfing here at the mouth of Laguna Creek. It's actually a pretty sketchy beach when the surf is up. It's not really up today. It drops off very steeply from the beach, and you can tell there's a lot of marine life, and the water's moving, and it's kind of one of those spots that you can say is sort of spooky. One day I was surfing by myself, trying to amp up the spooky factor, and a whale popped up next to me about as far away as you are, which is, you know, about six feet. It was probably about a thirty-foot whale, that I'm assuming was a gray whale given how close it was to the shore. And, you know, at first I gasped, and then I went, "Thank God, it's a whale!" because otherwise I probably never would have seen it, since it would have been a white shark. And it would have come up from beneath me and bounced me out of the water and chewed my leg off.

It's just one of those momentary brushes with wildlife that kinda makes you snap out of your everyday mundane 'I'm driving down the road,' and 'I'm gonna go to the bank, and I'm gonna go to work,' and just not paying attention to the world around you. It makes you appreciate your relatively small place in the food chain in the span of the universe and also appreciate that there are incredibly beautiful things happening all around you. And sometimes you have to be slapped in the face a little bit just to notice that.

The encounter probably only took ten seconds, but it's one of the most vivid memories of my life. I had that happen to me once again up at Ocean Beach, in San Francisco, and the second time, of course, it wasn't quite as startling, but it was still inspiring, especially with San Francisco right there, and an urban beach like that, and, "Oh, there's whales right here!" It's pretty amazing!

The whale was kind of my first, "Oh my God, I love Laguna Watershed, I love Laguna Beach." You know, it started me on that path. And then when I got to work for the city in the 1990s, my job involved implementing the Safe Drinking Water Act, which focused on watershed protection. The city had prioritized the use of the water from Laguna Creek, because it's the cleanest, cheapest water we have, so my work focused on one of my favorite watersheds. But the Safe Drinking Water Act exacerbated all of our problems with environmental regulatory compliance. In the mid-1990s, coho salmon and steelhead got listed under the Endangered Species Act. We were drying up the creek every summer. In fact, I remember the first time I drove up to the diversion and saw the stream totally dewatered below the diversion. I just couldn't believe it, and knowing where that water was going—this beautiful habitat down here—it was a little challenging protecting the habitat while providing water for people, all at the same time.

On the other hand, there are these greater values you have, these environmental values at work. And it's not like the city is some evil environmental villain. They're serving water to the customers of the City of Santa Cruz, who, by and large, have an environmental ethic. So that's how I kind of compartmentalized all that, and figured I'd take the long view. Perhaps over time things will change. I did bring a couple of photos to tell that story. In a nutshell, here we have the Laguna lagoon in 2004, which I believe was an average water year. You can see the creek flow doesn't make it to the ocean, and there's very little wet habitat back here on the back beach. In 2013, which was a historically dry year, we have a full lagoon, lots of inland wet habitat in the back as a result of the changes we had made. We now have had coho spawning here in the last two years. Coho are on the verge of extinction south of the Golden Gate. They are nearly extirpated now, so having them spawn here is kind of a big deal.

Things have improved since the early days. We've done a lot of work in the last ten years or so. Here's my other picture. Here's the day we started turning out water on Laguna Creek, in 2007. This was a pivotal moment in the city's history, believe it or not. It was as simple as turning a valve. The amount of work that went into that though was pretty huge. So that's our former Production Supervisor, Jim Bentley, releasing the first water out of the diversion from Laguna Creek.

You know, to a lot of folks that was a hard thing to do. We'd been diverting out of Laguna Creek for maybe a hundred years. But I think people are starting to see now that release of water has benefits, and we're planning around providing water for fisheries in the creek now, rather than trying to shoehorn fisheries into all of our other obligations.

Fisheries and natural resource protection have become coequal goals in our mission statement along with providing water to the City of Santa Cruz. That's been kind of a nice story there, although it still has its challenges. We have water rights issues from other users upstream that are challenging the fishery, as well as challenging the city water rights. And, of course, that affects the habitat in the stream, and that affects Monterey Bay. The coho are anadromous, so they are going in and out of the creek. We have a very healthy population of tidewater goby here as well, one that the U.S. Fish and Wildlife Service expects to use to reseed other adjacent creeks nearby, because this population is so robust just by virtue of the quality of this habitat here in the lagoon.

One of the other things about this watershed that I think is sort of fascinating and neat is that in Santa Cruz County we have sandhills, which are old marine deposits where there's unique biota. This watershed not only has sandhills at the headwaters, but it also has karst, which is metamorphosed limestone. It's geologically a unique and interesting watershed. It does have good flows during drought years because of that geology. You know it's got the redwood forest that Jodi's so aware of. It's got the maritime chaparral. It's got badgers up in some of the grasslands farther up the canyon, so it's just a really neat watershed.

Here's another little wildlife story I have, also in this watershed. The first time I was doing fish habitat typing on this creek, I had not only never seen an adult steelhead, but I don't think I'd ever seen a California red-legged frog. Lo and behold, somehow, right behind here, I'm talking about a mile up there, I came across an adult steelhead right there in a pool with a red-legged frog about six inches from its face sitting in the same pool. To me that was kind of like, 'you hit pay dirt there.' Again, it just sort of

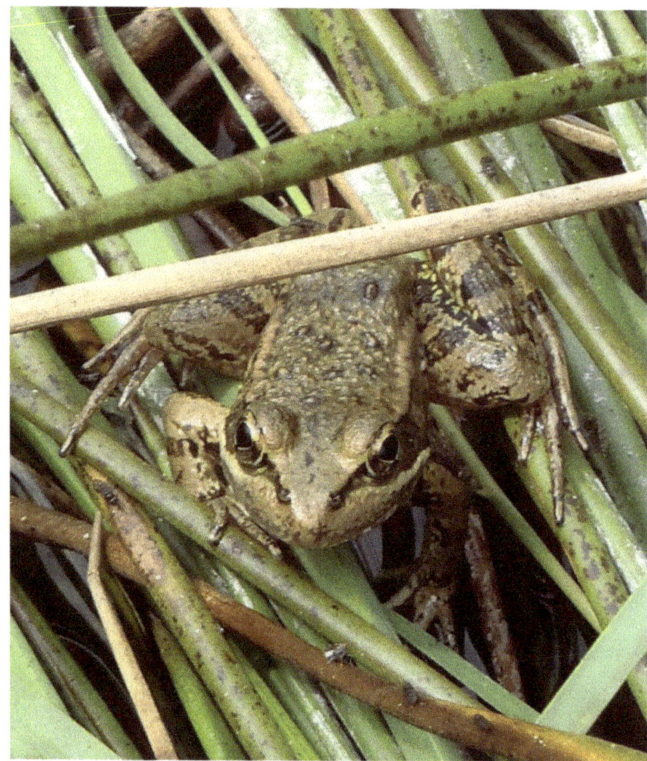

California red-legged frog © Chris Berry

added to the rich tapestry of interesting features, just the biodiversity and the story of Laguna Watershed, and, of course, its connectivity to the bay out there. We have Mount Hermon June beetle living up in the sandhills in the headwaters. We have snowy plovers out here on the beach. I've seen golden eagles out here, peregrine falcons, and western pond turtles in the lagoon as well.

In 2005, one of my favorite employees ever, Matt Baldzikowski, was out here and found a spawned-out coho salmon carcass. Live coho hadn't been seen out here. In fact, I don't think there was a record of a coho out here before then. Matt came back really excited. And he had the carcass in his hand, and said, "What do we do with this?" And I'm like, "I don't know, let's take it down to the [NOAA] Science Center at Terrace Point and see what they say." So that was kind of cool.

The next summer NOAA was doing some fish surveys and found a bunch of juvenile cohos, but after that we didn't see coho juveniles for another ten years until 2015. It's been pretty hard for the coho with the numbers being so low, and then we had the historic drought, but we did have spawning again in 2015 and 2016; 2015 was a superdry year. I don't think those fish would have survived if we hadn't been releasing the water we've been releasing for coho the last couple of years. So, it's a pretty cool place to get to work and I'm proud of what we have accomplished.

CHRIS BERRY

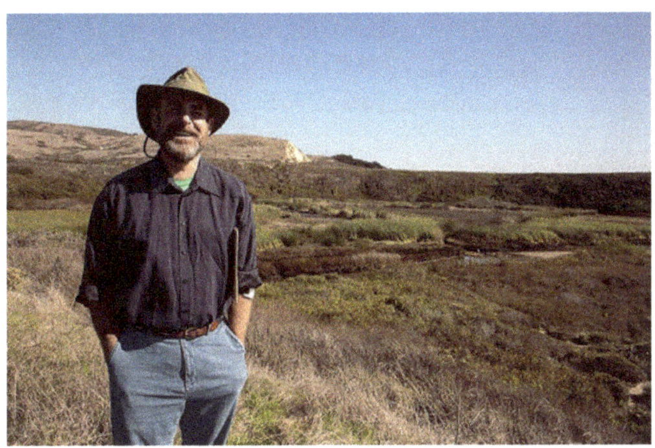

Chris Berry is the Watershed Compliance Manager for the City of Santa Cruz Water Department. He's involved primarily with environmental regulatory compliance work for the department, but he's also involved with Drinking Water Source Protection. Chris notes this is what the rest of the world knows as watershed protection, but in the context of the Safe Drinking Water Act, there's actually an emphasis on protecting the watersheds for the sake of drinking water quality.

Chris was born in Putnam, Connecticut. He grew up in northeastern Connecticut and central/north-central New Hampshire. Chris wasn't sure what he wanted to do when he grew up, though he thought he'd like to be some kind of conservationist. He knew he didn't want to work in an office; that is, he didn't want to work a traditional kind of job. Chris wanted to do something with social and environmental importance.

His brother, who was a real influence on him as a kid, is now an environmental attorney who runs a nonprofit land trust back East. Chris thought that might be a neat path to go down. At least, it looked like a good excuse to get out of his little hometown and come to Santa Barbara, California, where he enrolled as an undergraduate at the University of California (UC). He started studying aquatic biology in Santa Barbara.

Chris came to Monterey Bay as a twenty-two-year-old looking for a graduate school with surfable waves that were better than those in Santa Barbara. He landed at UC Santa Cruz (although he admits that, at the time, his first priority was to locate somewhere where the waves were good). By the time he was ready for grad school, there was a critical mass of people doing ocean-related things in the Santa Cruz area, and it was a time when watershed science was really starting to take off, too. Freshwater ecology and watershed science, as well as marine ecology, were both starting to pick up then. Santa Cruz had terrestrial and marine draws for Chris. He feels fortunate to have landed a nontraditional job that allowed him to work outside, and to do something with social and environmental importance.

References

Alaska Whale Foundation (AWF)	https://www.alaskawhalefoundation.org
American Cetacean Society (ACS)	https://www.acsonline.org
American Cetacean Society, Monterey Chapter	https://acsmb.org
Blue Ocean Whale Watch	https://www.blueoceanwhalewatch.com
California Department of Fish and Wildlife (previously Fish and Game)	https://wildlife.ca.gov/
California Killer Whale Project	https://tinyurl.com/2v36ahra
Cascadia Research	https://cascadiaresearch.org
CEBSE, Inc.	https://samana.org.do
Chris' Fishing and Whale Watching	https://www.chriswhalewatching.com
Discovery Whale Watch	https://discoverywhalewatch.com
Earthwatch	https://earthwatch.org
Elkhorn Slough Reserve	https://elkhornslough.org
FastRaft Ocean Safaris	https://www.fastraft.com
Happywhale	https://happywhale.com
Heirs To Our Ocean	https://h2oo.org
Hopkins Marine Station	https://tinyurl.com/3trnex3m
J&M Sport Fishing (previously Randy's Fishing)	https://jmsportfishing.com/about/
Joseph M. Long Marine Laboratory	https://tinyurl.com/2k2wtdsd
Marine Life Studies (MLS)	https://www.marinelifestudies.org
Marine Mammal Center	https://www.marinemammalcenter.org/
Marine Wildlife Veterinary Care Research Center	https://wildlife.ca.gov/OSPR/Science/MWVCRC
MBARI Data & Repositories	https://tinyurl.com/3rdehahs
Monterey Bay Aquarium	https://www.montereybayaquarium.org
Monterey Bay Aquarium Research Institute (MBARI)	https://www.mbari.org
Monterey Bay National Marine Sanctuary	https://montereybay.noaa.gov
Monterey Bay Whale Watch (MBWW)	https://tinyurl.com/2s3cw5nd
Moss Landing Marine Laboratories (MLML)	https://mlml.sjsu.edu
National Oceanic and Atmospheric Administration (NOAA)	https://www.noaa.gov
Oceana	https://oceana.org/
Ocean Conservancy	https://oceanconservancy.org/
Oceanic Society	https://www.oceanicsociety.org
Oceanswell	https://oceanswell.org
O'Neill Sea Odyssey	https://www.oneillseaodyssey.org
The Safina Center	https://www.safinacenter.org
Save Our Shores (SOS)	https://saveourshores.org
Soundscape Listening Room	https://tinyurl.com/2u94subh
Tiburon Marine Center	https://tinyurl.com/4j4m4r7t
The Whalenerd's Podcast	https://www.thewhalenerds.com
Whale-SETI	https://bmccowanlab.com/current-research/humpback-whale-research/